American Contract Bridge League

Introduction to Bridge
Bidding
"The Club Series"

by
Audrey Grant

FOREWORD

Why play bridge?

You may be a little confused — why is Martina Navratilova writing the introduction to a bridge book?

The answer is that I believe it takes a strong mind, as well as a strong body, to live life to its fullest.

Bridge is more than just a card game. *It's a cerebral sport.* Bridge teaches logic, reasoning, quick thinking, patience, concentration and partnership skills.

Once at Wimbledon, when we got rained out, I spent my time playing bridge to keep me sharp and on my toes. An evening of bridge at home with family and friends is so much more fulfilling than sitting around watching TV.

The American Contract Bridge League has commissioned one of the world's most successful bridge teachers, Audrey Grant, to write this book. Audrey has taken what many people consider a complex game and made it easy and fun to learn.

Bridge has meant a lot to me in my travels. No matter where I go, I can always make new friends at the bridge table.

You know, tennis is a sport for a lifetime, and bridge is a game for a lifetime. It can be enjoyed by young and old, male and female, weak and strong. It crosses all barriers!

Take this book home with you today. Start learning a game and a sport — to last a lifetime!

MARTINA NAVRATILOVA
World Tennis Champion

ISBN 0–943855–00–4

The American Contract Bridge League

The American Contract Bridge League (ACBL) is dedicated to the playing, teaching and advancement of contract bridge.

The current membership of 187,000 includes a wide range — from the thousands who are just learning the joys of bridge to the most proficient players in North America.

ACBL offers a variety of services. These include:

• Tournament play. Thousands of tournaments: — North American Bridge Championships (three a year), as well as tournaments at the regional, sectional, local and club levels are sanctioned annually.

• A monthly magazine. The BRIDGE BULLETIN offers articles on tournaments, card play, the Laws, personalities, special ACBL activities, etc.

• A ranking plan. Each time a member does well in any ACBL event, whether it be at the club level or at a North American Bridge Championship, that member receives a masterpoint award. Players achieve rankings and prestige as a result of their cumulative masterpoint holdings.

• A teaching program. ACBL has trained more than 3,000 people through the Teacher Accreditation Program (TAP) to effectively teach beginning bridge lessons.

• A novice program. ACBL offers special games and programs for players new to bridge and duplicate.

• A charity program. Each year the ACBL Charity Foundation selects a "Charity of the Year," which is the main beneficiary of ACBL charity games and general donations by the membership. All ACBL clubs participate to raise money for the charity.

• An education program. The ACBL Educational Foundation is dedicated to bringing the enjoyment of bridge to people of all ages and firmly believes this can be accomplished through bridge education. Grants are provided for special bridge projects.

• A college program. ACBL cooperates with the nation's colleges in making bridge instruction and play available to college students.

• A youth program (for players age 19 and under). ACBL offers a funded teaching program, youth membership, special events and a quarterly youth newsletter.

• Products. ACBL offers a wide variety of bridge supplies, books, clothing and bridge products for new players and teachers through its Customer Service Department.

• Membership in the World Bridge Federation. Each year ACBL sends premiere players to compete in the world championships. ACBL's Junior Team participates in the World Junior Team Competition in odd-numbered years.

• Membership benefits. Credit card programs, member discounts on product purchases, special hotel rates at tournaments, airline discounts for NABCs and supplemental insurances are offered.

ACBL has long been the center of North American bridge activity. In 1987 ACBL celebrated its 50th anniversary. We invite you to enjoy our second half-century with us.

TABLE OF CONTENTS

Introduction

The American Contract Bridge League's *Club Series* student text is the first in a series of bridge books for beginning players. It is followed by the *Diamond*, *Heart* and *Spade Series*. The books focus on introducing players to duplicate bridge.

This series of books is unusual in the field of bridge writing for several reasons. First, they were written by a professional educator, Audrey Grant, who also happens to be a bridge player. Accordingly these books encompass all of the sound principles that facilitate learning any subject and are built on the firm foundation of a basic understanding of the game of bridge.

Next, the technical approach to these books was determined by surveying a cross section of North American bridge teachers. This means that whether a student learns bridge from this book in Vancouver, British Columbia; St. Louis, Missouri; or Orlando, Florida, that student will be able to play bridge with virtually any other beginning bridge players in North America.

Third, the effectiveness of the teaching principles was field-tested in five cities prior to the publication of the first book in this series (*The Club Series, 1987*), with more than 800 actual bridge students and at least 25 bridge teachers involved.

Finally, it is the first time in the 50-year history of ACBL that the sanctioning body for bridge in North America has produced its own basic bridge texts. The end result of the joint effort of Audrey Grant and ACBL is this series that enables the reader to learn bridge or to review and improve bridge techniques in a logical and progressive fashion. More importantly, the reader will have fun while learning the fundamental concepts of good bridge bidding, play and defense which will be beneficial for a lifetime.

LESSON 1
Getting Started

Introductory Concepts

The Language of Bidding

Scoring

Guidelines for Play

Summary

Activities

INTRODUCTORY CONCEPTS

As early as the 16th century, Europeans were playing triumph, a game similar to bridge. Triumph evolved into the game of whist which Edmond Hoyle made internationally famous through his book, *A Short Treatise on the Game of Whist*, published in 1742. A later version of this book became the most widely circulated book of the 18th century next to the Bible. It brought the phrase "according to Hoyle" into the language. With the introduction of the *auction* concept at the end of the 19th century, whist evolved into auction bridge. Around 1925, Harold Vanderbilt refined the scoring to bring the game into its present-day format of contract bridge.

This game, popularized by Ely Culbertson in the 1930s and by Charles Goren in the 1950s, became the world's most popular card game. Home-style or *rubber bridge* is played by nearly 40 million people in North America. Duplicate bridge is played principally under the auspices of the American Contract Bridge League. It is enjoyed in over 3,800 bridge clubs and at hundreds of bridge tournaments held annually across the country.

Bridge is a game for four people. All you need is a deck of cards and a scorepad, and you are set to go.

The Players

Bridge is a *partnership* game. Partnerships may be arranged ahead of time as is commonly done in *duplicate bridge*, or players may draw for partners. To draw for partners, the cards are shuffled and fanned face down on the table. The two players drawing the higher cards form one partnership; the two players drawing the lower cards form the other partnership.

Partners sit opposite each other at the table. For convenience, players often are referred to by their compass direction. North and South play against East and West.

NORTH

WEST   EAST

SOUTH

Your relationship with your partner is a very important part of the game. You will get much better results if you learn to work with and appreciate your partner.

The Deck and the Deal

Bridge is played with a deck of 52 cards. There are four *suits*: clubs (♣); diamonds (♦); hearts (♥), and spades (♠). The cards are *ranked* within each suit. The ace is the highest card in each suit followed by the king, queen, jack, 10 . . . and on down to the 2.

RANK
OF THE
CARDS

The game starts when one of the players *shuffles* and deals the cards. In duplicate bridge, the *dealer* is predetermined. In home-style bridge, it is customary to determine the dealer on the first *deal* by having each player draw a card from the deck and turn it face up on the table. The player who draws the highest card deals.

Suppose you are the dealer. You give out the cards one at a time face down. You start with the player on your left and continue around the table clockwise until all of the cards are gone. Each player's 13 cards constitute a *hand*.

The players pick up their hands and fan them so they can see their cards. It is easier if the cards are sorted into suits, alternating colors, with the cards in each suit arranged from left to right according to rank. However, that is a matter of personal preference. A sorted hand might look like this:

SORTED
BRIDGE
HAND

When a hand is discussed in a textbook or newspaper, it is usually displayed in a symbolic fashion with letters and numbers for the cards (A – ace, K – king, Q– queen, J – jack, etc.). The suits are displayed one underneath another with the spades first, followed by the hearts, diamonds, and clubs. The previous hand looks like this:

♠ K 10 6 3
♥ Q J 9
♦ A Q 7 2
♣ 8 5

Sometimes symbols are used for the suits as in this textbook. Sometimes alphabetic abbreviations are used (S – spades, H – hearts, D – diamonds, C – clubs). When discussing a complete deal, all four hands are shown in the following manner:

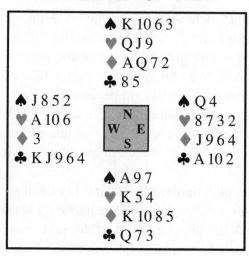

The Game's Two Stages

There are two stages in the game of bridge. First, there is *bidding*, as in an auction, to determine which partnership will undertake a *contract*. Second, the *play of the cards* follows where one side tries to fulfill the agreed contract while the other side tries to *defeat* it. Before looking at how the bidding works, it is helpful to understand something about how the cards are played out.

The Trick

The play of the cards starts when one player *leads* a card by placing it on the table and turning it face up. Each player, in clockwise rotation, plays a card of the same suit and puts it face up on the table. This is called *following suit*. The four cards played constitute a trick. The player who contributes the highest-ranking card wins the *trick*. This is a partnership game, so, if either you or your partner plays the highest card, your side wins the trick.

Here is an example of a trick.

2. North plays the ♦ 4.

1. West leads the ♦ J.

3. East plays the ♦ 9.

A
TRICK

4. South plays the ♦ A and wins the trick.

The player who wins the trick by playing the highest ranking card leads to the next trick. You must follow suit if you can. If you don't have any cards in the suit led, you play a card from another suit. This is called *discarding*. For example:

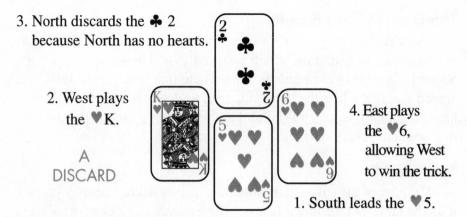

3. North discards the ♣ 2 because North has no hearts.

2. West plays the ♥ K.

A DISCARD

4. East plays the ♥ 6, allowing West to win the trick.

1. South leads the ♥ 5.

By the end of the deal, 13 tricks will have been played with one side having won more tricks than the other. Whenever your side wins a trick, place your card face down vertically in front of you. When your side *loses* a trick, place your card face down horizontally in front of you. By placing the card played to the first trick on your left and slightly offsetting each subsequent card to the right, at the end of the deal you will be left with a row of 13 cards in front of you. It will look like this:

Card played to the first trick

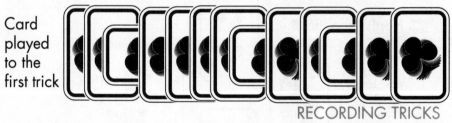

RECORDING TRICKS

This is a good way to record your winners and losers. At the end of the deal, you will have all of the cards you played in front of you. Now, you can have an instant replay. If you play other card games that have tricks, you may be accustomed to keeping track of winners by picking up all the cards in the trick, turning them over, and putting them in a stack in front of you. When you are learning bridge, it helps to keep your hand and look at it again when the play is over. This is also the required method of play in duplicate bridge.

Notrump and Trump

When the contract is played without a trump suit (notrump), the highest card played to a trick wins the trick provided it is of the same suit as the card led. On many deals, one suit is designated through the bidding as "wild" or as a *trump* suit. When there is a trump suit, a trump beats any card in another suit.

Here are some things to remember when playing a hand with a trump suit:

- You still have to follow suit if you can. You may play a trump if you have no cards left in the suit led. This is called *trumping* or *ruffing*.

- You do not have to trump. If your partner plays the ♦A and you have no diamonds, you may discard from another suit, since your partner's card will probably win the trick without your help.

- If more than one player puts a trump on a trick, the highest-ranked trump wins.

- The trump suit does not have to be led at any particular time. It is up to the discretion of each player to decide when to lead a trump.

Here is an example of a trick played with spades as the trump suit:

2. North, having no hearts left, trumps with the ♠7.

1. West leads the ♥A.

TRUMPING
A TRICK

3. East follows suit with the ♥10.

4. South plays the ♥8.

THE LANGUAGE OF BIDDING

Before the play of each deal, the contract must be determined. This is done through an *auction*. Having looked at the hands they were dealt, the members of each partnership would like the right to decide whether the deal is to be played in notrump or a particular trump suit.

To do this, each partnership must exchange information about their hands. They do this through the special language of bidding.

Bidding

After the cards have been dealt and the players have looked at their hands, the dealer starts the auction by making the first *call*. The dealer can either make a *bid* or refrain from bidding by saying "pass." The auction proceeds clockwise around the table with each player having an opportunity to bid or *pass*. This continues until three players in succession pass following a bid which now becomes the final contract.

A bid consists of two parts: a *level*, indicating the number of tricks the bidder proposes to take; and a *denomination*, indicating which suit or notrump the contract is to be played in. An example of a bid is:

ONE SPADE

Level   Denomination

The Level

Since the partnership that wins the auction must offer to take at least a majority of the 13 tricks available, the level named is in addition to the first six tricks. The first six tricks, called the *book*, is assumed as part of every bid. In other words, the one level represents $6 + 1 = 7$ tricks. Similarly, a bid at the two level is an undertaking to make $6 + 2 = 8$ tricks.

The highest level to which the bidding can proceed is the seven level. This implies a contract to take all 13 tricks. Thus, the level named in a bid is always a number from one to seven.

The Denomination

In addition to the level, a bid states whether the contract is to be played in a trump suit or in notrump. There are only five possible denominations — clubs, diamonds, hearts, spades, and notrump.

The Bidding Scale

As in an auction, each bid must be higher than the preceding bid. For this purpose, the denominations are ranked with clubs as the *lowest*, then diamonds, hearts, spades, and notrump as the highest. The suits are ranked in alphabetical order (♣, ♦, ♥, ♠).

The bids can be put on a scale called the *Bidding Scale*.

BIDDING SCALE			
SEVEN LEVEL			
7NT	SIX LEVEL		
7♠	6NT	FIVE LEVEL	
7♥	6♠	5NT	FOUR LEVEL
7♦	6♥	5♠	4NT
7♣	6♦	5♥	4♠
	6♣	5♦	4♥
		5♣	4♦
			4♣
THREE LEVEL			
3NT	TWO LEVEL		
3♠	2NT	ONE LEVEL	
3♥	2♠	1NT	
3♦	2♥	1♠	
3♣	2♦	1♥	
	2♣	1♦	
		1♣	

The bidding must always move up the bidding scale. If the preceding bid was 1 ♥, you can bid 1 ♠ since it is higher on the scale. However, you cannot bid 1 ♣. If you want to bid clubs, you would have to bid at the next higher level, 2 ♣. Of course, if at any point you do not want to bid any higher, you can pass.

Suppose North is the dealer. A typical auction might sound like this:

NORTH	EAST	SOUTH	WEST
(Dealer)			
Pass	Pass	1 ♥	Pass
2 ♥	Pass	Pass	Pass

Bidding is written across the page in this manner. You have to visualize it proceeding clockwise around the table.

The player who makes the first bid, South in the above example, is called the *opening bidder*. Note that the dealer is not forced to start the bidding. Also, although you have said pass, you may decide to bid later if you get another opportunity.

Three passes following a bid end the auction, and the final contract in the above example is 2 ♥. During the play, the partnership that won the auction becomes the offense and tries to take the number of tricks required to fulfill the contract. If the players on *offense* succeed, they *make* their contract. In the above example, North and South have contracted to make 2 ♥, a total of eight tricks (2 + 6 = 8) with hearts as the trump suit. The other partnership becomes the *defense* and tries to prevent the opponents from fulfilling their contract. If they succeed, they *defeat* or *set* the contract.

Declarer and Dummy

At the end of the bidding, the deal is played out. The member of the partnership who first suggested the denomination of the final contract is called the *declarer*. The declarer will play both of the partnership hands and try to fulfill the contract. Declarer's partner, who will not take part in the play of the cards, is appropriately called the *dummy*.

Here is how the play of a deal works:

The opponent to the *left of the declarer (LHO)* makes the *opening lead* by placing a card on the table and placing it face up. If you are declarer's partner, the dummy, you are next to play. You place all of your cards face up on the table in front of you and arrange them in four columns, one for each suit. If there is a trump suit, you place it on your right (declarer's left).

The table might look like this:

The Dummy

Opening Lead

DECLARER

The declarer now decides which card is to be played from dummy and names the card dummy is to play. For example, if you were declarer, you might say, "Play the queen of diamonds please, partner." Your *right-hand opponent (RHO)* then plays a card to the first trick, and you play a card from your hand. The play continues in this fashion with the lead to each subsequent trick coming from the hand, including dummy, which won the previous trick.

SCORING

At the end of the deal, points are awarded based on the final contract and whether or not it was fulfilled. Points can be earned in three ways:

> • *Trick score* for fulfilling a contract.
>
> • *Bonuses* for fulfilling special contracts.
>
> • *Penalties* for defeating the opponents' contract.

Trick Score

For each of the tricks bid and made (in excess of book), the partnership is awarded points based on the denomination of the contract.

> • 20 points per trick in clubs or diamonds *(Minor Suits)*
>
> • 30 points per trick in hearts or spades *(Major Suits)*
>
> • 40 points for the first trick in notrump, 30 points for each subsequent trick .

For example, making a contract of 2 ♠ is worth 60 points (30 + 30). Making a contract of 3NT is worth 100 points (40 + 30 + 30).

Bonuses

A large bonus is awarded if the partnership bids and makes a contract worth 100 or more points. This is called a *game* bonus. This can be earned by bidding to one of the following contracts:

> • 5 ♣ or 5 ♦ (20 + 20 + 20 + 20 + 20 = 100)
>
> • 4 ♥ or 4 ♠ (30 + 30 + 30 + 30 = 120)
>
> • 3NT (40 + 30 + 30 = 100)

Because of the possible bonus involved, a lot of the bidding centers around trying to reach one of these *game contracts*. This will be discussed in the next lesson.

A contract worth a trick score of less than 100 points is called a *partscore*. For example, a contract of 3 ♠ is a partscore since it is worth only 90 points (30 + 30 + 30). In duplicate bridge, a small bonus is awarded for bidding and making a partscore contract.

Note that you do not get the game bonus if you do not bid to a game contract, even if you take enough tricks. For example, if you are in a 3 ♠ contract and you take 10 tricks, the extra trick is worth the trick score (30 points) but does not entitle you to the game bonus. You must have bid 4 ♠ if you want to score the game bonus.

You receive an additional bonus if you bid and make a contract at the six level (12 tricks). This is called a *small slam*. An even larger bonus is awarded for bidding and making a contract at the seven level (all 13 tricks). This is called a *grand slam*.

The size of the bonuses is explained in the Appendix. For now, it is sufficient to know that there are certain key contracts on the Bidding Scale that are worth a large bonus in the scoring.

Penalties

If you do not make your contract, your opponents receive points for defeating you. The penalty for *going down* in your contract depends on the number of tricks by which your contract is defeated. (See the Appendix.)

At this point, it is only important to realize that you lose points if you bid too high and don't make your contract. This is why you shouldn't try for a game bonus with every hand. Sometimes, you have to stop in a partscore. Sometimes, rather than bid higher yourself, you have to let your opponents play in their contract and try to defeat them.

GUIDELINES FOR PLAY

The play of the hand, both from the declarer's and the defenders' points of view, is an exciting part of the game. It poses numerous challenges as to which card to play on each trick. For now, a few guidelines will get you started. The play is discussed in more detail in volume two, *The Diamond Series*.

The Opening Lead

The play starts with the player to the left of declarer making a lead. Entire books have been written on how to make good leads. Fortunately, there are a few simple rules that work splendidly to get you going.

When leading against a notrump contract, it is usually best to lead your longest suit. Long suits can be a good source of tricks. When choosing the card to lead, lead the top card if you have three or more high cards (A, K, Q, J, or 10) that are *touching* (e.g., K Q J or Q J 10). If you don't have touching high cards, lead a low card, (e.g., the 5 from K 10 7 5).

When leading against a suit contract, you can sometimes take advantage of your trumps by leading a short suit of one or two cards. You are hoping that, when the suit is led again, you will be able to win a trick by ruffing (playing a trump when you are out of the suit led). When leading from a two-card suit, lead the top card first.

Another good choice is a suit in which you have touching high cards. Lead the top of two or more touching high cards (e.g., K Q or Q J 10). Otherwise, lead a low card from a long suit.

Suppose you have the following hand:

♠ Q 6 3
♥ 5 2
♦ K Q J 7 6
♣ 9 5 3

If you are leading against a notrump contract, pick your longest suit, diamonds. Since you have touching high cards, lead the top card, the ♦ K. If you are leading against a contract with hearts as trump, the ♦ K would still be a good lead.

Suppose you have this hand:

$$\spadesuit \text{ K J 6 3}$$
$$\heartsuit \text{ 9 5 4 2}$$
$$\diamondsuit \text{ J 6 5 3}$$
$$\clubsuit \text{ 7}$$

If you are leading against a notrump contract, lead your longest suit. With a choice of long suits, it is usually best to pick your strongest suit. In this case, it would be spades. Since your high cards are not touching, lead low, the ♠3. If you are leading against a contract with hearts as trump, you also might lead a low spade. However, another good choice is the ♣7. You hope the club suit will be led again, and you will be able to win a trick by ruffing with one of your small trumps.

Subsequent Leads

When you win a trick during the play and have to lead to the next trick, the situation is a little different from the opening lead. In addition to the cards in your own hand, you can now see dummy's cards. You might also be able to remember some of the cards that have been played to previous tricks.

If you are defending, it is a good idea to return the suit that your partner led originally, unless you have a valid reason for not doing so.

If you are the declarer in a notrump contract, it's a good idea to lead a card from the longest *combined* suit between your hand and the dummy at your earliest opportunity. In a trump contract, you often lead the trump suit first and continue until the opponents have none left.

Second-Hand Play

If the opponent on your right leads a card, you have to play the second card to the trick. A general piece of advice, when you are not sure what to do, is to play a low card, second hand low.

The advantage of playing low is that your partner will be last to play to this trick. Partner will be in a better position to decide whether to play a high or low card after seeing the cards played by both opponents.

Third-Hand Play

If your partner leads a card, you will contribute the third card to the trick. If it doesn't look as though partner's card will win the trick, it is usually up to you to try to win the trick for your side by playing a high card, third hand high.

You only need to play as high a card as is necessary to win the trick. For example, if you have both the king and the queen, and two little cards have been played, you can play the queen. Either it will win the trick or it will force your left-hand opponent to play the ace, since you have the king. If either your partner or your RHO (right-hand opponent) has already played the ace, you don't need to play a high card. Play a low card instead.

Fourth-Hand Play

Usually it is easiest to decide what to do when you are last to play to a trick. You can see what has already been played, and you can decide whether you need to play a high card to win the trick or a low card if you can't (or don't wish to) win the trick. Don't forget to watch what your partner has played. Only one of you needs to win the trick, not both!

SUMMARY

Four players sit down to play a game of bridge and divide themselves into two partnerships, North and South against East and West. The cards are dealt out clockwise and face down. The players pick up their hands and sort the cards into suits.

The dealer starts the auction by making a bid or by saying "pass." A bid consists of a level which denotes the number of tricks to be taken (in addition to the six tricks called the book) and a denomination of clubs, diamonds, hearts, spades, or notrump. The auction continues clockwise. Each player either makes a bid that is higher on the bidding scale than the previous bid or says "pass." The auction ends when a bid is followed by three passes. The last bid becomes the final contract.

In the partnership that wins the auction, the player who first mentions the denomination of the final contract becomes the declarer. The opponent on declarer's left makes the opening lead, and then declarer's partner, the dummy, puts the dummy's hand face up on the table.

The declarer plays both of the partnership's hands and tries to take enough tricks to fulfill the contract. The opponents try to take enough tricks to defeat the contract. At the end of the deal, the partnerships are awarded a score depending upon whether or not the contract was made.

There are bonuses awarded for bidding and making special contracts. Most important are the game contracts of 3NT, 4♥, 4♠, 5♣, and 5♦. There are special bonuses for making small slams and grand slams.

ACTIVITIES

Exercise One — Taking Tricks

Dealer: North

Deal the cards face down starting with the player on your left. Continue around the table clockwise until all of the cards are dealt. Each player will have 13 cards.

The players pick up their hands and sort them into suits. The player to the left of the dealer leads any card by placing it face up on the table. All of the other players follow suit by playing a card of the same suit. If a player can't follow suit, a card from another suit should be put on the trick.

The highest-ranking card played of the suit led wins the trick. The player who wins leads to the next trick. If you win a trick, place your card vertically face down on the table in front of you. If you lose a trick, place it horizontally face down on the table in front of you. Try to take as many tricks as you can.

Exercise Two — Predicting Your Winners

Dealer: East

Leader: South

After you have sorted your hand into suits, estimate the cards in each suit that might win tricks. From the first exercise, you know that high cards and sometimes small cards from long suits win tricks. You can write an "x" rather than the specific small card you think will be a winner. Here is an example:

YOUR HAND	YOUR ESTIMATE	
♠ A K 4 3 2	♠ A K x	(3)
♥ K Q 8	♥ K or Q	(1)
♦ 9 8	♦ —	(0)
♣ Q J 10	♣ Q	(1)

After you have played the deal, turn over your winners and compare them with your estimate.

Exercise Three — The Opening Lead

Each player takes the cards for one of the suits and helps construct the following hand in the middle of the table:

♠ A 3 2
♥ A
♦ K Q J 10 9 8
♣ A 3 2

What would you lead if it were your turn. How many tricks would you expect to take with this hand?

Exercise Four — Playing with a Partner

Dealer: South

Leader: West

Work with the person sitting opposite you to take as many tricks as you can.

When West leads, all the other players turn their hands over and take a moment to look at the lead. What other card do you think West holds? What is West's longest suit? How many cards, at least, does West hold in that suit? What does the card led tell you about other cards West might hold in the suit?

Did you like working with a partner? What other things would you like to know that would help you when working with a partner?

Exercise Five — Playing in a Trump Contract

Dealer: West

Leader: North

The heart suit is wild or trump. Work with your partner to take as many tricks as you can. You must follow suit. When you can't, play a trump. Cards in the trump suit rank higher than cards in any of the other suits.

What did you think about playing in a trump suit? Why is having short suits valuable when playing in a trump suit?

Exercise Six — The Bidding

(E-Z Deal Cards: #1, Hand 1 – Dealer, North)

The Bidding

Each partnership uses a bidding conversation to agree on a trump or notrump contract.

Which suit do North and South like best? Who would suggest this suit first? Why would it benefit them to find they like this suit?

How many tricks could North estimate taking? How about South? How many tricks can North and South take as a partnership?

Answer all of the above questions for East and West.

```
Dealer: North
              ♠ A 9 4
              ♥ A 7 6
              ♦ 9 6
              ♣ A J 9 6 3
  ♠ 7 3                    ♠ 6 2
  ♥ J 10 9        N        ♥ 8 4 3 2
  ♦ K Q J 4 3  W     E     ♦ A 7 5 2
  ♣ Q 5 2         S        ♣ K 10 7
              ♠ K Q J 10 8 5
              ♥ K Q 5
              ♦ 10 8
              ♣ 8 4
```

Which partnership predicted the most tricks? In which contract?

Exercise Seven — The Play

Play the deal in Exercise Six.

Who first mentioned the suit that is trump? Who is the declarer? Who makes the opening lead? Which hand is dummy? What is the declarer's plan to make the contract?

Exercise Eight — Bidding and Playing a Complete Deal
(E-Z Deal Cards: #1, Hand 2 – Dealer, North)

The Bidding

Do North and South have a suit they would like to be trump? Do East and West have a suit they would like to be trump? If a partnership cannot agree on a trump suit, how do they decide on the final denomination for the contract?

How many tricks could North estimate taking? How many tricks could South estimate taking? What is the total number of tricks predicted by North and South? How many tricks could East estimate taking? How many tricks

```
Dealer: North
              ♠ J 5 2
              ♥ K Q J 8
              ♦ 9 3
              ♣ 10 8 6 4
♠ A K 8              ♠ 9 7 3
♥ 10 7 5      N      ♥ A 9 3
♦ A K Q    W   E    ♦ 7 5 4 2
♣ 9 5 3 2     S      ♣ A K Q
              ♠ Q 10 6 4
              ♥ 6 4 2
              ♦ J 10 8 6
              ♣ J 7
```

could West estimate taking? What is the total number of tricks predicted by East and West?

Which partnership predicted the higher number of tricks? What would the final contract be?

The Play

Which partner first suggested the denomination of the contract? This player will be the declarer.

The player to the left of the declarer makes the opening lead. The hand of the declarer's partner, the dummy, is placed face up on the table. The declarer tries to take as many tricks as the partnership predicted. How many tricks should the declarer end up with?

Exercise Nine — The Language of Bidding

How many tricks does each of the following bids represent?

1) 2♣   2) 4♠   3) 7NT
4) 3NT   5) 5♦   6) 1♥
7) 6♣

Exercise Ten — Trick Scores for Partscores and Games

What trick score would be given for making each of the following contracts?

1) 2♠   2) 4♥   3) 4♠
4) 5♣   5) 3♦   6) 1♥
7) 3NT   8) 4♣   9) 5♦

Circle the contracts with a trick score of at least 100 points. These are called game contracts.

Answers to Lesson 1 exercises are on pages 290–292.

LESSON 2
Objectives

Hand Valuation

The Golden Rules

The Roles of the Partners

Opening the Bidding

Responder's Approach to an Opening Bid of
One Notrump

Guidelines for Play

Summary

The Finer Points

Activities

You and your partner work together to reach your best contract. Through bidding, you decide the level to which you can afford to bid and the denomination, suit or notrump, that the partnership prefers. To make these decisions, you and your partner need to know the combined strength and the distribution of your hands. Then, you see how this strength and distribution relate to having a reasonable chance of making the various contracts on the Bidding Scale. The strength of your hand can be determined by using the *point-count* system popularized by Charles Goren.

HAND VALUATION

Tricks are taken with high cards and smaller cards in long suits. *Hand valuation* takes both into consideration. The features of your hand are assigned points. They are totaled together to give an estimate of the strength of your hand.

High-card points

Points are awarded for each of the four highest cards in a suit (ace, king, queen, and jack) on a 4-3-2-1 scale. These are referred to as *high-card points or HCP.*

Ace	4 points
King	3 points
Queen	2 points
Jack	1 point

Distribution Points

In addition, *distribution points (or length points)* are assigned for each suit of five cards or longer. One point is added for every card over four:

5-card suit	1 point
6-card suit	2 points
7-card suit	3 points
8-card suit	4 points

Hand Value

By adding together your high-card points and distribution points, you arrive at a total point count for your hand. Let's see how this works:

	High-Card Points	Distribution Points	Total Points
♠ A K 7	7	0	7
♥ Q J 10 9 8 7	3	2	5
♦ Q 7	2	0	2
♣ 10 9	0	0	0
	12	2	14

The value of the hand is 14 points.

	High-Card Points	Distribution Points	Total Points
♠ 10 9 8 6 5	0	1	1
♥ A Q 8 7 4	6	1	7
♦ A K	7	0	7
♣ A	4	0	4
	17	2	19

The value of the hand is 19 points.

Shape

The shape of your hand is also important. There are two general shapes — *balanced* and *unbalanced*. A balanced hand has no *voids* (zero cards in a suit), no *singletons* (one card in a suit), and no more than one *doubleton* (two cards in a suit).

The following three hand patterns are balanced:

x x x x	x x x x	x x x x x
x x x	x x x x	x x x
x x x	x x x	x x x
x x x	x x	x x
4-3-3-3	4-4-3-2	5-3-3-2

The numbers beneath each pattern refer to the number of cards in each suit: 4-3-3-3 means there are four cards in one suit and three cards in each of the other three suits. It doesn't matter which suit has the four cards. The second pattern, 4-4-3-2, describes a hand with four cards in each of two suits, three cards in one suit, and two cards in one suit. The last pattern, 5-3-3-2, describes a hand with one five-card suit, two three-card suits, and one two-card suit.

A hand that does not have one of the above hand patterns is said to be unbalanced.

THE GOLDEN RULES

The Game Bonus

Before considering how you and your partner exchange information about the strength and shape of your hands, let's look back at your objectives in the bidding. Bidding and making a game contract may give your partnership a large bonus. This goal is often within the reach of one of the pairs. Seeking the game bonus is a priority for your partnership. How many points in the combined partnership hands are needed for you to take enough tricks to make a game contract? Experience suggests the following guideline:

5 ♦ or 5 ♣ (Minor Suits)	29 combined points
4 ♠ or 4 ♥ (Major Suits)	26 combined points
3NT	26 combined points

You may wonder why you need 26 combined points for a 10-trick contract in the major suits, spades and hearts, and also for the nine-trick contract of 3NT. Because of the power of the trump suit, it is usually possible to make one extra trick in a trump contract with hands of equal strength. To make 5♦ or 5♣, however, requires 29 combined points since you need 11 tricks, two more tricks than you need to fulfill a 3NT contract.

The Golden Fit

There are two parts to making a bid — the level and the denomination. The level is generally determined by the combined strength of the partnership hands. The denomination represents the choice to play in a trump suit or in notrump. This decision is based on the partnership's combined distribution in each suit.

To name a suit as trump, you and your partner want a comfortable majority of cards in the suit. There are 13 cards in each suit. If you have six or fewer in the combined partnership hands, the opponents have the majority. Such a suit is unlikely to make a good trump suit for your side. If you have seven, the opponents have only six and you have a small majority. This might be adequate but it is cutting things a little close. If you have eight or more, this represents a comfortable majority since the opponents have five or fewer.

When you and your partner have at least eight combined cards in a suit, think of it as a *Golden Fit*. If you are going to play in a trump suit, you generally want to play in a Golden Fit. If you don't have an eight-card or longer fit in any suit, you generally want to play in notrump.

Partscores and the Golden Fit

If you have fewer than 26 combined points, you do not have enough strength for a game contract. You want to play in the best partscore contract. If you have a Golden Fit, play in that suit at as low a level as possible.

Games and the Golden Fit

With 26 or more combined points, you would like to try for a game bonus. With a Golden Fit in hearts or spades, you can bid 4♥ or 4♠. But, suppose you have between 26 and 28 combined points, and your only Golden Fit is in clubs or diamonds?

You are presented with an awkward choice. You could play in your Golden Fit in a partscore contract. This would be safe but would give up the opportunity for a game bonus. You could play in your Golden Fit at the game level. This would be risky since you generally need at least 29 points to make a contract of 5♣ or 5♦. A third choice is to play in a game contract of 3NT even though you have a Golden Fit in a minor suit. This should be about right as far as the strength goes, but it would ignore the principle of playing in a Golden Fit when you have one.

Experience has shown that you will achieve better results in the long run if you make the third choice. Play in 3NT when you have 26 or more combined points — even when you have a Golden Fit in a minor suit. There will be times when you could make either a partscore or a game in the minor suit, and you can't make 3NT. These occasions will be more than offset by the times this principle works for you (i.e., you make 3NT but can't make a minor suit game, or you get a game bonus in notrump rather than a partscore in the minor suit). The best bid is the one that works most of the time. There are no perfect bids that work all of the time!

For this reason, the partnership should always try to reach a game contract when there are 26 or more combined points. With a Golden Fit in hearts or spades, they should play in 4♥ or 4♠. Otherwise, they should play in 3NT. Three game contracts are Golden:

$$\left.\begin{array}{l} 4♠ \\ 4♥ \\ 3NT \end{array}\right\} \textit{Golden Games}$$

Only rarely should you consider playing in 5♣ or 5♦.

THE ROLES OF THE PARTNERS

You and your partner work together, through the bidding, to discover whether you have enough strength and the right distribution to go for one of the Golden Game bonuses.

The Opener

Each player has a role. The partner who opens the bidding gets the first opportunity to provide information to the partnership. The opening bidder does not know anything about partner's hand. Opener's best approach is to try and tell partner something about both the strength and the distribution of the hand. The opening bidder is sometimes referred to as the *describer*. The opening bid starts to paint a picture of the describer's hand for partner.

The Responder

The partner of the opening bidder is called the *responder*. As responder, you have the advantage of having heard your partner's first descriptive bid. You can see, in addition, what you have in your own hand, and, therefore, you can take the responsibility of guiding the partnership to its best contract. The responder is sometimes referred to as the *captain*. In general, it is up to the responder, or captain, to determine the contract. Responder does this by keeping two questions in mind:

- What Level?
- What Denomination?

What Level?

In deciding what level to bid to, the responder must try to do two things:

- Estimate the combined strength of the two hands, and

- Determine whether the partnership belongs in a partscore, game, or slam contract.

Slams are relatively rare. We can wait to consider them. Since the partnership should be in a game contract if there are 26 or more points, responder's decision boils down to determining whether the partnership has a combined total of 26 points. If it does, responder steers the partnership to the appropriate game contract. If it doesn't, responder steers the partnership to a partscore contract.

What Denomination?

In addition to determining the appropriate level, the responder must try to estimate the combined distribution of the two hands to determine whether the partnership should be playing in a suit or in notrump.

If responder knows that the partnership belongs in a partscore contract, responder wants to steer the partnership into a Golden Fit, if one can be found, otherwise, into notrump. If responder knows that there is enough combined strength for game, responder wants to steer the partnership into 4 ♥ or 4♠, if there is a Golden Fit in a major suit, otherwise, into 3NT. Remember that the partnership is generally interested only in the Golden Games, ignoring 5♣ and 5♦.

OPENING THE BIDDING

Once you know the strength and shape of your hand, you are ready to decide whether to open the bidding. The dealer has the first opportunity and will either pass or make a bid at the one level. Since your partnership needs 26 or more combined points for one of the game bonuses, you need at least half of that, 13 points, to consider opening with a bid of one.

Opening 1NT

How does the opener decide on the best opening bid? Since the opener is the describer, the opening bid should give as much information as possible to partner about the strength and distribution of the hand. One of the most descriptive opening bids in bridge is 1NT. Notrump bids take up all of the bidding room at the one level. They require more than a minimum number of points to take the same number of tricks as a suit bid at the same level. Suits usually produce one more trick because of trumps.

REQUIREMENTS FOR OPENING THE BIDDING ONE NOTRUMP

- 16, 17 or 18 points
- A balanced hand

The following hands would qualify as 1NT opening bids because they have both the strength and distribution required for the bid.

♠ J 10 9	♠ Q 9 8 7	♠ J 7 3
♥ A 7 6	♥ K J	♥ A Q 9
♦ K 8 7 2	♦ A J 6 2	♦ K Q 10 8 5
♣ A K J	♣ K Q J	♣ A J

The following hands, however, would not qualify:

♠ J 10 9	♠ A Q 8 7	♠ J
♥ A 7 6	♥ K J	♥ A Q 9 3
♦ 9 8 7 2	♦ A J 6 2	♦ K Q 10 8 5
♣ A K J	♣ K Q J	♣ A J 7

The first hand is balanced but contains only 13 points, not enough strength to open the bidding 1NT. The second hand is also balanced but contains 21 points, too much to open 1NT. The third hand contains 18 points, but it is not balanced since it has a singleton. Remember that opener is trying to paint a picture for responder.

Opening a Suit at the One Level

To open a suit at the one level requires 13 to 21 points (combining high-card points and distribution points). If you have 22 or more points, you start at the two level. Hands with 22 or more points are uncommon and will be discussed briefly in the Appendix.

You need five or more cards in a major suit to open the bidding 1 ♥ or 1 ♠. You have seen that 4 ♥ and 4♠ are Golden Games. Opener wants to paint as clear a picture as possible of the cards for partner. When opener starts with 1 ♥ or 1 ♠, the bid describes a hand that has at least 13 points and at least five cards in the suit bid.

REQUIREMENTS FOR OPENING THE BIDDING ONE IN A SUIT

- With fewer than 13 points, pass.
- With 13 to 21 points
    - With a five-card or longer suit:
        - Bid your longest suit.
        - Bid the *higher ranking* of two five-card or six-card suits.
    - With no five-card or longer suit:
        - Bid your longer minor suit.
        - Bid the higher ranking of two four-card minor suits or the lower ranking of two three-card minor suits.

Let's see how this works:

	HCP + Distribution Points	
♠ A Q J 4 3	8	You have 14 points, enough to open the bidding.
♥ 5 3 2	0	You have a five-card suit, so open your longest
♦ K Q 7	5	suit, 1♠.
♣ J 7	1	
	14	

HCP +
Distribution Points

♠ A 2	4	You have 16 points and an unbalanced hand.
♥ K 9 8 7 3	4	With two five-card suits, open the higher-rank-
♦ Q J 9 8 7	4	ing suit, 1 ♥.
♣ A	4	
	16	

♠ 9 8	0	You have a balanced hand but only 15 points,
♥ A K Q	9	not enough to open 1NT. With no five-card suit,
♦ K Q 10 9	5	open a minor suit. With two four-card suits, bid
♣ J 10 9 8	1	the higher-ranking, 1 ♦.
	15	

♠ K Q 3	5	With only 6 points, you do not have enough to
♥ 9 8 7 6 3	1	open the bidding. You would pass.
♦ 8 4 2	0	
♣ 10 6	0	
	6	

♠ Q J 10 9	3	With 13 points and no five-card suit, open a
♥ A 9 8	4	minor suit. With a choice of three-card suits,
♦ Q 4 3	2	open the lower-ranking, 1 ♣.
♣ A 9 7	4	
	13	

♠ A 9 8 7 6	5	With enough to open the bidding and a hand con-
♥ 6	0	taining a five-card or longer suit, open the longer
♦ 4	0	suit, 1 ♣.
♣ K Q J 9 8 3	8	
	13	

RESPONDER'S APPROACH TO AN OPENING BID OF ONE NOTRUMP

If your partner opens the bidding, you as responder have a picture of opener's hand. You also know what you have in your own hand. Your objective is to put this information together and decide both the level and the denomination of the final contract.

If opener starts the bidding with 1NT, that bid gives responder a very clear description of opener's hand — 16, 17, or 18 points and balanced shape. Let's see how responder can use this information.

Responder Decides What Level

When your partner opens the bidding 1NT, you as responder know that opener has 16, 17, or 18 points. By adding your strength to that of opener's, you usually can tell whether the partnership has at least 26 points, enough for a game contract, or fewer than 26 points, enough for only a partscore contract.

Let's look at some sample hands you might hold as responder:

HCP +
Distribution Points

♠ A 8 7	4	With 12 points, responder knows the combined
♥ A Q 8 7 6 3	8	strength is either 28 (12 + 16), 29 (12 + 17), or
♦ 8 6 2	0	30 (12 + 18) points. Responder is sure there is
♣ 7	0	enough combined strength for game and should
	12	steer the partnership toward one of the Golden Games.

HCP +
Distribution Points

♠ J 10 9	1	With only 6 points, responder knows that the
♥ 9 8 7	0	combined strength lies between 22 (6 + 16) to
♦ Q 9 7 4	2	24 (6 + 18) points. The partnership has fewer
♣ K 4 2	3	than the 26 points needed for a game contract.
	6	Responder would pass.

♠ Q 8 5	2	With 9 points, responder knows the combined
♥ K 6	3	strength could be as little as 25 (9 + 16) points
♦ K J 4 2	4	or as much as 27 (9 + 18) points. Responder
♣ 10 9 5 3	0	will have to get more information from opener
	9	before deciding whether the partnership should
		be in game. Bid 2NT.

Responder Decides What Denomination

In addition to deciding the level of the contract, responder decides the denomination. To do this, responder first must determine whether there is a Golden Fit.

It is important to recall that an opening 1NT bid shows one of three hand patterns — 4-3-3-3, 4-4-3-2 or 5-3-3-2 (see page 26). When opener bids 1NT, opener always has at least two cards in each suit and usually at least three cards. **Sometimes opener has four or more cards in a suit and occasionally five cards.** Let's look at some examples to see how responder uses this information to decide if there is a Golden Fit.

♠ J 9 8 7 4 2	Responder has a six-card spade suit. Opener has at
♥ Q J 2	least two cards in spades, so responder can be sure
♦ A K	that there is a Golden Fit in spades. Bid 4♠.
♣ 7 4	

♠ 9 6 3
♥ J 8 5
♦ 8 7 5
♣ Q 7 6 3

Since opener rarely has a five-card suit, it is unlikely that there is a Golden Fit in spades, hearts, or diamonds. There is some possibility that opener has a four-card club suit, but responder can't be very sure of a Golden Fit. Pass.

♠ A 4
♥ K Q 9 7 6
♦ J 6 3
♣ 9 8 3

With a five-card heart suit, it is very likely that there is a Golden Fit. Only in the rare cases where opener has a doubleton heart will there not be a Golden Fit. Bid 3♥.

Responder Decides What Level and What Denomination

Let's see how responder puts the pieces together to steer the partnership to an appropriate contract.

HCP +
Distribution Points

♠ J 8	1	
♥ K Q J 9 8 2	8	
♦ 9 2	0	
♣ K 8 3	3	
	12	

With 12 points, responder knows the combined strength is at least 28 (12 + 16) points, more than enough for a game contract. With a six-card heart suit, responder knows there is a Golden Fit in hearts. Responder can take the partnership directly to its final contract of 4♥.

♠ J 5 3	1	
♥ 10 7	0	
♦ J 8 7 5 4 2	3	
♣ 9 8	0	
	4	

With only 4 points, responder knows that there are at most 22 (4 + 18) points, only enough for a part-score. With a six-card diamond suit, responder can be assured of a Golden Fit and confidently put the partnership in a safe contract of 2♦.

HCP +
Distribution Points

♠ J 2	1	Holding 10 points, responder knows that there
♥ 9 3	0	are at least 26 (10 + 16) points, enough for game.
♦ A K 9 6 4 2	9	With a six-card diamond suit, responder can be
♣ 8 6 3	0	assured of a Golden Fit in diamonds. However,
	10	5 ♦ is not one of the Golden Games. Instead, responder steers the partnership into a final contract of 3NT.

GUIDELINES FOR PLAY

The opening lead is made, partner puts down the dummy, and you, as declarer, have to play the hand. How do you go about it? Playing a hand is an exciting exercise. As with all tasks of this nature, you should start by making a *plan*. The first step is to pause to consider your objective: how many winners must you take, or how many losers can you afford if you are to make your contract. Then, you need to assess your current position — look at your winners and losers. How close are you to fulfilling your objective? Once you have done this, you will be in a better position to decide what to do next. On many deals, you will be able to meet your objective with little extra effort.

Declarer's Objective

Declarer's objective is to make the contract by taking the required number of tricks. First, declarer must determine how many tricks are required. This is calculated by adding six tricks (book) to the level of the final contract. For example:

CONTRACT	NUMBER OF TRICKS REQUIRED
2♦	6 + 2 = 8 tricks
3NT	6 + 3 = 9 tricks
4♥	6 + 4 = 10 tricks

Counting Winners

After determining your objective, you as declarer must see how close you are to achieving it. You do this by examining your combined holding in each suit to see how many *sure tricks* you have. A sure trick is one that you can take without giving up the lead to your opponents. Let's look at some examples.

DUMMY: 7 4   With this combination of cards in a suit, you can take one trick, the ace. Once you take the
DECLARER: A 5   ace, the opponents have the remaining high cards in the suit.

DUMMY: A 6 4   You have two sure tricks. You can take one trick with dummy's ace, playing a small card
DECLARER: K 5 2   from your hand. You can then lead one of dummy's small cards to your king.

DUMMY: Q 8 3   You have three sure tricks. You can take two tricks with your ace and king, playing the small
DECLARER: A K 4   cards from dummy. Next, lead the 4 to dummy's queen. With the same number of cards in both hands, it does not matter in what order you take your sure tricks. For example, you could win the first trick with dummy's queen and the last two with your ace and king.

| DUMMY: | Q 8 | This looks similar to the previous example, but you can take only two sure tricks. When you play your ace and king, you will have to follow suit by playing dummy's 8 and queen. |
| DECLARER: | A K | |

| DUMMY: | Q 8 | You have three sure tricks but must be careful in the order in which you take them. If you play the ace and king first, you will have to play dummy's queen on one of these tricks. When the suit is unevenly divided between the two hands, you should take your sure tricks by playing the high card from the short side first. Win the first trick with dummy's queen, and then play the 8 to your ace and king. |
| DECLARER: | A K 4 | |

Taking Your Tricks

After determining the number of sure tricks in each suit, add them together to see if you have enough tricks to make the contract. If you do, playing the hand is merely a matter of taking your tricks. As you saw in the last example, you sometimes must be careful of the order in which you take your tricks, playing the high cards from the short side first.

There is a further consideration when you are playing in a trump contract. If you have enough tricks to make your contract, you start by playing the trump suit until the opponents have no cards left in the trump suit. This is referred to as *drawing trumps*. You do this to make certain that the opponents cannot play a trump on one of your sure tricks, turning a winning trick into a losing trick.

If you add up your sure tricks and find that you don't have enough to fulfill the contract, there is some work to do. In future lessons, we'll examine ways to establish the additional tricks.

SUMMARY

Your hand value is calculated by combining your high-card points and distribution points using the following scale:

HIGH-CARD POINTS		DISTRIBUTION POINTS	
Ace	4 points	Five-card suit	1 point
King	3 points	Six-card suit	2 points
Queen	2 points	Seven-card suit	3 points
Jack	1 point	Eight-card suit	4 points

Each hand is either balanced or unbalanced. There are only three balanced hand patterns. All others are unbalanced.

THE BALANCED PATTERNS:

x x x x	x x x x	x x x x x
x x x	x x x x	x x x
x x x	x x x	x x x
x x x	x x	x x
4-3-3-3	4-4-3-2	5-3-3-2

One of the main objectives of the partnership is to bid to a game contract when there is sufficient combined strength.

THE APPROXIMATE REQUIREMENTS FOR A GAME CONTRACT ARE:

5 ♦ or 5 ♣ (Minor Suits)	29 combined points
4 ♠ or 4 ♥ (Major Suits)	26 combined points
3NT	26 combined points

A second objective is to reach the right denomination by looking for a Golden Fit of at least eight cards in the combined hands. If there is no Golden Fit, then the contract should be played in notrump.

If you and your partner have fewer than 26 combined points, play a partscore in a Golden Fit or notrump or let the opponents play the contract. If you have 26 or more points, play in one of the Golden Games:

4 ♠
4 ♥ } GOLDEN GAMES
3NT

OPENING THE BIDDING

Opener is describer. The rules for opening the bidding at the one level are:

- With 16 to 18 points and a balanced hand, bid 1NT.
- With 13 to 21 points:
  - With a five-card or longer suit:
    - Bid your longest suit
    - Bid the higher ranking of two five-card or two six-card suits
  - With no five-card or longer suit:
    - Bid your longer minor suit
    - Bid the higher ranking of two four-card minor suits or the lower ranking of two three-card minor suits

RESPONDER'S DECISIONS

Responder is the captain. Responder decides:

WHAT LEVEL?
- With 26 or more combined points, bid a Golden Game.

WHAT DENOMINATION?
- With a Golden Fit in a major suit, play with that suit as trump in a partscore or game contract.
- With a Golden Fit in a minor suit, play with that suit as trump in a partscore contract. Play 3NT rather than a minor suit game.

When playing a hand, first determine the number of tricks you need to make your contract. Then, count the number of sure tricks in the combined hands. If you have enough tricks, take them. Be careful to play the high card from the short side first when a suit is unevenly divided between the two hands. In a trump contract, draw trumps before taking sure tricks in the other suits.

THE FINER POINTS

Distribution Points

Void	3 points
Singleton	2 points
Doubleton	1 point

While the use of high-card points in hand valuation is a commonly accepted standard, there are two common ways of valuing distribution when opening the bidding.

In this text, we recommend that you add points for long suits (1 point for a five-card suit, 2 points for a six-card suit, etc.). Another method is to add points for short suits according to the following scale:

This point scale is usually adjusted when you have high cards in a short suit (for example, a singleton king) and can become quite complex.

When you first pick up your hand, the value of short suits may not be apparent. It is often easier to see that long suits are valuable because of their extra trick-taking potential. Since the two methods result in approximately the same value (if you have a long suit somewhere, you have a short suit somewhere else), we suggest that you count for long suits when opening the bidding. Later in the text you will see that points are given for short suits once the partnership finds a Golden Fit.

Opening 1NT

DUPLICATE PREVIEW

RULES FOR OPENING 1NT

15 to 17 POINTS

BALANCED HAND

A common variation is to open the bidding 1NT with 15, 16, or 17 points rather than 16, 17, or 18. It is easy to adjust to this style (or even other ranges for 1NT) but this text is consistent with the 16 to 18-point range.

Some players do not like to open 1NT with two small cards in a suit ("worthless doubleton") or when they have a five-card major suit. While this style has some merit, it can make later bidding awkward. For the beginning student, the more straightforward requirements in the text are recommended.

Opening a Suit at the One Level

The requirements given in the text ensure that an opening bid of 1 ♥ or 1 ♠ shows at least a five-card suit. This is the basis for a *Five-Card-Major* System of bidding. A more classic approach is always to open the bidding in your longest suit, which sometimes means opening with a four-card major suit. While such a *Four-Card Major System* simplifies the rules for opening the bidding, this text has been written to conform with the more modern style of five-card majors. Once you are familiar with the basic bidding concepts, it is easy to adjust to the style of your choice with your favorite partner.

Some authorities recommend opening the bidding with fewer than 13 points in certain situations. Since this involves additional consider- ations such as opener's position at the table or the location of the high cards in specific suits, it is beyond the scope of this text. As you gain experience, you will be able to introduce more judgment into deciding when to open the bidding. When getting started, 13 points is an excellent minimum requirement for opening the bidding.

ACTIVITIES

Exercise One — Hand Valuation

Add up the high-card points (HCP) and the distribution points on each of the following hands. What is the total point value for each hand?

1) ♠ 10 9 8 6 5 3
   ♥ A K Q
   ♦ 9 8
   ♣ Q J

2) ♠ A Q J
   ♥ 9 6 4 3 2
   ♦ J 9 4 3
   ♣ 9

3) ♠ 8 6 3
   ♥ A Q J 9
   ♦ K 9 8
   ♣ A K Q

HCP: _____   HCP: _____   HCP: _____

Distr. Points: _____   Distr. Points: _____   Distr. Points: _____

Total Points: _____   Total Points: _____   Total Points: _____

Exercise Two — Hand Shapes

A balanced hand has no voids, no singletons, and no more than one doubleton. Which of the following hands are balanced?

1) ♠ K J 7 3
   ♥ A 9 5
   ♦ Q J 6
   ♣ A J 10

2) ♠ J 7
   ♥ K 9 7 4
   ♦ K Q 10 5
   ♣ A J 8

3) ♠ K Q 3
   ♥ A
   ♦ Q 8 6 4 2
   ♣ K J 6 5

4) ♠ K 8
   ♥ A K 8 6 2
   ♦ K Q 7 3
   ♣ 9 5

5) ♠ K 8
   ♥ 9 5 2
   ♦ A Q 8
   ♣ K Q J 7 3

6) ♠ Q 6
   ♥ K 4 2
   ♦ A J 8 7 5 2
   ♣ K 3

Exercise Three — What Level?

How many points do you need in the combined hands to make the following contracts?

1) 3NT   2) 4♥   3) 4♠

4) 5♣   5) 5♦

Exercise Four — What Denomination?

Take all the cards in a single suit (e.g., the heart suit) and spread them face down on the table. By separating the cards into various groupings, discuss the following questions as a group.

How many cards must a partnership hold to have a majority of the cards in the suit? Would a minimum majority of cards in a suit be adequate in a trump suit? Why? How many cards of a suit should a partnership hold to be comfortable making it the trump suit? In how many ways can eight cards in a suit be divided between the partnership hands? Are the specific high cards you hold in a suit important when choosing the trump suit? (You might try turning the cards face up when answering the last question.)

Exercise Five — Opening the Bidding

How many total points are in each of the following hands? Determine the proper opening bid.

1) ♠ 9 6 4
   ♥ Q J 9 8
   ♦ A K 4
   ♣ A Q J

HCP: _____
Distr. Points: _____
Total Points: _____
Opening Bid _____

2) ♠ A J 9 8 7
   ♥ K 7
   ♦ K J 8 2
   ♣ 9 8

HCP: _____
Distr. Points: _____
Total Points: _____
Opening Bid _____

3) ♠ 10 9 8
   ♥ Q 9 8 7 6
   ♦ A Q J
   ♣ 8 5

HCP: _____
Distr. Points: _____
Total Points: _____
Opening Bid _____

4) ♠ 3
   ♥ A J 8 6 5
   ♦ K 4
   ♣ A K J 7 3

HCP: _____
Distr. Points: _____
Total Points: _____
Opening Bid _____

5) ♠ A Q 7 3
   ♥ A 9 5
   ♦ 7 6
   ♣ K J 6 2

HCP: _____
Distr. Points: _____
Total Points: _____
Opening Bid _____

6) ♠ A J 6 3
   ♥ 5
   ♦ K J 9 4
   ♣ A 8 6 2

HCP: _____
Distr. Points: _____
Total Points: _____
Opening Bid _____

7) ♠ K 4 3
   ♥ A K 8 6
   ♦ A Q 5
   ♣ K J 2

HCP: _____
Distr. Points: _____
Total Points: _____
Opening Bid _____

8) ♠ Q 8 5 3
   ♥ Q 9 6 3
   ♦ A J 10
   ♣ A 6

HCP: _____
Distr. Points: _____
Total Points: _____
Opening Bid _____

9) ♠ 4
   ♥ A Q 9 6 3
   ♦ 5
   ♣ A K 10 7 5 2

HCP: _____
Distr. Points: _____
Total Points: _____
Opening Bid _____

Exercise Six — Responder, the Captain, Decides What Level

Your partner opens the bidding 1NT. You as responder decide at what level to play the contract. On the following hands, would you play at a game, partscore, or possibly a game?

1) ♠ A 8 7
   ♥ K Q 9 8 6 4
   ♦ J 3
   ♣ 10 2

2) ♠ Q J 9
   ♥ K 5 3 2
   ♦ 9 7 5
   ♣ 8 3 2

3) ♠ 10 7 5
   ♥ K J 2
   ♦ A 8 6
   ♣ J 9 6 3

Exercise Seven — Responder, the Captain, Decides What Denomination

Your partner opens the bidding 1NT. Would you like to play with spades or hearts as the trump suit? Answer yes, no, or possibly. Give reasons for your decision.

1) ♠ 8 2
   ♥ 10 9
   ♦ A K 8 7 6
   ♣ Q J 9 8

2) ♠ 9 8 3
   ♥ K Q 10 7 6 2
   ♦ 6 3
   ♣ J 4

3) ♠ A K 9 7 4
   ♥ Q 7
   ♦ J 7 6
   ♣ Q 9 8

Exercise Eight — Counting Winners

How many sure tricks can you take with each of the following suit combinations?

	1)	2)	3)	4)
DUMMY:	A 7 2	K 6 4	A 4	Q 5
DECLARER:	9 6 3	A Q 5	K Q	A K 6

Exercise Nine — Taking Tricks
(E-Z Deal Cards: # 2, Hand 1 — Dealer, North)

You know how to value both partnership hands, and you know that you need 26 combined points to make a Golden Game. Let's see how this works. Turn up all of the cards on the first pre-dealt hand. Put each hand dummy style at the edge of the table in front of each player.

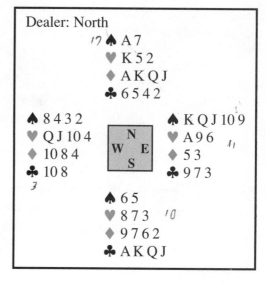

Dealer: North

North
♠ A 7
♥ K 5 2
♦ A K Q J
♣ 6 5 4 2

West
♠ 8 4 3 2
♥ Q J 10 4
♦ 10 8 4
♣ 10 8

East
♠ K Q J 10 9
♥ A 9 6
♦ 5 3
♣ 9 7 3

South
♠ 6 5
♥ 8 7 3
♦ 9 7 6 2
♣ A K Q J

The Bidding

How many combined points are there in each partnership? Does one partnership have enough combined strength for a Golden Game? Does the partnership have a Golden Fit in a major suit?

North is the dealer. Which player would open the bidding? What would the opening bid be? Which player would be the describer? Which player would be the responder? Which player would be the captain? What should the contract be? Which player would be the declarer?

The Play

Suppose that North is the declarer in a contract of 3NT. Which player would make the opening lead? What would the opening lead be? How many tricks must declarer take to fulfill the contract?

Look at each combined suit in the North and South hands and determine how many sure tricks there are. There is a bridge saying, take your tricks and run, that applies to this hand. Why would this be good advice? What might happen if you do not take your tricks when you have the opportunity?

Exercise Ten — High Card from the Short Side
(E-Z Deal Cards: # 2, Hand 2 — Dealer, East)

When a partnership has fewer than 26 combined points, they should play in a partscore. If there is no Golden Fit, the partnership should play in notrump. Let's see how this works. Turn up all of the cards on the second pre-dealt hand, and arrange them as in the previous exercise.

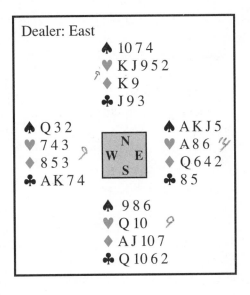

Dealer: East

♠ 10 7 4
♥ K J 9 5 2
♦ K 9
♣ J 9 3

♠ Q 3 2   ♠ A K J 5
♥ 7 4 3   ♥ A 8 6
♦ 8 5 3   ♦ Q 6 4 2
♣ A K 7 4   ♣ 8 5

N
W   E
S

♠ 9 8 6
♥ Q 10
♦ A J 10 7
♣ Q 10 6 2

The Bidding

How many points are there in each partnership? Does either partnership have enough strength for a Golden Game? Does either partnership have a Golden Fit? Which partnership has the majority of the strength?

East is the dealer. Which player would open the bidding? What would be the opening bid? Which player would be the describer? Which player would be the responder? Which player would be the captain?

If East and West bid to a contract, should it be a game contract or a partscore contract? What should be the denomination of the contract? What might be a reasonable contract? Must East end up as the declarer? If not, how might West become declarer?

The Play

Suppose that West is the declarer in a contract of 1NT. Which player would make the opening lead? What would be the opening lead be? How many tricks must declarer take to fulfill the contract?

Look at each combined suit in the East and West hands and determine how many sure tricks there are. There is a bridge saying, play the high card from the short side, that applies to this hand. Why would this be good advice? What might happen if declarer does not follow this advice?

Exercise Eleven — Playing in a Golden Fit
(E-Z Deal Cards: #2, Hand 3 — Dealer, South)

You know that the partnership needs eight or more cards in a suit for a Golden Fit. Let's see how this works. Turn up all the cards on the third pre-dealt hand and arrange them as in the previous exercise.

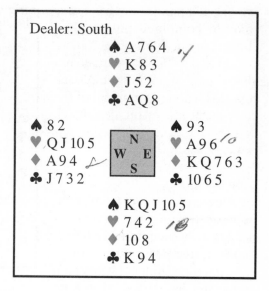

Dealer: South

♠ A 7 6 4
♥ K 8 3
♦ J 5 2
♣ A Q 8

♠ 8 2   ♠ 9 3
♥ Q J 10 5   ♥ A 9 6
♦ A 9 4   N   ♦ K Q 7 6 3
♣ J 7 3 2   W E ♣ 10 6 5
              S

♠ K Q J 10 5
♥ 7 4 2
♦ 10 8
♣ K 9 4

The Bidding

How many points are there in each partnership? Does either partnership have enough combined strength for a Golden Game? Does either partnership have a Golden Fit? Which partnership has the majority of the high card strength?

South is the dealer. Does the dealer always open the bidding? Which player would open the bidding? What would the opening bid be?

If North and South bid to a contract, should it be a game contract or a partscore contract? What should the denomination of the contract be? What might be a reasonable contract?

The Play

Suppose that South is the declarer in a contract of 2♠. Which player would make the opening lead? What would the opening lead be? How many tricks must declarer take to fulfill the contract?

Look at each combined suit in the North and South hands. Determine how many sure tricks there are. What is the advantage of playing in a Golden Fit? What might happen if North and South played in a notrump contract instead of their Golden Fit?

Exercise Twelve — Drawing Trumps
(E-Z Deal Cards: #2, Hand 4 — Dealer, West)

When the partnership has 26 or more combined points and a Golden Fit in a major suit, it should play in a Golden Game contract in the major suit. Let's see how this works.

Turn up all the cards on the fourth pre-dealt hand and arrange them as in the previous exercise.

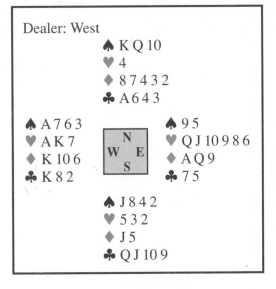

Dealer: West

♠ K Q 10
♥ 4
♦ 8 7 4 3 2
♣ A 6 4 3

♠ A 7 6 3   ♠ 9 5
♥ A K 7   ♥ Q J 10 9 8 6
♦ K 10 6   ♦ A Q 9
♣ K 8 2   ♣ 7 5

♠ J 8 4 2
♥ 5 3 2
♦ J 5
♣ Q J 10 9

The Bidding

How many points are there in each partnership? Does either partnership have enough strength for a Golden Game? Does either partnership have a Golden Fit? Which partnership has the majority of the high card strength?

West is the dealer. Which player would open the bidding? What would the opening bid be? After West's opening bid, how does East know there is enough combined strength for a game contract? How does East know there is a Golden Fit in a major suit? What contract would East steer the partnership to?

The Play

Suppose that East is the declarer in a contract of 4♥. Which player would make the opening lead? What would the opening lead be? How many tricks must declarer take to fulfill the contract?

Look at each combined suit in the East and West hands. Determine how many sure tricks there are. Another saying, get the kiddies off the street (play the trump suit as soon as you get the lead), applies to this hand. Why? What would happen if declarer did not play the trump suit before trying to take the other sure tricks?

Answers to Lesson 2 exercises are on pages 292–297.

LESSON 3
Responses to 1NT Opening Bids

Responder's Decision with 0 to 7 Points

Responder's Decision with 8 or 9 Points

Responder's Decision with 10 to 14 Points

The Bidding Messages

Opener's Rebid after a 1NT Opening Bid

Guidelines for Play

Summary

Activities

The opener is the describer and tries to paint a clear picture of the hand. Responder, the captain, uses the information to steer the partnership to the best contract. When the opening bid is 1NT, opener is off to a good start. The bid shows 16, 17, or 18 points, and a balanced hand. Responder then decides the level and denomination of the contract. Let's see how you, as responder, make these decisions after an opening bid of 1NT.

RESPONDER'S DECISION WITH 0-7 POINTS

What Level?

When responder has 0 to 7 points, the contract should be played in a partscore. Even if opener has 18 points and responder has a maximum of 7 points, there are only 25 (18 + 7 = 25) combined points, not enough for game.

What Denomination?

Responder wants to play a partscore in a Golden Fit if one can be found; otherwise, in notrump. If there is a Golden Fit, the cheapest level available for bidding is the two level. After an opening 1NT bid, there are no longer any one-level bids available on the Bidding Scale. If responder determines there is no Golden Fit, responder can pass and leave the contract in 1NT.

With only 0 to 7 points, you, as responder, can't afford to get the partnership higher than the two level. This limits your options. You can't make any exploratory bids. You must decide immediately on the best partscore contract. To do this, you look at the long suits in your hand and decide whether there is likely to be a Golden Fit.

If you have a six-card suit, you are certain that there is a Golden Fit.

Opener has promised a balanced hand with a minimum of two cards in each suit.

If you have a five-card suit, a Golden Fit is highly likely. As we saw in Lesson Two, opener is most likely to hold three or more cards in a given suit. Since there is no room on the Bidding Scale to make an exploratory bid, you assume there is a Golden Fit. Even if you happen to find opener with only a doubleton, the partnership will still have a majority of the trump suit (5+2 = 7).

If you have only a four-card suit, opener would also need at least a four-card suit to have a Golden Fit. This is less likely than opener's having two or three cards in the suit. With 0 to 7 points, your hand is so weak that you can't afford the bidding space to get more information about opener's hand. You will have to make an on-the-spot decision and go with the odds. Settle for a partscore in notrump by passing.

If you have fewer than four cards in a suit, there is virtually no chance of a Golden Fit. You should leave the denomination in notrump.

2♣, The Stayman Convention

There is another point responder must take into account when deciding the denomination. A bid of 2♣ in response to an opening bid of 1NT is reserved for a special purpose, the *Stayman convention*. The use of this bid is described in the Appendix. For now, you only need to know that a 2♣ response, after a 1NT opening bid, has nothing to do with the club suit.

Therefore, you do not respond 2♣ with 0 to 7 points even when you know there is a Golden Fit in clubs. Instead, you pass and play a partscore in 1NT.

Putting It Together

> **IN SUMMARY, WHEN RESPONDING TO A 1NT OPENING BID WITH 0-7 POINTS:**
>
> - Bid 2♠, 2♥, or 2♦ with a five-card or longer suit (2♣ is reserved for the Stayman convention).
> - Otherwise, pass.

Let's look at some examples. Your partner opens the bidding 1NT, and you hold:

♠ J 8 7 5 4 2 ♥ Q 10 2 ♦ J 7 6 ♣ 9	You know you belong in a partscore, so play in your Golden Fit. Your partnership has at least eight cards in spades in the combined hands since opener has at least two. Respond 2♠.
♠ J 5 3 ♥ Q 7 3 ♦ K 9 8 7 2 ♣ 10 4	You have at least a seven-card fit in diamonds and very likely eight or more. Quite often opener will have three or more diamonds. Respond 2♦.
♠ Q 6 2 ♥ 8 7 4 ♦ J 10 8 2 ♣ 9 7 3	With only one four-card suit, it is unlikely there is a Golden Fit. Opener will have four or more diamonds less than half the time. Pass and play in 1NT.
♠ Q 6 ♥ J 4 ♦ 9 6 5 3 ♣ 10 8 7 6 2	As in the second example, you are likely to have a Golden Fit. Here you have a five-card club suit. Unfortunately, you can't play a partscore in 2♣ (Stayman convention). Pass and play in 1NT.

RESPONDER'S DECISION WITH 8-9 POINTS

What Level?

When responder has 8 or 9 points opposite opener's 16, 17, or 18, there are possibly enough points for a game contract. The partnership has a combined strength of 24 to 27 points. Half of the time, there are 26 or more combined points. Responder needs more information. Responder would like to know whether opener has specifically 16, 17, or 18 points.

A 2NT response is used to ask opener to tell responder more about opener's hand. With 16 points, opener can pass and the partnership will stay safely in partscore. With 17 or 18 points, opener can bid 3NT, and the partnership will play in game.

What Denomination?

By bidding 2NT, responder is heading toward a Golden Game in notrump. If there are 26 or more combined points, responder wants to play 3NT, even if there is a Golden Fit in diamonds or clubs.

If there is a Golden Fit in spades or hearts, however, responder would like to play in a major suit game. In addition to more information about opener's strength, responder also might like more information about opener's length in the major suits. But, when responder holds only 8 or 9 points, bidding space is limited. Here, the Stayman convention comes in handy. Responder can first bid 2♣ to ask opener about the number of cards opener has in the major suits. Opener answers this question at the two level. There is still room to ask the next question: what is the exact strength of opener's hand?

For now, a *raise* to 2NT can be used to show any hand with 8 or 9 points. You can read about the Stayman convention in the Appendix and learn to use it at your leisure.

Putting It Together

> ### IN SUMMARY, WHEN RESPONDING TO A 1NT OPENING BID WITH 8-9 POINTS:
>
> • Bid 2NT.

Let's look at some examples. Your partner opens the bidding 1NT, and you hold:

♠ K 8 7
♥ A 3
♦ J 9 8 7
♣ J 10 9 8

With 9 points, you can't rule out the possibility of a game contract. However, you don't have to bid game without further information from opener. Respond 2NT to ask opener to further describe the strength of the hand.

♠ Q 8
♥ A 10 9
♦ J 3
♣ 10 9 8 6 5 3

With 9 points, you want to look for a Golden Game. Ignore the Golden Fit in your minor suit since there cannot be enough combined strength to make 5♣. Respond 2NT.

♠ 9 8 5
♥ Q 7 6
♦ J 9 8 4 3
♣ A 7

With 8 points, respond 2NT to try to get to a Golden Game.

RESPONDER'S DECISION WITH 10-14 POINTS

What Level?

When responder has 10 or more points, even if opener has only 16 points, there are enough combined points for game. With more than 14 points, responder is probably interested in a slam contract. Slam bidding is briefly discussed in the Appendix. In the meantime, let's consider the range of 10 to 14 points for which responder wants to choose one of the Golden Games — 4♠, 4♥, or 3NT.

What Denomination?

Responder's first choice is to play in a major suit game if there is a Golden Fit (eight or more cards in the suit). If not, responder wants to play in 3NT.

If you, as responder, have a six-card or longer major suit, you know for sure there is a Golden Fit. In this case, you can bid game directly, 4♥ or 4♠.

If you have a five-card major suit, you know there will be a Golden Fit unless opener has only two cards in the suit. Unlike the situation when you had 0 to 7 points and merely had to assume that there was a Golden Fit, here you have some room to explore on the way to your game contract. You can bid at the three level, 3♥ or 3♠. These bids ask opener to bid game in the major suit with three or more cards and to bid 3NT with only two. Thus, responder is assured of getting to the right Golden Game.

When you have a four-card major suit, opener must have at least four cards for there to be a Golden Fit. Once again you start to run out of bidding room. You cannot bid your major at the two level since that would show 0 to 7 points. You cannot bid it at the three level since, as you've just seen, that shows a five-card suit. You cannot bid it at the four level since that shows a six-card or longer suit (and also gets the partnership past 3NT).

This is another situation in which the Stayman convention is used. A 2♣ response asks whether opener has four or more cards in a major suit. If opener does have a four-card major, opener bids it at the two level, and responder bids on accordingly. The details of this convention will not be discussed here. For now, you only need to know that responder has a way to find out whether opener has a four-card major suit. In the meantime, until you understand this convention, you can assume that there is no Golden Fit and bid game in notrump.

When responder has three or fewer cards in a major suit, a Golden Fit is highly unlikely. Responder can bid game in 3NT.

Putting It Together

IN SUMMARY, WHEN RESPONDING TO A 1NT OPENING BID WITH 10-14 POINTS:

- Bid 4♡ or 4♠ with a six-card or longer major suit.
- Bid 3♡ or 3♠ with a five-card major suit
- Otherwise, bid 3NT.

Here are some examples. Your partner opens 1NT, and you hold the following hands:

♠ A K 9 7 5 4
♥ Q 7 6
♦ J 9
♣ 8 7

With 12 points, you want to play in a game contract. With a six-card spade suit, you know you have a Golden Fit. Place the final contract in 4♠.

♠ 10 9
♥ Q 2
♦ A 9 8 6 4
♣ K J 5 3

You have 11 points, enough for game. With only two cards in each major, there is no possibility of a Golden Fit in a major suit. Respond 3NT.

♠ 9 8 6
♥ A J 9 6 2
♦ K Q 3
♣ Q 7

With 13 points and a five-card major suit, you want to play game in 4♥ if opener has three or more; otherwise, in 3NT. Respond 3♥. This bid asks opener to bid 4♥ with three or more hearts, otherwise, to bid 3NT.

♠ A Q J 8
♥ J 10 9
♦ Q 9 8 4
♣ 3 2

With 10 points and a four-card major suit, you could use the Stayman convention, 2♣, to ask if opener has a four-card major. Since this bid hasn't been discussed in detail yet, assume there is no Golden Fit in a major suit and respond 3NT.

♠ A 9
♥ K 7 6
♦ Q J 9 8 5 4
♣ 10 2

With 12 points and no likely major suit fit, respond 3NT. Ignore the Golden Fit in diamonds since 5♦ isn't one of the Golden Games.

THE BIDDING MESSAGES

Suppose you open the bidding 1NT, and your partner responds. What do you do now? How do you know whether or not you should bid again?

The Stop Light

Every bid carries one of three *messages* to your partner:

(1) Stop: don't bid any more.
(2) Proceed with Caution: pass or bid depending on your strength.
(3) Go: you must bid again.

The messages can be compared to a traffic light:

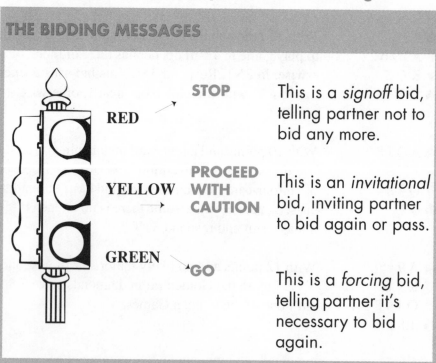

THE BIDDING MESSAGES

RED	**STOP**	This is a *signoff* bid, telling partner not to bid any more.
YELLOW	**PROCEED WITH CAUTION**	This is an *invitational* bid, inviting partner to bid again or pass.
GREEN	**GO**	This is a *forcing* bid, telling partner it's necessary to bid again.

For example, opening bids at the one level are all yellow, invitational bids. Responder may either bid or pass depending on the strength of the hand.

Signoff Bids in Response to 1NT

A 1NT opening bid paints a very clear picture of opener's hand. Most of the time, responder can ascertain both the level and the denomination of the final contract without further information from the opener. Usually responder decides between game or partscore and signs off.

The partscore signoff bids are:

- Pass (1NT becomes the contract)
- 2♦, 2♥, 2♠

The game signoff bids are:

- 3NT
- 4♥, 4♠
- 5♣, 5♦ (Rarely)

After a signoff bid, opener is expected to pass. Responder, as captain, has made the decision.

Invitational Bids in Response to 1NT

Responder makes an invitational bid by asking for further clarification of opener's strength. Opener passes with a minimum hand and bids on with a maximum. The invitational response after 1NT is:

- 2NT

Forcing Bids in Response to 1NT

Responder may have the answer to one question, the level, but want more information from partner before being able to answer the second question, the denomination. For example, if responder holds 10 or more points, responder knows there is enough strength for a game contract. With five cards in a major suit, responder wants to find out whether there is a Golden Fit. It's necessary to find out if opener has three or more cards in the major suit.

Responder has to make a forcing bid. Responder wants to make sure that the partnership ends up in either 3NT or four of the major, but a question must be asked on the way. The forcing bid is different from the invitational bid because opener is not invited to pass. Opener is forced to bid again.

The forcing bids after a 1NT opening bid are:

- 3 ♥, 3 ♠

With three cards or more in the major suit, opener goes on to game in the major. With only two cards in the suit, opener bids 3NT. Opener does not pass since responder gave a forcing message!

There is another forcing bid in response to 1NT:

- 2 ♣ (the Stayman convention)

This response of 2 ♣ after a 1NT opening bid asks opener to bid a four-card or longer major suit if opener has one. Opener cannot pass.

OPENER'S REBID AFTER A 1NT OPENING BID

Opener's second bid is called *opener's rebid*. If responder makes a signoff bid, opener passes at the next turn. If responder makes an invitational bid, opener can either pass or bid again. If responder makes a forcing bid, opener must bid again.

Suppose you open the bidding 1NT with the following hand:

♠ K Q 8 5

♥ A K 3

♦ K 4 2

♣ J 6 3

If responder bids 2♠, you pass on your rebid. Even though you have attractive spades, you can't bid more. Partner has made a signoff bid and expects you to pass.

If responder bids 2NT, you can either pass or bid 3NT. Responder is making an invitational bid. With only 16 points, you would decline the invitation and pass.

If responder bids 3♥, this is a forcing bid, and you must bid again. Since you have three hearts, bid a game in hearts, 4♥. If you held only two hearts, you would bid 3NT.

GUIDELINES FOR PLAY

In the previous lesson, we saw that declarer makes a plan by first pausing to consider the objective (how many tricks are needed to make the contract) and then by looking at the winners and losers (counting the number of sure tricks in the combined hands). If there are enough sure tricks to make the contract, declarer can go ahead and take them. However, on most deals, there will not be enough sure tricks, and declarer will have to analyze the alternatives to figure out how to develop the extra tricks that are needed. One of the most common techniques for developing extra tricks is through the promotion of high cards.

Developing Tricks Through Promotion

A card is *promoted* into a sure trick when all the higher-ranking cards in the suit have been played. Sometimes the opponents will promote some tricks for you by taking their sure tricks in a suit, but usually you will have to do the work. Let's look at some examples.

DUMMY: 5 4

DECLARER: K Q

You do not have a sure trick in this suit. You can establish one by leading the king (or queen) to make an opponent play the ace in order to win the trick. Your remaining high card is now promoted into a sure trick.

DUMMY: Q 6

DECLARER: K J 5

You can develop two sure tricks in this suit. Lead one of your high cards to drive out the opponents' ace, your two remaining high cards are promoted into winners. Because the suit is unevenly divided between the two hands, you should follow the principle of playing the high card from the short side first — the queen in this example.

DUMMY:	Q J 10	You can develop one trick. Start by leading the queen to drive out the opponents' ace or king. When you have another opportunity to lead, play the jack to drive out the opponents' remaining high card. You have now promoted your 10 into a trick.
DECLARER:	8 5 3	

DUMMY:	7 5 4 2	With this suit, you have a lot of work to do — the opponents have the ace, king, and queen. However, by leading one of your high cards at every opportunity, you eventually can promote a trick in the suit.
DECLARER:	J 10 9 8	

Losing Tricks to the Opponents

When developing tricks through promotion, you have to give up the lead to the opponents. There is nothing wrong with losing a trick to the opponents, provided that they cannot take enough tricks to defeat your contract. You often have to lose tricks to the opponents, either because you have no choice or because you are trying to develop the tricks needed to make your contract.

If you have to give up the lead while developing additional tricks, you want to be able to regain the lead to take the tricks you have developed. It's generally a good idea to keep sure tricks in other suits to help you regain the lead and maintain control of the hand. In other words, when developing tricks in a suit, follow the guideline "take your losses early" while you still have winning tricks in other suits. Do not take all of your sure tricks in other suits first — you may develop sure tricks for your opponents.

SUMMARY

RESPONSES TO 1NT

After your partner opens the bidding 1NT, put your hand into one of three categories:

0 to 7
- Bid 2♦, 2♥, or 2♠ with a five-card or longer suit (2♣ is reserved for the Stayman convention).

- Otherwise, pass.

8 or 9
- Bid 2NT (2♣ can be used to uncover an eight-card major suit fit).

10 to 14
- Bid 4♥ or 4♠ with a six-card or longer suit.

- Bid 3♠ or 3♥ with a five-card suit.

- Otherwise, bid 3NT (2♣ can be used to uncover an eight-card major suit fit).

Each bid carries one of three possible bidding messages:

BIDDING MESSAGES

Red	Stop	Signoff
Yellow	Proceed with Caution	Invitational
Green	Go	Forcing

THE BIDDING MESSAGES IN RESPONSE TO A 1NT OPENING BID ARE:

Signoff:
   • Pass
   • 2♦, 2♥, 2♠
   • 3NT, 4♥, 4♠
   • 5♣, 5♦ (Rarely)

Invitational:
   • 2NT

Forcing:
   • 3♥, 3♠
   • 2♣ (the Stayman convention)

REBIDS BY OPENER AFTER A 1NT OPENING BID

After responder's signoff:
   • Pass.

After responder's invitational bid of 2NT:
   • Pass with 16 points.
   • Bid 3NT with 17 or 18 points.

After responder's forcing bid of 3♥ or 3♠:
   • Bid four of the major with three or more cards in the major.
   • Bid 3NT with two cards in the major.

When playing a hand, you sometimes need to develop additional tricks in order to make the contract. One technique for doing this is promotion: playing high cards to drive out the opponents' higher-ranking cards until your lower-ranking cards become sure tricks. Promotion involves giving up the lead to the opponents. It is a useful technique as long as you have enough sure tricks in other suits to regain the lead before the opponents can take enough tricks to defeat the contract.

ACTIVITIES

Exercise One — Responding with 0 to 7 Points

You are the responder after your partner opens 1NT. Value the hand and decide the level, the denomination, and the response for each of the following hands:

1) ♠ 10 8 6 5 4 2	2) ♠ J 9 8	3) ♠ Q J
♥ J 7 5	♥ A 9 6 2	♥ 9 8
♦ 8	♦ J 7 6	♦ Q 9 8
♣ J 6 2	♣ 10 9 4	♣ 10 9 7 6 3 2

Points: _4_	Points: _6_	Points: _7_
Level: _____	Level: _____	Level: _____
Denomination: _____	Denomination: _____	Denomination: _____
Response: _2s_	Response: _Pass_	Response _Pass_

What do all of the hands have in common?

Exercise Two — Responding with 10 to 14 Points

You are the responder after your partner opens 1NT. Value the hand and decide the level, the denomination, and the response for each of the following hands.

1) ♠ Q J 9 7 6 4	2) ♠ A 8 2	3) ♠ Q J
♥ K 8 6	♥ A Q 9 8 3	♥ K Q
♦ K 4 3	♦ 9 4 2	♦ Q 9 8
♣ 5	♣ 10 9	♣ J 9 7 6 3 2

Points: _11_	Points: _11_	Points: _13_
Level: _____	Level: _____	Level: _____
Denomination: _____	Denomination: _____	Denomination: _____
Response: _4s_	Response: _3H_	Response _3N_

What do all of the hands above have in common? How do they differ from the hands in Exercise One?

Exercise Three — Responding with 8 or 9 Points

You are the responder after your partner opens the bidding 1NT. Construct a hand with which you would respond 2NT.

Exercise Four — The Bidding Messages

Each bid has a message. Your partner opens the bidding 1NT.
What are seven signoff responses you can make?
What invitational response can you make?
What are two forcing responses you can make?

Exercise Five — Playing in the Golden Fit

Construct the following hands for North and South:

Randomly deal the remaining cards to East and West. Have South play the hand as declarer in a contract of 1NT. When you are finished, record the number of tricks taken by South. Then, play the hand again. This time make North the declarer in a contract of 2♠. Record the number of tricks taken by North.

When the opening bid is 1NT, why is it important that responder, holding 0 to 7 points, steer the partnership into a Golden Fit whenever possible?

NORTH
♠ 10 9 8 7 6 5
♥ 7 3 2
♦ 8 7
♣ 4 3

SOUTH
♠ Q J
♥ A K 4
♦ A 6 5 3
♣ A 8 6 2

Exercise Six — Promoting Tricks

How many tricks can be developed with each of the following suit combinations?

DUMMY:	1) K Q J	2) K 5	3) J 8 4	4) 10 8 6 3
DECLARER:	7 4 2	Q 4	Q 10 3	J 9 5 2

Exercise Seven — Promoting Winners in Notrump
(E-Z Deal Cards: #3, Hand 1 — Dealer, North)

Turn up all of the cards on the first pre-dealt hand. Put each hand dummy style at the edge of the table in front of each player.

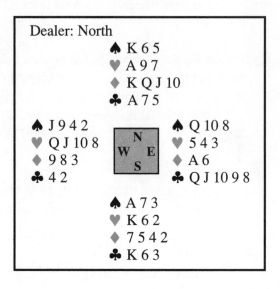

Dealer: North

North:
♠ K 6 5
♥ A 9 7
♦ K Q J 10
♣ A 7 5

West:
♠ J 9 4 2
♥ Q J 10 8
♦ 9 8 3
♣ 4 2

East:
♠ Q 10 8
♥ 5 4 3
♦ A 6
♣ Q J 10 9 8

South:
♠ A 7 3
♥ K 6 2
♦ 7 5 4 2
♣ K 6 3

The Bidding

North is the dealer. Which player would open the bidding? What would the opening bid be? Which player would be the describer? Which player would be the responder? Which player would be the captain?

Look at responder's hand. At what level should the contract be played? In what denomination should the contract be played? What would the response be? What is the bidding message given by responder's bid? What would opener do? What would the contract be? Who would be declarer?

The Play

Which player would make the opening lead? What would the opening lead be?

How many tricks must declarer take to fulfill the contract? How many sure tricks does declarer have? Which suit provides declarer with the opportunity to develop the additional tricks needed to make the contract? Which suit should declarer play after winning the first trick? Why?

Bid and play the deal. Did declarer make the contract?

Exercise Eight — Promoting Winners in a Suit Contract
(E-Z Deal Cards: #3, Hand 2 — Dealer, East)

Turn up all of the cards on the second pre-dealt hand and arrange them as in the previous exercise.

```
Dealer: East
                ♠ K 2
                ♥ A 7
                ♦ 9 8 6 4
                ♣ Q J 10 9 7
♠ Q J 10 9 8 7              ♠ 6 5 3
♥ 8 4 2        ┌─────┐      ♥ K Q J
♦ A J          │ N   │      ♦ K 7 5 2
♣ 5 4          │W   E│      ♣ A K 6
               │  S  │
               └─────┘
                ♠ A 4
                ♥ 10 9 6 5 3
                ♦ Q 10 3
                ♣ 8 3 2
```

The Bidding

East is the dealer. Which player would open the bidding? What would the opening bid be? Which player would be the describer? Which player would be the responder? Which player would be the captain?

Look at responder's hand. At what level, should the contract be played? In what denomination should the contract be played? What would the response be? What is the bidding message given by responder's bid? What would opener do? What would the contract be? Who would be declarer?

The Play

Which player would make the opening lead? What would the opening lead be?

How many tricks must declarer take to fulfill the contract? How many sure tricks does declarer have? How can declarer develop the tricks needed to make the contract? Which suit should declarer develop first? Why? What would happen if declarer played the other suits first?

Bid and play the deal. Did declarer make the contract?

Exercise Nine — High Card From the Short Side
(E-Z Deal Cards: #3, Hand 3 — Dealer, South)

Turn up all of the cards on the third pre-dealt hand, and arrange them as in the previous exercise.

The Bidding

South is the dealer. Which player would open the bidding? What would the opening bid be?

Look at responder's hand. At what level, should the contract be played? In what denomination, should the contract be played? What would the response be? What is the bidding message given by responder's bid? What would opener do? What would the contract be? Who would be declarer?

```
Dealer: South
                    ♠ 7 6 2
                    ♥ 8 7 3
                    ♦ K J 10 3
                    ♣ A 4 2
    ♠ Q J 10 8              ♠ 9 4
    ♥ K 10          N       ♥ Q J 9 5
    ♦ A 6 2      W     E    ♦ 9 8 7 4
    ♣ 10 8 5 3      S       ♣ J 9 7
                    ♠ A K 5 3
                    ♥ A 6 4 2
                    ♦ Q 5
                    ♣ K Q 6
```

The Play

Which player would make the opening lead? What would the opening lead be?

How many tricks must declarer take to fulfill the contract? How many sure tricks does declarer have? How can declarer develop the tricks needed to make the contract? Which suit should declarer play after winning the first trick? Which card should declarer play first in the suit? Why? What might happen if declarer played the suit differently?

Bid and play the deal. Did declarer make the contract?

Exercise Ten — Patience When Promoting
(E-Z Deal Cards: #3, Hand 4 — Dealer, West)

Turn up all of the cards on the fourth pre-dealt hand, and arrange them as in the previous exercise.

The Bidding

West is the dealer. Which player would open the bidding? What would the opening bid be?

Look at responder's hand. At what level, should the contract be played? In what denomination, should the contract be played? What would the response be? What is the

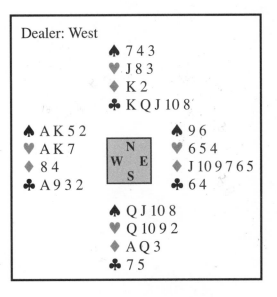

Dealer: West

♠ 7 4 3
♥ J 8 3
♦ K 2
♣ K Q J 10 8

♠ A K 5 2   ♠ 9 6
♥ A K 7   ♥ 6 5 4
♦ 8 4   ♦ J 10 9 7 6 5
♣ A 9 3 2   ♣ 6 4

♠ Q J 10 8
♥ Q 10 9 2
♦ A Q 3
♣ 7 5

bidding message given by responder's bid? What would opener do? What would the contract be? Who would be declarer?

The Play

Which player would make the opening lead? What would the opening lead be?

How many tricks must declarer take to fulfill the contract? How many sure tricks does declarer have? How can declarer develop the tricks needed to make the contract? Which suit should declarer play after winning the first trick? How often will declarer have to give up the lead before developing sure tricks in the suit?

Would it be better to play the hand in a notrump contract? If not, why not?

Bid and play the deal. Did declarer make the contract?

Answers to Lesson 3 exercises are on pages 297–300.

LESSON 4
Responses to Opening Bids of One in a Suit

RESPONDER'S GENERAL APPROACH

A 1NT opening bid, which shows 16, 17, or 18 points and balanced distribution, paints a clear picture of opener's hand. Responder, the captain, usually has enough information to decide the level and the denomination of the contract. As a result, many of responder's bids after a 1NT opening bid are signoffs.

When the opening bid is one of a suit, opener has not given as well–defined a picture of the hand. There could be anywhere from 13 to 21 points, balanced or unbalanced. Before deciding the best place to play the contract, responder needs more information from opener. Most of responder's bids are now forcing, waiting for opener to give a more specific description of the hand.

Responder's Use of the Bidding Messages

Signoff Bids: After an opening bid of one in a suit, the only signoff bid a responder can make holding a very weak hand (0 to 5 points) is pass. There is no likelihood of a game contract. Responder doesn't know enough about opener's strength and distribution to be able to make a decision about the level and denomination of the contract. In addition, responder doesn't hold enough points to ask opener to further describe the hand.

Invitational Bids: With a minimum hand (6 to 10 points), responder may want to make an invitational bid. This would give opener a chance to either bid again or accept the option to pass. When responder makes an invitational bid, responder must be willing to play at the level and the denomination of that bid because opener may pass. Responder can make an invitational bid (1) by showing support for opener's suit at the cheapest available level or (2) by bidding notrump at the cheapest available level.

Forcing Bids: Most of the time, responder makes a forcing bid. Responder usually wants more information from opener. Responder does this by bidding a new suit. With a minimum hand, 6 to 10 points, responder can only afford to bid a new suit at the one level. With a stronger hand (11 or more points), responder can afford to bid a new suit at the two level, if necessary.

How Responder Categorizes Strength

0 to 5
6 to 10
11 or 12
13 or more

As responder, you put your hand into one of four categories according to its value:

Once you have categorized your strength, we'll see how you go about steering the partnership to the appropriate level and denomination when you hold each of these point ranges.

Roles of the Partners

Opener is the describer, and the responder is the captain. The conversation works best when opener paints a picture for responder, and responder makes the decision. Responder's bids are designed to get more information from the opener so responder can make an appropriate decision.

RESPONDER'S DECISION WITH 0–5 POINTS

What Level?

When responder has 0 to 5 points, the contract will be a partscore. Opener shows from 13 to 21 points, so there is only a remote chance (if opener has specifically 21 points) that the partnership has 26 combined points.

The response to a bid of one of a suit differs from the response to 1NT. Responder could pass with 0 to 7 points after a 1NT opening bid because opener's top limit was 18 points (7 + 18 = 25), not enough for game. When opener bids one of a suit, the top limit is 21 points. There is a chance for 26 combined points if responder has as few as 6 or 7 points.

What Denomination?

After a 1NT opening bid, a suit bid at the two level is a signoff. Opener is expected to pass. There is no signoff bid after an opening bid of one of a suit — a new suit by responder is forcing. This means that even with a long suit, responder should pass with 0 to 5 points and leave opener to play the contract in the suit opener bid. After all, opener's suit could be as long as or longer than responder's suit. Responder has no room to find out without getting the partnership too high.

Putting It Together

In summary, when responding to an opening bid of one in a suit with 0 to 5 points:

> • Pass

Let's look at an example. Your partner opens the bidding 1 ♥, and you have the following hand:

♠ J 9 8 5 3 2	Even though you have long spades, pass. A new
♥ 5 2	suit by responder is forcing, and opener would bid
♦ 9 5 4	again. This probably would get the partnership too
♣ 8 2	high.

RESPONDER'S DECISION WITH 6-10 POINTS

What Level?

Until responder has more information from opener, the level is unknown. Opener has from 13 to 21 points; responder has from 6 to 10 points. Even if responder has a minimum response, there is still a chance for the game bonus if opener has the top range for an opening bid at the one level. On the other hand, even if responder has the top of the range, there will not be enough combined strength for game if opener has a minimum hand.

Responder must keep the auction going when holding 6 to 10 points in case there is a game. However, responder cannot afford to get the partnership too high until more is known about opener's hand.

What Denomination?

The main priority when searching for the right denomination is to uncover a major suit Golden Fit if one exists. A suit contract is usually better than notrump when there is a major suit Golden Fit.

When opener starts the bidding with 1 ♥ or 1 ♠, responder knows this shows a hand with at least five cards in the major suit and from 13 to 21 points. To be sure there is a Golden Fit, responder needs at least three cards in the suit. With three or more cards in opener's major, responder raises, or *supports*, the major suit. For example, if partner opens 1 ♥, responder could raise to 2 ♥ to show a Golden Fit. The level to which responder raises depends on the strength of the hand.

When opener starts the bidding with 1 ♣ or 1 ♦, responder knows that opener has at least three cards in the minor suit and from 13 to 21 points. In this case, responder would need five cards in opener's minor to be sure of a Golden Fit. However, opener could have four cards in a major suit and, since finding a Golden Fit in a major suit is important, responder must look for one before raising opener's minor.

Because of the difference involved when responding to opening bids of one of a major suit and one of a minor suit, we will look at the two cases separately.

RESPONDING TO A MAJOR SUIT

Dummy Points

Suppose your partner is the dealer, and this is your hand:

♠ —
♥ J 7 5 3
♦ K 9 6 4 2
♣ 10 8 6 3

DUMMY POINTS	
Void	5 Points
Singleton	3 Points
Doubleton	1 Point

If partner's opening bid is 1♠, your hand is not as valuable as it would be if the opening bid was 1♥. Valuing your hand with *dummy points* takes this into consideration. If hearts are trump, the void in the spade suit is very useful. It's more useful than the ♠A would be. Having a singleton or a doubleton is also an advantage after you have discovered a Golden Fit.

When counting dummy points, value your distribution as follows:

Use dummy points instead of distribution points for length when raising partner's major suit. By adding together your high–card points and dummy points, you arrive at a total point count value for your responding hand.

Let's see how this is done.

Partner opens the bidding 1 ♥, and you hold the following hand:

	HIGH–CARD POINTS	DUMMY POINTS	TOTAL POINTS
♠ —	0	5	5
♥ J 7 5 3	1	0	1
♦ K 9 6 4 2	3	0	3
♣ 10 8 6 3	0	0	0
	4	5	9

Once you see that you can raise your partner's major, value your hand using dummy points before deciding what response to make. Dummy points are not used when raising partner's minor suit. Often a partnership will play game in 3NT even when there is a Golden Fit in a minor. In notrump, short suits will be a disadvantage rather than an advantage.

RESPONDING TO A MAJOR SUIT WITH 6–10 POINTS

When your partner opens 1 ♥ or 1 ♠ and you have 6 to 10 points, you have three choices in order of priority.

The First Choice

Your first priority is to raise or support partner's major with three cards or more in the suit. With only 6 to 10 points, raise to the cheapest level, the two level. This is an invitational bid. If the opener has a minimum hand, opener can pass. With additional strength, opener can bid again.

For example, your partner opens 1♥, and you have the following hand:

♠ 6 4	You know there is a Golden Fit in hearts since partner's
♥ Q J 9	opening bid shows at least five cards in the major.
♦ 10 8 2	You have 6 high-card points and 1 for the doubleton
♣ K 8 7 5 3	in spades, a total of 7 points. Raise to the cheapest
	level, 2♥.

The Second Choice

If you don't have support for partner's major suit, you can bid a new suit — but only at the one level, since your hand is minimum (6 to 10 points). If partner has opened the bidding 1♥, the only suit you can bid at the one level is spades. If partner has opened 1♠, you won't be able to bid a suit at the one level.

To bid a new suit at the one level, you need a four-card or longer suit. Let's look at an example. Your partner opens the bidding 1♥, and you have the following hand:

♠ J 9 7 3	Your first choice is to support partner's hearts if you
♥ Q 7	can, but you have only two hearts. Your next choice
♦ A 6 4 3 2	is to bid a new suit at the one level. With a four-card
♣ 10 6	spade suit, you can bid 1♠. This is a forcing bid, and
	opener will bid again.

The Third Choice

If you cannot support partner's major and you cannot bid a new suit at the one level, your only remaining option is to bid 1NT. This does not promise a balanced hand. It shows a hand with 6 to 10 points with which you are unable to raise partner's major or bid a new suit at the one level.

For example, your partner opens the bidding 1♠, and you have the following hand:

♠ 10 5
♥ J 8 6 5 3 2
♦ A 7
♣ 6 3 2

You can't support opener's major or bid a new suit at the one level. The hearts are attractive, but you don't have enough strength to bid a new suit at the two level. The only choice left is 1NT. Unlike an opening bid of 1NT, a response of 1NT does not describe a balanced hand. Instead, it shows a minimum hand for responder of 6 to 10 points.

Putting It Together

RULES FOR RESPONDING TO A MAJOR SUIT OPENING BID WITH 6–10 POINTS

- Raise partner's major suit to the two level with at least three–card support.

- Bid a new suit at the one level.

- Bid 1NT.

Let's look at some examples. Your partner opens the bidding 1♥, and you hold the following:

♠ 10 9 7 3
♥ Q J
♦ A 7 3
♣ J 10 6 3

You cannot support partner's major since you have only two cards in hearts. However, your second choice, bidding a new suit at the one level, is possible because you have a four–card spade suit. Respond 1♠.

♠ 7 5 4
♥ K 6
♦ Q J 9 8 6 4
♣ J 8

You don't have the requirements to either support your partner's heart suit or bid a new suit at the one level. You have an attractive-looking diamond suit, but you can't bid it at the one level. With only 9 points, you respond 1NT.

♠ A 9 8 7
♥ K 6 3 2
♦ 9 8 6
♣ 10 3

You could bid a new suit at the one level, but your first priority is to support partner's major. With 7 high-card points and 1 for the doubleton club, raise partner to 2 ♥, telling partner you have found a Golden Fit.

RESPONDING TO A MINOR SUIT WITH 6-10 POINTS

The First Choice

The priorities in bidding revolve around uncovering a Golden Fit in a major suit to play in at the partscore or game level. This priority guides your thinking after an opening bid in a minor suit. Suppose your partner opens 1 ♦, and you have the following hand:

♠ K 7 6 3
♥ 8 5
♦ Q 7 6 5 3
♣ A 2

You have diamond support, but supporting partner's minor suit is not a priority. You can afford to bid a new suit at the one level, and you have a four-card major suit. Bid 1 ♠. This keeps the search for the major suits open. Since a new suit by responder is forcing, opener must bid again. Thus, you will still have an opportunity to support diamonds if you cannot find a fit in a major suit.

In summary, when your partner starts the bidding with 1♣ or 1♦, your first priority is to bid a new suit at the one level if you can. If you have a choice of suits, there are guidelines:

- Bid your longest suit.
- Bid the higher-ranking of two five-card suits.
- Bid the lower-ranking of two four-card suits.

Your partner opens the bidding 1♣. Let's see what you do with each of the following hands:

♠ Q 8 6 5 3
♥ A 8 7 4
♦ J 7
♣ 6 3

You have two suits that you could bid at the one level. In this case, you bid the longer suit, 1♠.

♠ 8
♥ K 10 8 5 2
♦ A J 5 4 2
♣ 5 4

With a choice of two five-card suits to bid at the one level, bid the higher-ranking. Respond 1♥.

♠ J 8 6 4
♥ A 9 7 6
♦ K 2
♣ 10 9 5

With a choice of two four-card suits to bid at the one level, bid the lower-ranking. Respond 1♥.

The Second Choice

If you can't bid a new suit at the one level, your second choice is to support your partner's minor suit if you can. Remember that partner may have only three cards in the suit when opening with a minor. You should prefer to have five-card support when you raise. If you do have five or more of partner's suit, raise to the two level.

For example, your partner opens 1 ♦ , and you have the following hand:

♠ 8 3   You don't have a four-card or longer suit to bid at the
♥ K 9 7   one level. However, you do have five cards in your
♦ Q 10 8 7 4   partner's minor suit. Raise to 2 ♦ .
♣ K J 3

The Third Choice

If you can't bid a new suit at the one level or support your partner's minor suit, bid 1NT. Again, this has nothing to do with the shape of your hand, only with the point count. It shows 6 to 10 points. It tells partner that you can't bid a new suit at the one level, and you can't support partner's suit.

For example, partner opens 1 ♦ , and you have the following hand:

♠ K 7 6   You don't have a four-card or longer suit to bid at the
♥ Q 8 2   one level, and you don't have five cards in your
♦ J 5   partner's minor suit. Fall back to your third choice
♣ Q 9 6 4 2   and respond 1NT.

Putting It Together

> ### RULES FOR RESPONDING TO A MINOR SUIT OPENING BID WITH 6–10 POINTS
> - Bid a new suit at the one level.
> - Raise partner's minor suit.
> - Bid 1NT.

You can see that the first two priorities are in the reverse order to those for responding to a major suit. Also, to raise a major suit to the two level, you need only three cards in the suit; to raise a minor suit to the two level, you need five. Avoid using dummy points when valuing your hand to support opener's minor suit because you may be headed for a notrump contract.

Here are some examples after partner opens 1♣:

♠ 9 8 6 5
♥ Q 10 8 6 3
♦ K 5
♣ Q 6

Your first priority is to bid a new suit at the one level if you can. With a choice of suits, bid your longer suit, 1♥.

♠ 8 5
♥ Q J 7
♦ J 9 3
♣ K 10 8 7 3

You cannot bid a new suit at the one level. With five-card support for your partner's suit, move to your second choice and raise to 2♣.

♠ K 9 3
♥ Q 10 8
♦ A J 2
♣ 7 5 4 2

With no suit to bid at the one level and only four cards in partner's minor, exercise your third option. Respond 1NT.

RESPONDER'S DECISION WITH 11-12 POINTS

With 11 or 12 points, responder knows the partnership has at least 24 (11 + 13 = 24) points and is close to the strength required for game. Responder's first priority is to support opener's major suit. If responder cannot support opener's major, responder can bid a new-suit — at the two level if necessary.

Partner Opens a Major Suit

Suppose opener bids 1♠, and responder has the following hand:

♠ 9 8 7 3
♥ K 6
♦ Q J 10 4
♣ A 9 4

With support for opener's major suit, responder can value the hand using dummy points. There are 10 HCP plus 1 point for the doubleton heart. With 11 points, responder can bid 3♠. This is an invitational bid. It tells opener three things: responder has support for opener's suit; responder is too strong to raise to 2♠ (6 to 10 points); responder is not strong enough to commit the partnership to game. If opener has a minimum hand of 13 or 14 points, opener can pass and play in the partscore. With more, opener can bid on to game.

Suppose opener bids 1♠, and responder holds this hand:

♠ 7 3
♥ A Q 9 8 3
♦ J 6 3
♣ K J 10

Responder can't support opener's major but does have a suit that is biddable. With 12 points, responder has enough strength to bid at the two level when necessary and can respond 2♥. Because 2♥ is a new-suit bid, it is forcing, and opener will have to bid again.

Responding to a Minor Suit Opening

If opener bids a minor suit, responder's priority is still to look for a major suit. Whether or not responder has support for opener's minor suit, responder will bid a four–card or longer major suit rather than raise opener's minor suit. There is time enough for showing the minor suit support later.

For example, suppose the opening bid is 1♦, and responder holds the following hand:

♠ J 9 7 5   Responder bids a new suit, 1♠, and waits to hear a
♥ Q 4   further description of opener's hand. If there is no
♦ Q 10 8 5 3   Golden Fit in spades, responder can show diamond
♣ A Q   support at the next opportunity.

If responder does not have a new suit to bid, responder can raise opener's minor suit to the three level with 11 or 12 points, inviting opener to bid game with more than 13 or 14 points.

For example, suppose the opening bid is 1♣, and responder has the following hand:

♠ 9 6   Responder raises opener's suit to the three level, 3♣,
♥ 7 4 2   to show 11 points and to invite partner to bid game
♦ A J 7   with more than 13 or 14 points.
♣ K Q 9 7 5

RESPONDER'S DECISION WITH 13 OR MORE POINTS

What Level?

When responder has at least 13 points, responder knows there are enough points for a game contract. As captain, responder must make sure the partnership does not stop below the level of game. If responder bids below the level of game, responder must make a forcing bid.

Since responder raises opener's major to the two level with 6 to 10 points and the three level with 11 or 12 points, it would seem natural to raise to the four level when responder has support and 13 or more points. While this is the most natural approach, it uses up a lot of room on the Bidding Scale. Opener has little opportunity to finish describing the hand. This can be important when opener is interested in getting to a slam contract, for which there is a big bonus. The more modern approach is for responder to bid a new suit first and show support for opener's suit at responder's next opportunity to call.

Partner Opens a Major Suit

Opposite an opening bid of one of a major, responder has two choices with 13 or more points:

- With a balanced hand, bid 2NT.
- Bid a new suit.

All of responder's bids are forcing.

Let's look at some examples in response to an opening bid of
1♠:

♠ Q 10 ♥ K J 10 ♦ A K 5 4 ♣ J 10 6 3	With 14 points and a balanced hand, responder can bid 2NT. This is a forcing bid.

♠ 3 ♥ A 3 ♦ A K J 9 7 4 ♣ Q 10 8 3	Responder does not have a balanced hand and bids a new suit, 2♦. After hearing opener's next bid, responder will be in a better position to decide on the denomination and level of the contract.

♠ Q J 9 3 ♥ 8 7 ♦ A J 9 8 ♣ A Q 3	Responder could support opener's major suit holding 15 points, counting 1 for the doubleton heart, but that is too much to raise to the three level. A raise to the four level would not leave the partnership much room to explore the possibility for a slam contract. Instead, responder bids a new suit, 2♦, giving opener the opportunity to further describe the hand. Responder can show spade support by jumping to game at the next opportunity to bid.

Partner Opens a Minor Suit

Once again responder's first priority is to bid a new suit, a major if possible, looking for a Golden Fit. With 13 or more points, responder has enough strength to explore. Responder has the following choices.

- Bid a new suit, a major if possible.

- With a balanced hand, bid 2NT.

All of responder's bids are forcing. Let's look at some examples in response to an opening bid of 1 ♦:

♠ A Q 8 7   Responder could support opener's minor. However,
♥ K 3   looking for a Golden Fit in a major takes priority.
♦ K J 9 5 2   Responder should bid a new suit, preferring a major,
♣ 7 5   if one is available. Bid 1 ♠.

♠ A J 10   With no new suit to bid and not enough diamonds to
♥ K J 9   raise opener's minor, responder bids 2NT. This is a
♦ K 10 7 3   forcing bid, and opener may not pass.
♣ Q 9 6

GUIDELINES FOR PLAY

Declarer often needs to analyze the alternatives to develop additional tricks in order to make the contract. As we saw in the previous lesson, one method for developing extra tricks is through promotion of high cards. Another common technique makes use of the power of long suits.

Developing Tricks Through Length

In each suit there are 13 cards. The more cards you have in a suit, the fewer the opponents have. After a suit has been led a couple of times, it is possible that the opponents will have no cards remaining in the suit. In that case, whenever the opponents are out of trumps or the contract is notrump, any remaining cards you have in the suit will be sure tricks, even if they are small cards. Let's look at some examples.

DUMMY: 7 6 4 3

DECLARER: A K Q J 2

You have nine cards in the suit, and the opponents have four (13 − 9 = 4). Even if one opponent has all four of the missing cards, that opponent will not have any left after you play the ace, king, queen, and jack. Your 2 will be a sure trick, and you will end up taking five tricks in the suit.

DUMMY: 5 4 3 2

DECLARER: A K Q 6

You have eight cards in the suit, and the opponents have five (13 − 8 = 5). When you play the ace, king, and queen, your remaining card, the 6, will be a sure trick if one of the opponents started with three cards and the other with two cards in the suit. If one opponent started with four or five cards, your 6 will not be a winning trick.

DUMMY: 5 4 3 2

DECLARER: A K 7 6

You have eight cards in the suit. The best you can hope for is that one opponent has three and the other has two. In that case, you can play the ace and king and lead the suit again, giving up a trick to the opponents' remaining high card. Your remaining card has been developed into a winning trick.

DUMMY: 9 5 3

DECLARER: A 8 6 4 2

It is possible to develop two additional tricks if the opponents' cards are divided three and two. Play the ace, and lead the suit a second time, losing a trick to the opponents. Remember to maintain your high cards in the side suits for entries while establishing your long suit. After regaining the lead, give up another trick to the opponents. Both of your remaining cards have become sure tricks.

Giving Up the Lead

As the last couple of examples show, you often have to give one or more tricks to the opponents when developing additional tricks through length. This is not a problem provided the opponents can't take enough tricks to defeat your contract when they get the lead. Also, you must have sure tricks in other suits. You will need to regain the lead in order to play the winners you have developed.

This is similar to the situation we saw in the last lesson when you were promoting high cards. You want to keep your sure tricks in other suits whenever possible while developing the extra tricks you need. Once again, the guideline "take your losses early" is useful when developing tricks.

Distribution of the Opponents' Cards

When developing tricks through length, the way in which the missing cards are distributed in the opponents' hands can be very important. For example, if you are missing five cards, you may have to hope that the missing cards are divided favorably: three in one hand and two in the other. This is called a 3–2 *break* or *split*.

Sometimes the opponents' cards will break unfavorably. For example, five missing cards could break 4–1 or 5–0. As you play the suit, you should watch to see how the missing cards are divided. In general, an odd number of missing cards will usually divide as evenly as possible. An even number of missing cards will usually divide slightly unevenly. You can see this in the following table:

NUMBER OF MISSING CARDS	MOST LIKELY DISTRIBUTION
3	2–1
4	3–1
5	3–2
6	4–2
7	4–3
8	5–3

Here are a couple of examples:

DUMMY: 6 4 2

DECLARER: A K Q 3

You are missing six cards. The most likely distribution of the opponents' cards is 4–2. After you play the ace, king, and queen, your 3 will not be a sure trick unless you are lucky and the suit breaks 3–3.

DUMMY: A K 7 4 2

DECLARER: 6 5 3

You normally can expect to take four tricks with this suit. After you play the ace and king, you can give up a trick. (High cards in the side suits will be needed for entries.) The remaining cards will be winners if the suit breaks 3–2. If the suit breaks 4–1, you will have to give up two tricks, and you will end up with only three tricks. If the suit breaks 5–0 — too bad!

SUMMARY

RESPONSES TO OPENING BIDS OF ONE OF A SUIT

0 to 5 • Pass

6 to 10 **Responding to a major suit**
- Raise to the two level with three-card support.
- Bid a new suit at the one level.
- Bid 1NT.

Responding to a minor suit
- Bid a new suit at the one level.
- Raise to the two level with five-card support.
- Bid 1NT.

11 or 12 **Responding to a major suit**
- Raise to the three level with three-card or longer support.
- Bid a new suit.

Responding to a minor suit
- Bid a new suit.
- Raise to the three level with five-card or longer support.

13 or more **Responding to a major suit**
- Jump to 2NT with a balanced hand.
- Bid a new suit.

Responding to a minor suit
- Bid a new suit.
- Jump to 2NT with a balanced hand.

When playing a hand, one way to develop additional tricks is by taking advantage of your long suits. If the missing cards in the opponents' hands are distributed favorably, you often can develop tricks by continuing to play the suit, even if you have to give up one or more tricks to the opponents.

THE FINER POINTS

Dummy Points When Raising Partner's Minor Suit

Because 5♣ and 5♦ are not Golden Games, the partnership will usually play in 3NT with 26 or more combined points. In notrump contracts, short suits are a disadvantage rather than an advantage. This explains why dummy points are usually not counted when raising partner's minor suit. The partnership does not want to get to 3NT with only 26 points when some of the points come from valuing short suits.

However, if the partnership is not headed for a notrump contract, dummy points can be used when supporting partner's minor suit. This is the case in these situations: when the partnership is going to play in a partscore contract in a minor suit; when the partnership is going to play game in a minor suit because the combined hands are not suited for notrump; when the partnership is going to play a slam contract in a minor suit.

You usually do not know exactly where the partnership is headed early in the auction. For this reason, it is recommended that you do not initially value your hand using dummy points when raising partner's minor suit. Value your hand using dummy points only when raising partner's major suit. As your experience grows, you will learn to spot those situations when using dummy points will give you a better estimate of the value of the hand.

Raising Partner's Suit — Forcing Raises

When responder has support for partner's suit, the text recommends the following framework based on the value of responder's hand:

0 to 5	Pass.
6 to 10	Raise to the two level.
11 or 12	Raise to the three level.
13 or more	Bid a new suit, intending to raise partner's suit later.

A popular style in many areas is to reverse the last two actions, so the framework becomes:

0 to 5	Pass.
6 to 10	Raise to the two level.
11 or 12	Bid a new suit, intending to raise partner's suit later.
13 or more	Raise to the three level.

The major difference is in the message given by the immediate raise to the three level. In the first framework the raise to the three level is only an invitational (yellow) bid. Since responder is limited to at most 12 points, opener does not need to carry on with only a minimum opening bid. This style is referred to as a *Limit Raise*.

In the second framework, responder is saying that there is enough combined strength for a game contract. This is a forcing (green) bid, and opener must bid again. This style is referred to as a *Forcing* (Jump) *Raise*.

The choice of styles is a matter of partnership preference. Each has advantages and disadvantages. While the text is consistent with the more modern approach of limit raises, it is simple to adapt to the style that is popular in your area or that your partner prefers.

Even within the two frameworks, there are many possible variations. Most authorities recommend that responder always have four–card support when raising to the three level. Others give special meanings to certain responses to fill out the framework. Such special *conventions* and *treatments* are not recommended for new players.

It might seem that the simplest framework for raising opener's suit is the following:

0 to 5	Pass.
6 to 10	Raise to the two level.
11 or 12	Raise to the three level.
13 or more	Raise to the four level.

This is certainly a playable system, but the classic use of the raise to the four level is as a *preemptive bid,* showing fewer than 10 points and at least five–card support. Preemptive bids are discussed briefly in the Appendix but are really beyond the scope of this text.   (SEE P.274)

When to Respond 2NT

With no support for opener's suit and 13 to 15 points, responder has two options. Responder can bid a new suit or bid 2NT. With an unbalanced hand, responder always bids a new suit. With a balanced hand, responder has a choice. For example, if the opening bid is 1♥, does responder bid 2NT or a new suit (2♣) with this hand?

> ♠ A J 3
> ♥ 10 5
> ♦ K 9 7 5
> ♣ A K 10 3

Responder can use the following guidelines:
- With a five-card suit, bid the suit.
- With a four-card suit, bid the suit if it can be bid at the one level.
- Otherwise, bid 2NT.

Thus, on the above hand, responder would bid 2NT.

Responder's Jump Shift

When responder bids a new suit, the text indicates that responder always bids it at the cheapest available level. With very strong hands, usually 19 or more points, responder can show the extra strength by jumping a level. Since responder is changing (shifting) the suit and jumping a level, this is referred to as a *jump shift*. For example, in response to an opening bid of 1♥, responder could jump shift by bidding 2♠, 3♣, or 3♦. The jump shift is a forcing (green) bid. It tells opener that the partnership belongs at least at the game level and likely at the slam level.

A jump shift occurs rarely, and, since a new suit by responder is forcing even when responder does not jump, it is not needed even when responder has a powerful hand. However, in the next lesson, you will see that opener often makes use of the jump shift to show a powerful opening bid.

ACTIVITIES

Exercise One — Responding to a Major Suit Opening with 6 to 10 Points

Partner opens the bidding 1♥. Add up the high-card points and the dummy or distribution points on each of the following hands, and decide what you would respond.

1)	♠ 3	2)	♠ J 10 7 6	3)	♠ K 3 2
	♥ Q J 10		♥ Q 3		♥ J 10
	♦ Q 8 7 6 2		♦ K Q 8 7 4		♦ Q J 9 6 4
	♣ J 10 9 8		♣ 9 6		♣ 5 3 2

HCP:	_6_	HCP:	_8_	HCP:	_7_
Dummy/ Distr. Points:	_3_	Dummy/ Distr. Points:	_1_	Dummy/ Distr. Points:	_1_
Total Points:	_9_	Total Points:	_9_	Total Points:	_8_
Response:	_2 H_	Response:	_1.5_	Response:	_1NT_

What do all three hands have in common? For which of the three hands do you count dummy points?

Exercise Two — Priorities when Responding with 6 to 10 Points

If partner opens the bidding with one of a major, you have three choices with 6 to 10 points. Arrange the following choices in order of their priority:

- a) Bid 1NT.
- b) Bid a new suit at the one level.
- c) Raise partner's major suit to the two level.

If partner opens the bidding with one of a minor suit, your priorities change. Again, arrange the following choices in order of their priority:

- a) Raise partner's minor suit to the two level.
- b) Bid a new suit at the one level.
- c) Bid 1NT.

Exercise Three — Responding to a Minor Suit Opening with 6 to 10 Points

Your partner opens the bidding 1♦. What would you respond on each of the following hands?

1)	♠ 9 8 4 2	2)	♠ J 10	3)	♠ 9 5 3
	♥ Q 8 7		♥ J 4 3		♥ Q J 10 8 7
	♦ K J 4 3		♦ Q 9 8		♦ Q 6
	♣ J 3		♣ K 9 7 5 3		♣ J 5 3

Response: ___*1 S*___   Response: ___*1NT*___   Response: ___*1 H*___

Exercise Four — Responding with 11 or 12 Points

With 11 or 12 points, responder raises partner's major with three–card or longer support; otherwise, responder bids a new suit. What would responder bid with each of the following hands after partner starts the bidding with 1♠?

1)	♠ J 9	2)	♠ J 9 8 4	3)	♠ 8
	♥ A Q J 6 5		♥ K Q		♥ J 6 3
	♦ K 4		♦ J 6		♦ Q J 10 8 6
	♣ 8 6 4 3		♣ K 10 7 5 3		♣ A Q J 9

Response: ___*2 H*___   Response: ___*3S*___   Response: ___*2D*___

It is important to remember the roles of each player. What role does the responder have? What will the opener do on the next bid?

Exercise Five — Responding with 13 or More Points

If responder has 13 or more points, what will the level of the contract be? What bidding message will responder give with all responses?

Your partner opens the bidding 1♠. What would you respond on each of the following hands?

1)	♠ A Q 8 3	2)	♠ J 7	3)	♠ 8
	♥ A 5		♥ K Q 10		♥ K 5 3
	♦ Q J 10 6		♦ A J 8 4		♦ A Q 10 8 6
	♣ 7 6 4		♣ K J 6 3		♣ K 9 6 3

Response: _2◇_   Response: _2♠_   Response: _2◇_

In the first example, how can responder be certain opener will not pass and leave the partnership to play in diamonds rather than spades?

Exercise Six — Developing Tricks Through Length

How many tricks can be developed with each of the following suit combinations if the opponents' cards are divided as favorably as possible?

	1)	2)	3)	4)
DUMMY:	A 9 6 3	A 7 6 4 2	K 7 4	7 4
DECLARER:	K 8 4 2	9 5 3	A Q 6 3	A K 8 6 5 2
	3	3	4	5

Exercise Seven — Developing Winners in Notrump
(E–Z Deal Cards: #4, Hand 1 — Dealer, North)

Turn up all the cards on the first pre-dealt hand. Put each hand dummy style at the edge of the table in front of each player

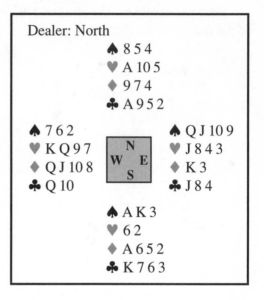

Dealer: North

♠ 8 5 4
♥ A 10 5
♦ 9 7 4
♣ A 9 5 2

♠ 7 6 2   ♠ Q J 10 9
♥ K Q 9 7   ♥ J 8 4 3
♦ Q J 10 8   ♦ K 3
♣ Q 10   ♣ J 8 4

♠ A K 3
♥ 6 2
♦ A 6 5 2
♣ K 7 6 3

The Bidding

North is the dealer. Which player would open the bidding? What would the opening bid be?

Look at responder's hand. Can responder support opener's suit? Can responder bid a new suit? What would responder bid? What is the bidding message given by responder's bid? Does opener have to bid again? If opener does not bid again, what will the contract be? Who will be declarer?

The Play

Suppose that North is declarer in a contract of 1NT. Which player would make the opening lead? What would the opening lead be?

How many tricks must declarer take to fulfill the contract? How many sure tricks does declarer have? Which suit provides declarer with the opportunity to develop the additional tricks needed to make the contract? Which suit should declarer play after winning the first trick? Why?

Bid and play the deal. Did declarer make the contract?

Exercise Eight — Developing Winners in the Trump Suit
(E–Z Deal Cards: #4, Hand 2 — Dealer, East)

Turn up all the cards on the second pre-dealt hand and arrange them as in the previous exercise.

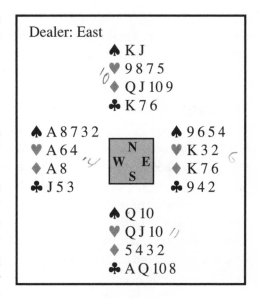

Dealer: East

♠ K J
♥ 9 8 7 5
♦ Q J 10 9
♣ K 7 6

♠ A 8 7 3 2   N   ♠ 9 6 5 4
♥ A 6 4   W E   ♥ K 3 2
♦ A 8   S   ♦ K 7 6
♣ J 5 3   ♣ 9 4 2

♠ Q 10
♥ Q J 10
♦ 5 4 3 2
♣ A Q 10 8

The Bidding

East is the dealer. Which player would open the bidding? What would the opening bid be?

Look at responder's hand. Can responder support opener's suit? What is the value of responder's hand? What would responder bid? What is the bidding message given by responder's bid? Does opener have to bid again? If opener does not bid again, what will the contract be? Who will be declarer?

The Play

Suppose that West is declarer in a contract of 2♠. Which player would make the opening lead? What would the opening lead be?

How many tricks must declarer take to fulfill the contract? How many sure tricks does declarer have? Which suit provides declarer with the opportunity to develop the additional tricks needed to make the contract? Which suit should declarer play after winning the first trick? Will declarer have to be lucky to make the contract? If so, why?

Bid and play the hand. Did declarer make the contract?

Exercise Nine — Developing a Side Suit
(E–Z Deal Cards: #4, Hand 3 — Dealer, South)

Turn up all the cards on the third pre-dealt hand and arrange them as in the previous exercise.

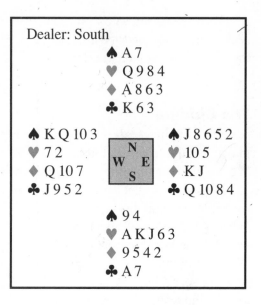

Dealer: South

♠ A 7
♥ Q 9 8 4
♦ A 8 6 3
♣ K 6 3

♠ K Q 10 3   ♠ J 8 6 5 2
♥ 7 2   ♥ 10 5
♦ Q 10 7   ♦ K J
♣ J 9 5 2   ♣ Q 10 8 4

♠ 9 4
♥ A K J 6 3
♦ 9 5 4 2
♣ A 7

The Bidding

South is the dealer. Which player would open the bidding? What would the opening bid be?

Look at responder's hand. What is the value of responder's hand? Although responder can support South's major, what would responder bid first to show the strength of the hand? What is the bidding message given by responder's bid? What would opener rebid? What would the final contract be, most likely? Who would be declarer?

The Play

Suppose that South is declarer in a contract of 4 ♥. Which player would make the opening lead? What would the opening lead be?

How many tricks must declarer take to fulfill the contract? How many sure tricks does declarer have? Which suit provides declarer with the opportunity to develop the additional tricks needed to make the contract? Which suit should declarer play after winning the first trick?

Bid and play the deal. Did declarer make the contract?

Exercise Ten — Patience When Developing a Long Suit
(E–Z Deal Cards: #4, Hand 4 — Dealer, West)

Turn up all the cards on the fourth pre-dealt hand and arrange them as in the previous exercise.

The Bidding

West is the dealer. Which player would open the bidding? What would the opening bid be?

Look at responder's hand. What is the value of responder's hand? Can responder support opener's suit? Can responder bid a new suit? What would responder bid? What is

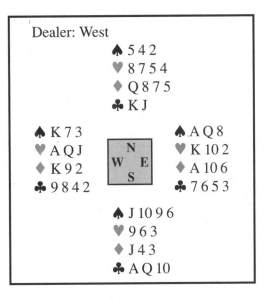

Dealer: West

```
                    ♠ 5 4 2
                    ♥ 8 7 5 4
                    ♦ Q 8 7 5
                    ♣ K J

   ♠ K 7 3                      ♠ A Q 8
   ♥ A Q J         N            ♥ K 10 2
   ♦ K 9 2      W     E         ♦ A 10 6
   ♣ 9 8 4 2       S            ♣ 7 6 5 3

                    ♠ J 10 9 6
                    ♥ 9 6 3
                    ♦ J 4 3
                    ♣ A Q 10
```

the bidding message given by responder's bid? Does opener have to bid again? If opener has to bid again, what would the contract be, most likely? Who would be declarer?

The Play

Suppose that East is declarer in a contract of 3NT. Which player would make the opening lead? What would the opening lead be?

How many tricks must declarer take to fulfill the contract? How many sure tricks does declarer have? Which suit provides declarer with the opportunity to develop the additional tricks needed to make the contract? Which suit should declarer play after winning the first trick? What will have to happen for declarer to make the contract?

Bid and play the deal. Did declarer make the contract?

Answers to Lesson 4 are on pages 300–304.

LESSON 5
Rebids by Opener

Opener's General Approach to the Second Bid

Opener's Rebid after Responder Makes
an Invitational Bid

Opener's Rebid after Responder Makes
a Forcing Bid

Guidelines for Play

Summary

The Finer Points

Activities

OPENER'S GENERAL APPROACH
TO THE SECOND BID

Opener's first bid of one of a suit paints a broad picture. It shows a hand between 13 and 21 points that could be balanced or unbalanced. Responder does not have enough information to decide the level and the denomination of the contract. Opener's hand could have as few as 13 points or as many as 21 points. It could have a wide range of distributional patterns.

Opener's second bid, the rebid, gives responder a clearer picture of the strength (point-count value) and shape (whether it is balanced or unbalanced) of the hand. Opener categorizes the hand according to its strength and shape.

Opener Categorizes the Strength

Opener puts the hand into one of three categories according to its point count:

Minimum Hand	13 to 16 points
Medium Hand	17 or 18 points
Maximum Hand	19 to 21 points

The more points opener has for the opening bid, the higher opener can go when making a rebid.

Opener Categorizes the Shape

Opener puts the hand into one of two categories according to the shape of the hand.

Balanced	No voids, no singletons, no more than one doubleton
Unbalanced	A void, a singleton or more than one doubleton

With a balanced hand, it would seem that opener should always rebid notrump. However, responder is interested in uncovering any Golden Fit to help decide the denomination of the contract. Thus, if a Golden Fit has not yet been found, opener will bid a new suit of at least four cards at the one level if possible. Otherwise, opener will rebid in notrump and let responder take it from there.

With an unbalanced hand, if a Golden Fit has not yet been found, opener will show a second suit of four cards or longer when there is one that can be shown without getting the partnership too high on the Bidding Scale. Otherwise, opener will rebid the suit with which the auction was started.

Opener's Use of the Bidding Messages

Opener is the describer. Opener watches the bidding messages that responder, the captain, gives.

Sign-off Bids: If opener starts the bidding with 1NT, many of responder's bids are signoff bids asking opener to pass. The opening bid is so specific, 16 to 18 points and a balanced shape, that responder can usually decide the level and the denomination without further information from opener.

However, an opening bid of one in a suit is made on so many different kinds of hands that responder needs more information before making a decision. None of responder's bids are sign-offs, and opener is never in the position of being forced to pass on the second time it's opener's turn to bid.

Invitational Bids: There are three invitational bids that responder can make. First, there are the raises of opener's suit. For example:

OPENER	RESPONDER
1♥	2♥
OPENER	RESPONDER
1♥	3♥

When responder holds either a minimum hand with 6 to 10 points and supports opener's suit with a simple raise to the two level or a medium hand of 11 or 12 points and supports opener's suit with a limit raise to the three level, responder cannot insist that opener pass on the second round of bidding. Responder doesn't know the strength of opener's hand. Opener could have a hand as big as 21 points. Therefore, a single raise or a double raise (limit raise) of opener's suit *invites* opener either to pass or bid again depending on the strength of opener's hand.

The other invitational bid that responder has available is a response of 1NT. For example:

OPENER	RESPONDER
1♦	1NT

This bid shows a minimum hand of 6 to 10 points. Opener is invited to pass if opener is content with the contract of 1NT, or to bid again if not.

Forcing Bids: Most of the time, responder is looking for more information from opener. The bid of a new suit by responder is forcing. For example:

OPENER	RESPONDER
1 ♥	1 ♠

Responder's hand is no longer limited to 6-10 points. Responder could have as few as 6 points but might have 13 or more. Opener is being asked to bid again; opener must continue to describe the hand.

Another forcing bid by responder is a jump to 2NT:

OPENER	RESPONDER
1 ♥	2NT

The Role of the Players

The role of each player is important. After opener hears responder's bidding message, opener focuses on the best descriptive rebid for the hand. Responder, the captain, will put the pieces of the puzzle together. Responder will consider opener's description and combine it with the known strength and shape of the hand responder is holding. After consulting what is required for the various bids on the Bidding Scale, responder will decide the level and denomination and steer the partnership to a contract (Lesson 6).

Keep It Simple

It would be easy, at this point, to become so concerned with the memory work involved that the joy of the game of bridge would escape. Just remember to keep it simple — the more strength opener has for the opening bid, the further opener can move up the Bidding Scale on the rebid. At the same time, opener tries to describe the shape of the hand to responder. Opener always keeps the goals of the partnership in mind: to find out whether or not there is a Golden Game and a Golden Fit.

OPENER'S REBID AFTER RESPONDER MAKES AN INVITATIONAL BID

Responder Raises a Major Suit Opening

Consider opener's action after responder has made a single raise of opener's bid of one of a major suit. For example:

OPENER	RESPONDER
1 ♠	2 ♠

The denomination for the contract has been decided. Opener suggested a major suit, and responder confirmed that there is a Golden Fit. Opener doesn't need to show another suit or describe whether the hand is balanced or unbalanced. There is no need to search further for the denomination. Responder's only uncertainty is whether the contract should be a partscore or game. To decide this, responder may need more information about the strength of opener's hand.

♠ A K 10 9 8 2
♥ J 10 9
♦ 5 3
♣ K 3

Opener has 11 HCP and 2 points for the six-card spade suit, a total of 13 points. This is a minimum hand (13 to 16 points). Responder's raise is invitational, and opener may pass or bid again. On this hand, opener has no extra strength and will pass, leaving the partnership in a partscore. Even if responder has as many as 10 points, there will not be enough combined strength for game.

♠ A Q J 7 4 2
♥ A 9
♦ 7 4 2
♣ A 6

Opener has 15 HCP and 2 points for the six-card suit, a total of 17 points. This is a medium hand (17 or 18 points). With some extra strength, opener moves higher on the Bidding Scale to three. The decision as to whether there is enough combined strength for game will be left to responder. If responder has 6, 7, or 8 points, there will not be enough combined strength for game. If responder has 9 or 10 points, the partnership will have enough.

♠ K Q 10 7 6 2
♥ Q 4
♦ A K
♣ A J 8

Opener has 21 points, 19 HCP and 2 points for the six-card suit. This is a maximum hand (19 to 21 points). With this much extra strength, opener can jump one level on the bidding scale and rebid 4♠, putting the partnership in game. Even if responder has as few as 6 points, there will be enough combined strength for a game contract.

The more strength opener has for the original opening bid, the higher opener rebids. After responder raises a major suit opening bid to the two level, opener passes with a minimum hand (13 to 16 points), raises to the three level with a medium hand (17 or 18 points), and jumps to the four level (game) with a maximum hand (19 to 21 points).

Similarly, consider opener's action after responder raises the opening bid to the three level. For example:

OPENER	RESPONDER
1 ♥	3 ♥

Again, the denomination has been decided. Responder is making an invitational bid. The only decision left is whether or not there is enough combined strength for game:

♠ K 9 5
♥ K J 7 5 3
♦ A 8 2
♣ J 7

Opener has 12 HCP and 1 point for the five-card heart suit. Since responder has at most 12 points, there will not be enough combined strength for game. Opener must decline responder's invitation and pass.

♠ 10 6
♥ A Q 10 6 5 3
♦ A Q J 8
♣ 5

With 13 HCP and 2 points for the six-card suit, opener has enough to accept the invitation. Opener bids 4♥. There is no need to bid another suit since the denomination has already been decided.

When responder raises opener's suit to the three level, opener passes with a minimum of 13 or 14 points but bids game with 15 or more.

Responder Raises a Minor Suit Opening

Consider opener's action after responder has made a single raise of opener's bid of one of a minor suit. For example:

OPENER	RESPONDER
1♦	2♦

In this case, the denomination for the contract has not yet been decided. Opener suggested a minor suit. Responder has confirmed a Golden Fit in the minor suit and likely no Golden Fit in a major suit. (Responder would have bid a four-card or longer major suit at the one level if responder had one.) If the contract is to be a partscore, playing in the minor suit Golden Fit will be fine. However, if the contract is to be game, it probably should be played in 3NT rather than 5♦. Opener will need to keep this in mind when choosing a rebid.

♠ Q 9 7
♥ J 10
♦ A 9 8 7 6 3
♣ K Q

Opener has 12 HCP and 2 points for the six-card diamond suit, a total of 14 points. This is a minimum hand (13 to 16 points). Responder's raise is invitational, and opener may pass or bid again. On this hand, opener has no extra strength and will pass, leaving the partnership in a partscore. Even if responder has as much as 10 points, there will not be enough combined strength for game.

♠ 9 8
♥ 9 7
♦ K Q J 6 4 2
♣ A K Q

Opener has 15 HCP and 2 points for the six-card suit, a total of 17 points. This is a medium hand (17 or 18 points). With some extra strength, opener moves higher on the Bidding Scale to 3 ♦. The decision on whether or not there is enough combined strength for game will be left to responder. If responder has only 6, 7, or 8 points, there will not be enough combined strength for game. If responder has 9 or 10 points, the partnership will have enough.

♠ A Q 7
♥ K 10
♦ K J 10 7 4
♣ K Q 9

There are 19 points — 18 HCP and 1 for the five-card suit. This is a maximum hand (19 to 21 points). With this much extra strength, opener can jump to game. However, opener should jump to 3NT, the Golden Game, rather than 5 ♦. Unless responder has the maximum of 10 points, there is unlikely to be enough combined strength for a 5 ♦ contract.

Opener's rebid when responder raises a minor suit to the two level is similar to that when responder raises a major suit to the two level. Opener passes with a minimum hand, raises to the three level with a medium hand, and jumps to game (3NT) with a maximum hand.

Similarly, when responder raises opener's minor suit to the three level, opener passes with only 13 or 14 points but bids game (3NT) with 15 or more.

Responder Bids 1NT

After an opening bid of one in a suit, a 1NT response shows 6 to 10 points. It is an invitational bid, and opener can either pass or bid again. This time, however, the denomination has not been decided, so opener has to consider both the strength and shape of the hand when making the next bid.

Suppose the auction starts this way:

OPENER	RESPONDER
1♥	1NT

The following hands for opener fall into the minimum range (13 to 16 points). Opener cannot move too far up the Bidding Scale because opener does not want to show responder any extra strength. At the same time, opener wants to describe the shape of the hand as accurately as possible.

♠ K 7 3
♥ A Q 10 9 5
♦ K 10 3
♣ 8 2

Opener has 12 HCP and 1 point for the five-card heart suit, a total of 13 points. Opener knows there is no Golden Fit in hearts because responder would have raised to 2♥ with three or more. Since the contract is already in notrump and opener has a balanced hand with no extra strength, opener can best describe the hand by saying pass. The partnership cannot make game since responder has a maximum of 10 points.

♠ Q 9 8
♥ K Q 6 4 3
♦ A J 8 4
♣ 3

Again opener has 13 points. This time, however, the hand is unbalanced since opener has a singleton club. To finish describing the hand, opener rebids 2♦, showing the second suit. Responder can now choose whether to pass or go back to 2♥.

♠ 9 6 2
♥ A K 10 8 6 2
♦ A J 4
♣ 6

Opener has 12 HCP and 2 for the six-card heart suit, making a total of 14 points. Opener's hand is unbalanced, but there is no second suit to show. In this case, opener rebids the original suit, 2 ♥.

♠ K 10 6 4
♥ A Q J 7 6 3
♦ Q 10
♣ 5

Once again opener has a minimum hand of 14 points but this time there is a second suit that could be shown, spades. However, there are two reasons why opener should not show this suit. First, if opener bids 2 ♠ to show the second suit and an unbalanced hand, responder will have to choose between spades and hearts. If responder prefers hearts, the bid has to be 3 ♥ and, with both partners having minimum hands, the partnership might be too high on the Bidding Scale. Second, opener knows there can't be a Golden Fit in spades since responder would have bid 1 ♠ with four or more spades rather than 1NT. Opener should rebid the original suit, 2 ♥.

The last example illustrates a general principle. When holding a minimum hand, opener should not rebid at the two level a suit that ranks higher than the original suit bid by opener. It is fine to bid a lower-ranking suit, as in the second example.

When opener has a medium strength hand (17 or 18 points) and responder bids 1NT, there is still some possibility of a game contract if responder has the top of the range (9 or 10 points). If responder is at the bottom of the range (6, 7, or 8 points), game is unlikely. The partnership should rest in a partscore contract.

Suppose the auction starts this way:

OPENER	RESPONDER
1 ♦	1NT

♠ 2
♥ A 8 3
♦ A K J 9 7 6
♣ A 4 2

Opener has 16 HCP and 2 points for the six-card dia-mond suit, a total of 18 points. Opener has an unbal-anced hand with no second suit. To describe the shape of the hand, opener must rebid the original suit. But with extra strength, opener does not rebid the suit at the two level as opener would holding a minimum hand. Instead, opener jumps to the three level and bids 3♦.

♠ 9
♥ A K 7 2
♦ K J 10 8 4
♣ A J 5

Opener has 16 HCP and 1 point for the five-card dia-mond suit, a total of 17 points. This puts the hand in the medium category. Again the hand is unbalanced, but this time opener has a second suit. Opener can show this by bidding 2♥ to tell responder this is an unbalanced hand with at least five diamonds and four hearts. Opener also shows a medium-strength hand by bidding a higher-rank-ing suit at the two level. Opener wouldn't do this with a minimum hand. Opener has enough strength to push the partnership to the three level if necessary.

♠ 4
♥ K J 5
♦ K Q 10 6 3
♣ A Q J 8

This is similar to the previous example, except that opener's second suit is lower-ranking than the original suit. Opener, with 16 points plus 1 for the five-card dia-mond suit, can describe the hand by rebidding 2♣. This shows an unbalanced hand. It will sound exactly the same to responder as if opener had a minimum hand with dia-monds and clubs. Unfortunately, there is no way around this. If opener jumps to 3♣ to show the extra strength, the partnership might get too high on the bidding scale. As we'll see in the next section, a jump in a new suit is used to show a maximum hand. Nothing's perfect!

You might have noticed that the previous examples contain no balanced hands of medium strength. With a balanced hand of medium strength, opener would start the bidding with 1NT rather than one of a suit.

When opener has a maximum strength hand (19 to 21 points) and responder shows a minimum hand of 6 to 10 points, the partnership has enough combined strength for game.

Opener's rebid will guarantee that the partnership reaches a game contract.

Suppose the auction starts as follows:

OPENER	RESPONDER
1 ♠	1NT

♠ A K J 8 7
♥ 10 4 2
♦ A Q 7
♣ A 10

Opener has 18 HCP and 1 point for the five-card spade suit, a total of 19 points. Opener has a balanced hand and can show this by jumping to 3NT.

♠ K Q J 9 7 6 3
♥ 5
♦ A J
♣ A Q J

With 18 HCP and 3 points for the seven-card spade suit, opener has 21 points. With an unbalanced hand and no second suit to show, opener rebids the original suit. Opener jumps right to a game of 4 ♠ to show the great strength of the hand.

♠ A Q 10 5 3
♥ 9 5
♦ A K J 6
♣ A 3

Opener has 19 points — 18 HCP and 1 for the five-card spade suit. This is an unbalanced hand with a second suit that can be shown. To do this, opener rebids 3 ♦. This jump in a new suit is called a jump shift. It is a forcing bid by opener describing a maximum unbalanced hand. Responder will use this information to determine the appropriate contract.

In the last example, opener's second suit was lower-ranking than the original suit, and opener jumped to show the extra strength. If opener's second suit were higher-ranking than the original suit, it would take up a lot of room on the bidding scale if opener were to jump. For example:

OPENER	RESPONDER
1 ♦	1NT
3 ♠	

Responder, having responded 1NT rather than 1 ♠, is known not to have four spades. If responder now wanted to show diamond support, the bid would have to be 4 ♦, getting the partnership past 3NT. As you saw in the discussion on medium strength hands, opener can show extra strength by bidding a suit higher-ranking than the original suit at the two level. Opener just needs to bid 2 ♠ in the above example to show extra strength. Responder will not know whether opener has a medium or maximum hand but will bid again to give him an opportunity to further describe the hand.

Putting It Together

In summary, when the opening bid is one of a suit and responder makes an invitational response, opener chooses a rebid following these guidelines:

OPENER'S REBID AFTER RESPONDER RAISES OPENER'S MAJOR SUIT TO THE TWO LEVEL

With 13 to 16 points (minimum hand):

- Pass.

With 17 or 18 points (medium hand):

- Raise to the three level.

With 19 to 21 points (maximum hand):

- Jump raise to the four level (game).

OPENER'S REBID AFTER RESPONDER RAISES OPENER'S MINOR SUIT TO THE TWO LEVEL

With 13 to 16 points (minimum hand):
* Pass.

With 17 or 18 points (medium hand):
* Raise to the three level.

With 19 to 21 points (maximum hand):
* Jump to 3NT (game).

OPENER'S REBID AFTER RESPONDER RAISES OPENER'S SUIT TO THE THREE LEVEL

With 13 or 14 points (minimum hand):
* Pass.

With 15 or more points:
* Bid game.

OPENER'S REBID AFTER RESPONDER BIDS 1NT

With 13 to 16 points (minimum hand):
* Pass with a balanced hand.
* Bid a second suit of four cards or longer if it is lower-ranking than the original suit.
* Rebid the original suit at the two level.

With 17 or 18 points (medium hand):
* Bid a second suit of four cards or longer, even if it is higher-ranking than the original suit.
* Rebid the original suit at the three level.

With 19 to 21 points (maximum hand):
* Bid 3NT with a balanced hand.
* Bid a second suit of four cards or longer, jumping a level (jump shift) if it is lower-ranking than the original suit.
* Rebid the original suit, jumping to game.

Let's see how this works.

OPENER	RESPONDER
1♠	2♠

♠ K J 9 8 5 4
♥ A 8 6
♦ K 9
♣ Q 4

With 13 HCP and 2 for the six-card suit, you have a minimum hand of 15 points. Pass and rest in a partscore.

♠ A K J 7 5 3
♥ K Q
♦ A Q 8
♣ 5 3

With 19 HCP and 2 points for the six-card spade suit, you have a maximum hand of 21 points. Jump to game, 4♠.

♠ K Q 10 9 6 2
♥ 5 4
♦ K Q 8
♣ A J

This hand is worth 17 points — 15 HCP and 2 for the six-card suit. With a medium hand, raise to 3♠ and leave the final decision to responder.

Let's see what you do with the following hands when the auction starts:

OPENER	RESPONDER
1♣	2♣

♠ A Q 8 5
♥ K 10 6 3
♦ J 9
♣ Q J 2

With a minimum hand of 13 points, pass and stop in a partscore. Remember that responder will hold five clubs when raising your minor suit so you will be playing in a Golden Fit.

♠ K 3 2
♥ A 7 3
♦ 3
♣ A K J 8 6 2

With a medium hand of 17 points — 15 HCP plus 2 for the six-card suit — raise to the three level, 3♣. Responder will decide whether to stay in a partscore or carry on to game.

♠ A J 10
♥ K J
♦ 9 7 3
♣ A K Q J 8

With a maximum hand of 20 points — 19 HCP and 1 for the fifth club — jump to game. In this case, rebid 3NT since this is the Golden Game, not 5♣.

Let's see what you rebid on each of the following hands when the auction starts:

OPENER	RESPONDER
1♦	1NT

♠ 9 3
♥ A
♦ A 10 8 7 3
♣ K Q 6 4 3

You have 13 HCP and 1 point for each of the five-card suits. That puts this hand in the minimum range. With an unbalanced hand and a second suit that is lower-ranking than your original suit, rebid 2♣.

♠ A 5
♥ K J 9
♦ A K J 7 3
♣ A 5 2

You have 20 HCP and a balanced hand that was too strong to open 1NT. You can show the strength on your rebid by jumping to 3NT.

♠ A Q 3
♥ J 8 7
♦ A K Q 10 6 3
♣ 6

This is a medium sized unbalanced hand of 18 points. With no second suit, show your strength by jumping in your original suit, 3♦.

♠ Q J 10 9
♥ A 3
♦ K Q 9 7 6 4
♣

With 12 HCP and 2 for the six-card diamond suit, your hand falls in the minimum category. It is an unbalanced hand but you are not strong enough to bid a second suit at the two level that is higher-ranking than your first suit. Instead, rebid your first suit, 2♦.

♠ A Q
♥ 6 2
♦ A Q J 8 7
♣ K Q J 9

This hand contains 20 points — 19 HCP and 1 for the five-card suit — putting it in the maximum category. With an unbalanced hand, you want to show your second suit. To do this, you jump shift to 3♣, telling responder you are in the maximum range.

♠ K 7
♥ Q J 9 2
♦ A 8 7 4
♣ Q J 3

This time you have a minimum hand, 13 points, that is balanced. You can describe your hand best with a pass, leaving the contract in notrump at the cheapest level. Remember that the response of 1NT is invitational only, not forcing.

OPENER'S REBID AFTER RESPONDER MAKES A FORCING BID

Responder Bids a New Suit at the One Level

A new-suit bid by responder is forcing. Opener can no longer show a minimum hand by passing. Responder has at least 6 points but could have considerably more. Since opener cannot tell how many points responder has, opener must continue to describe the hand. The partnership's priority is still to look for a Golden Game, in spades or hearts with a Golden Fit, otherwise in notrump. If there are not enough combined points for a game contract, the partnership settles for a partscore in a Golden Fit or notrump.

Opener uses the familiar guidelines. Opener classifies the strength and shape of the hand and describes them with a carefully selected rebid. When planning to raise responder's major, opener falls into the position of becoming a dummy for partner. When classifying the strength of the hand, opener should then use dummy points for shortness in place of distributional points for length.

DUMMY POINTS	
Void	5 Points
Singleton	3 Points
Doubleton	1 Point

This is similar to the case where responder raises opener's major (Lesson 4). Since opener is showing a five-card suit by opening the bidding in a major suit, responder needs only three-card support to raise. However, when responder bids a major suit at the one level, responder may only have four cards in the suit. Thus, opener needs four-card support to raise.

Suppose the auction starts:

OPENER	RESPONDER
1 ♦	1 ♥

Let's see how opener approaches the rebid when holding a minimum hand (13 to 16 points).

♠ A 9 3
♥ K 7 6 4
♦ A Q 7 3 2
♣ 9

Opener has started the bidding with 1 ♦. On hearing the response of 1 ♥, opener knows the partnership has a Golden Fit in a major suit. Opener's first priority is to inform responder of opener's support for hearts. Since opener is planning to support responder's major suit, opener revalues the hand using dummy points. Opener has 13 HCP plus 3 points for the singleton — a total of 16 points. Opener raises to the cheapest level, bidding 2 ♥. Note that opener does not pass, even knowing the partnership has found a Golden Fit. Responder's bid is forcing, and opener must keep the auction going to allow responder to determine the appropriate level for the contract.

♠ Q J 9 4
♥ J 8 2
♦ A K J 4
♣ Q 5

Opener cannot support responder's major suit with this hand. Responder may have only a four-card suit, so opener needs four-card support to ensure a Golden Fit. However, opener does not give up on the search for a Golden Fit in a major suit. Opener can conveniently show the spade suit at the one level and rebids 1♠. It is quite possible that responder has a four-card spade suit (or five hearts). With four hearts and four spades, responder would bid hearts first, showing the suits up the line (Lesson 4).

♠ K J 10
♥ J 5
♦ A J 10 9 4
♣ A 6 2

Opener cannot raise responder's major suit and does not have another suit to bid at the one level. However, the hand is a balanced minimum hand. Opener can describe this type of hand to responder by bidding 1NT. Since opener would have started the bidding with 1NT holding a balanced hand with 16 to 18 points, this sequence tells responder that opener has a minimum balanced hand, too weak to open 1NT.

♠ A 10 8
♥ 5
♦ K Q 10 7 3
♣ A J 4 2

Again opener has a minimum hand, but it is not balanced. Opener can describe the hand by rebidding 2♣, showing the second suit. As discussed in the section on rebids by opener after a 1NT response, it is all right for opener to bid a second suit at the two level with a minimum hand if it is lower-ranking than the original suit. Opener would need a medium hand if the second suit were a higher-ranking suit.

♠ A 10
♥ 10 4
♦ A Q J 8 5 3
♣ 7 5 4

Opener has a minimum unbalanced hand with no second suit to bid. In this case, opener can rebid the original suit at the cheapest available level, 2♦. Rebidding the suit without a jump tells responder that opener is in the minimum range.

Suppose the auction starts this way:

OPENER	RESPONDER
1 ♣	1 ♠

Let's see the effect on opener's rebid when holding a medium hand (17 or 18 points).

♠ A K 6 4
♥ 9 3
♦ J 8
♣ A K J 6 3

Having heard partner's response of 1 ♠, opener intends to describe the hand further by showing support for partner's suit. But before raising responder's major, opener values the hand using dummy points. Opener has 16 HCP and 1 for each of the doubletons, a total of 18 points. With more than minimum strength, opener can describe the hand to responder by jumping a level and raising to 3 ♠. Responder, knowing that opener has medium strength, will decide whether there is enough combined strength for game.

♠ 7 2
♥ A Q J 5
♦ K 5
♣ K Q J 10 8

This hand is worth 17 points, 16 HCP plus 1 for the five-card club suit. It is unbalanced. Opener wants to show the second suit whenever possible to give responder a good description of the hand. Opener can bid 2 ♥ on this hand because there is extra strength. Even if responder has only 6 points and prefers clubs to hearts, the partnership should not be too high on the Bidding Scale in a contract of 3 ♣.

♠ 10 4
♥ A K 6
♦ J 2
♣ A K J 9 6 2

Opener has a medium-strength unbalanced hand with no second suit to show. In this case, opener rebids the original suit with a jump, 3 ♣. This tells responder about the extra strength since, with a minimum hand, opener would have rebid 2 ♣.

With a medium-strength hand, opener sometimes will be able to describe the shape by bidding a second suit at the one level or bidding a lower-ranking second suit at the two level. When opener does this, responder will assume that opener has a minimum strength hand. It is not always possible for opener to describe both the strength and the shape. As the auction continues, opener may get an opportunity to show the extra strength.

Opener does not have to worry about what to rebid with a balanced hand of medium strength. All such hands would be opened 1NT (Lesson 3).

Let's move on to opener's rebid when holding a maximum hand (19 to 21 points). Suppose the auction starts:

OPENER	RESPONDER
1♥	1♠

♠ K Q 9 3
♥ A Q J 7 5
♦ A 4
♣ K 2

Hearing a response of 1♠, opener knows there is a Golden Fit in a major suit. Before deciding how high to raise responder's suit, opener revalues the hand using dummy points. With 19 HCP and 1 point for each doubleton, opener has 21 points. To show this much strength, opener jumps all the way to game, 4♠. Even if responder has only 6 points, there should be enough combined strength for the partnership to make game.

♠ A Q 10
♥ K Q J 10 5
♦ K 9 3
♣ K J

Opener has a balanced hand and cannot support responder's suit (responder may have a four-card suit). Opener can show this by jumping a level to 2NT. It may seem strange that opener does not jump all the way to game, 3NT, but remember that opener is merely describing the hand. Responder will make the decision of where to play the contract after getting sufficient information about opener's hand.

♠ A Q
♥ A K J 8 2
♦ K Q 10 6 3
♣ 5

Opener, with a maximum unbalanced hand with a second suit to show, jump shifts to 3 ♦. Responder will know that opener has a hand in the range of 19 to 21 points and will ensure that the partnership reaches a game contract.

♠ A 4
♥ A Q J 9 7 5 3
♦ K 3
♣ K 2

Opener has 17 HCP and 3 points for the seven-card suit, a maximum hand. With no second suit to show, opener rebids the original suit with a jump to game, 4 ♥, to show a hand in the maximum range.

Responder Bids a New Suit at the Two Level

To bid a new suit at the two level, responder must have at least 11 points. As with a new suit at the one level, responder's bid is forcing — opener cannot pass. Opener uses the same principles in choosing a rebid, but, since the auction is already at the two level, opener's rebid is often higher on the bidding scale than if responder had bid at the one level. This can be illustrated with a few examples.

Suppose the auction starts this way:

OPENER	RESPONDER
1 ♠	2 ♥

♠ A K 9 8 4 ♥ Q J 8 6 ♦ K 5 ♣ 10 2	Since opener can support responder's major, opener revalues the hand using dummy points. With 13 HCP and 1 point for each of the doubletons, opener has 15 points, a minimum hand. To show this, opener raises to the cheapest level (opener cannot pass since responder's bid is forcing) and bids 3♥.
♠ A Q 10 7 4 ♥ A Q 9 3 ♦ K J ♣ 9 3	Opener has a medium strength hand of 18 points in support of responder's suit — 16 HCP and 1 for each doubleton. To show the extra strength, opener jumps one level and bids 4♥. This gets the partnership to game when opener has only a medium hand, but responder must have at least 11 points to have bid a new suit at the two level.
♠ K J 10 8 4 ♥ J 7 ♦ K J 9 ♣ A 10 2	Opener has a minimum hand but cannot raise responder's suit. With a balanced hand, opener can rebid notrump at the cheapest available level, 2NT. Since opener did not jump, responder will know that opener has a minimum balanced hand, too weak to open 1NT.
♠ A J 9 7 4 ♥ A J ♦ K Q 6 ♣ Q J 10	Opener has a maximum balanced hand of 19 points. To show this, opener jumps to 3NT. Responder knows that opener has a maximum balanced hand too strong to open 1NT.

Responder Jumps to 2NT

By jumping to 2NT in response to an opening bid of one in a suit, responder shows a balanced hand of 13 to 16 points without support for opener's major suit (if opener bid a major). Responder has announced that the partnership holds enough combined strength for a game contract. Responder's bid has left room for opener to further describe the hand.

Suppose the auction starts this way:

OPENER	RESPONDER
1 ♠	2NT

♠ A J 7 6 3
♥ K 9 5
♦ 8 4 2
♣ A 3

Opener has a minimum hand of 13 points — 12 HCP plus 1 for the five-card spade suit. With a balanced hand, opener can simply raise to 3NT. Note that opener cannot pass since responder's bid is forcing. Opener also knows that there is no Golden Fit in spades because responder did not raise them.

♠ A J 7 6 3
♥ K 9 5 4 2
♦ 8
♣ A 3

Opener has a minimum hand, but it is unbalanced. Opener can rebid 3♥, showing the second suit and leaving it up to responder to place the contract.

♠ A J 7 6 3 2
♥ K 9 5
♦ 8 4 2
♣

Opener has a minimum unbalanced hand but knows there is a Golden Fit in spades. Responder is showing a balanced hand and cannot have a singleton spade. Opener can simply bid a game contract in the known fit, 4♠.

Putting It Together

In summary, when responder makes a forcing response, opener cannot pass. Opener considers the strength and shape of the hand and rebids accordingly.

OPENER'S REBID AFTER RESPONDER BIDS A NEW SUIT AT THE ONE LEVEL

With 13 to 16 points (minimum hand):
- Raise partner's major to the cheapest available level with four-card support (count dummy points).
- Bid a second suit of four cards or longer if it can be bid at the one level. A lower-ranking suit than the original one can be bid at the two level.
- Bid notrump at the cheapest available level with a balanced hand.
- Rebid the original suit at the cheapest available level.

With 17 or 18 points (medium hand):
- Raise partner's major, jumping one level, with four-card support (count dummy points).
- Bid a second suit of four cards or longer (even if it is higher-ranking than the original suit and must be bid at the two level).
- Rebid the original suit, jumping one level.

With 19 to 21 points (maximum hand):
- Raise partner's major, jumping two levels, with four-card support (count dummy points).
- Bid a second suit of four cards or longer, jumping one level (jump shift) if it is lower-ranking than the original suit.
- Bid notrump with a balanced hand, jumping one level.
- Rebid the original suit, jumping to game.

OPENER'S REBID AFTER RESPONDER BIDS 2NT

- With a balanced hand, raise to 3NT.
- With an unbalanced hand, bid a second suit of four cards or longer or rebid the original suit.

Suppose you open the bidding 1♣ and your partner responds 1♠.

♠ 10 9 7 3
♥ A Q 5
♦ 4 3
♣ A K 6 2

You have support for partner's major suit, so revalue the hand using dummy points. You have 13 HCP and 1 point for the doubleton diamond, making a total of 14 points. With a minimum hand, raise to the cheapest available level, 2♠.

♠ Q 6 3
♥ A J 4 2
♦ J 8 7
♣ A Q 5

With a minimum hand, you can't support responder's major suit with only three cards, and you can't bid a new suit that is higher-ranking than your original suit at the two level. You describe a minimum balanced hand by rebidding 1NT.

♠ 3
♥ K 10 2
♦ J 8 4
♣ A K Q 7 5 3

You have an unbalanced hand with no second suit, and it lies in the minimum range. Describe this to responder by rebidding your suit at the cheapest available level, 2♣.

♠ A J 10 6
♥ —
♦ K 9 3
♣ A Q J 7 5 3

You can support responder's major suit. You have a hand worth 20 points counting dummy points — 15 HCP and 5 points for the void in hearts. That makes this a maximum hand. Raise to game, 4♠.

♠ K 3
♥ A Q J
♦ Q 10 5
♣ A K 9 3 2

With a maximum balanced hand, jump to 2NT to describe your strength and shape.

♠ 4 2
♥ Q 2
♦ A Q
♣ K Q J 8 6 3 2

With a medium unbalanced hand and no second suit, rebid your original suit, jumping a level. Bid 3♣.

GUIDELINES FOR PLAY

When you don't have enough tricks to make your contract, you have to "analyze your alternatives." Sometimes, you can try to win a trick with one of your high cards even if the opponents have a higher-ranking card. To do this, you will need a little luck. The higher-ranking card must be favorably placed in an opponent's hand. If it is, careful play will let you develop an extra trick.

The Finesse

Consider the following suit:

DUMMY:　　　K 4

DECLARER:　　3 2

If you had the queen, you could lead the king to drive out the opponent's ace. The queen would be promoted to a sure trick. Without the queen, leading the king will do no good. The opponents will win the ace, and now, their queen will be a sure trick. In such situations, you can sometimes get a trick by leading toward the high card. This is called taking a *finesse*. You have to hope that the opponents' cards are favorably placed. For example:

K 4

A J 9 7 5　W　E　Q 10 8 6
N / S

3 2

When you lead from your hand toward dummy, you will be able to get a trick if the opponent on your left holds the ace. Your left-hand opponent has to play before the dummy. If the ace is played, you put in the 4 from dummy, and the king has become a sure trick. If the ace isn't played, you select dummy's king. It will win the trick because the opponent on your right does not have the ace.

A finesse will not always work. For example, the opponents' cards could be placed in this fashion:

K 4

J 9 7 5   W E   A Q 10 8 6

3 2

You lead a small card toward dummy. The opponent on your left plays a small card, and you try a finesse by playing dummy's king. Unfortunately, the opponent on your right wins the trick with the ace, and your finesse fails. However, you gave it your best shot. You couldn't take a trick no matter how you played the suit. The ace was unfavorably placed.

Here is another example of a finesse:

DUMMY: A Q

DECLARER: 3 2

You always have one sure trick, the ace. If you need two tricks from this suit, you follow the principle of leading toward high cards by leading toward the ace and queen. If the opponent on your left plays a small card, you play dummy's queen. You are hoping that your left-hand opponent holds the king.

For example:

A Q

K J 8 7   W E   10 9 6 5 4

3 2

The player on your right does not have a higher card than your queen, and you win the trick. Of course, if your right-hand opponent did have the king, your finesse would lose. You would be back to the one sure trick you started with.

Entries

In the above examples, you had to lead from the appropriate hand to give yourself the best chance to get an extra trick. There are many times when you want to be in a specific hand. For example, if you have sure tricks in one hand, you want to be able to get to that hand in order to take them.

A card or a combination of cards, which lets you get from one hand to the other, is called an entry. There are two parts to an *entry* — you need a sure trick in one hand and a smaller card of the same suit in the other hand. The smaller card enables you to cross over to the sure trick. Here is a simple example:

DUMMY: A

DECLARER: 2

This combination of cards provides an entry to dummy's hand. You have a small card in your hand which you can lead to the sure trick in dummy.

Here is another example:

DUMMY: K 4 2

DECLARER: A 6 5

This suit provides an entry to either hand. You can play one of your small cards to dummy's king, or you can lead one of dummy's small cards over to your ace.

Entries are very useful. They let you to be in the right place at the right time. As declarer, you should always watch your entries, being careful not to squander them.

SUMMARY

When making a rebid, opener puts the hand into one of the following categories according to the point count value. (Remember to use dummy points if you are planning to support responder's major suit.)

Minimum Hand	13 to 16 points
Medium Hand	17 or 18 points
Maximum Hand	19 to 21 points

Next, opener chooses the rebid that best describes the hand. Opener takes into account the nature of responder's bid, using the following guidelines.

OPENER'S REBID AFTER RESPONDER RAISES OPENER'S MAJOR SUIT TO THE TWO LEVEL

With 13 to 16 points (minimum hand):
- Pass.

With 17 or 18 points (medium hand):
- Raise to the three level.

With 19 to 21 points (maximum hand):
- Jump raise to the four level (game).

OPENER'S REBID AFTER RESPONDER RAISES OPENER'S MINOR SUIT TO THE TWO LEVEL

With 13 to 16 points (minimum hand):
- Pass.

With 17 or 18 points (medium hand):
- Raise to the three level.

With 19 to 21 points (maximum hand):
- Jump to 3NT (game).

OPENER'S REBID AFTER RESPONDER RAISES OPENER'S SUIT TO THE THREE LEVEL

With 13 or 14 points:
- Pass.

With 15 or more points:
- Bid game.

OPENER'S REBID AFTER RESPONDER BIDS A NEW SUIT AT THE ONE LEVEL

With 13 to 16 points (minimum hand):
- Raise partner's major to the cheapest available level with four-card support (count dummy points).
- Bid a second suit of four cards or longer if it can be bid at the one level. A lower-ranking suit than the original one can be bid at the two level.
- Bid notrump with a balanced hand at the cheapest available level.
- Rebid the original suit at the cheapest available level.

With 17 or 18 points (medium hand):
- Raise partner's major, jumping one level, with four-card support (count dummy points).
- Bid a second suit of four cards or longer, even if it is higher-ranking than the original suit and must be bid at the two level.
- Rebid the original suit, jumping one level.

With 19 to 21 points (maximum hand):

- Raise partner's major, jumping two levels, with four-card support (count dummy points).
- Bid a second suit of four cards or longer, jumping one level (jump shift) if it is lower-ranking than the original suit.
- Bid notrump with a balanced hand, jumping one level.
- Rebid the original suit, jumping to game.

OPENER'S REBID AFTER RESPONDER BIDS 1NT

With 13 to 16 points (minimum hand):

- Pass with a balanced hand.
- Bid a second suit of four cards or longer if it is lower-ranking than the original suit.
- Rebid the original suit at the two level.

With 17 or 18 points (medium hand):

- Bid a second suit of four cards or longer, even if it is higher-ranking than the original suit.
- Rebid the original suit at the three level.

With 19 to 21 points (maximum hand):

- Bid 3NT with a balanced hand.
- Bid a second suit of four cards or longer, jumping a level (jump shift) if it is lower-ranking than the original suit.
- Rebid the original suit, jumping to game.

OPENER'S REBID AFTER RESPONDER BIDS 2NT

- With a balanced hand, raise to 3NT.
- With an unbalanced hand, bid a second suit of four cards or longer or rebid the original suit.

A good guideline for declarer when playing a hand is to lead toward the high cards. To do this, you may need an entry to allow you to get to the appropriate hand.

THE FINER POINTS

The text recommends categorizing opener's strength into one of the following ranges:

Minimum Hand	13 to 16 points
Medium Hand	17 or 18 points
Maximum Hand	19 to 21 points

The ranges are slightly uneven. Some authorities find it easier to use a series of 3-point ranges:

Minimum Hand	13 to 15 points
Medium Hand	16 to 18 points
Maximum Hand	19 to 21 points

This is certainly reasonable although a little aggressive when starting out. Opener always bids again with a medium strength hand, even when responder shows a hand in the 6 to 10 point range. For example:

OPENER	RESPONDER
1♥	2♥
3♥	

If opener has 16 points, the only time the partnership belongs in game is when responder has exactly 10 points. If responder has 6, 7, 8, or 9 points, the partnership should stop in partscore! With only 16 points, opener risks getting the partnership too high for the one chance in five that there is game. For this reason, the text recommends the higher range for a medium hand, even though it makes it a little more difficult to memorize the ranges.

The Reverse

The text points out that opener can show a medium strength hand by bidding a second suit at the two level that is higher-ranking than the original suit. For example:

OPENER	RESPONDER
1♣	1♠
2♥	

Such a sequence is called a *reverse*. The text also states that opener can reverse with a maximum hand instead of jump shifting in the second suit. The jump shift is used only with a maximum hand when opener's second suit is lower-ranking than the original suit.

A reverse requires more than a minimum hand. Responder may have as few as 6 points but will have to bid again in case opener has a maximum hand. (This will be discussed in the next lesson.) Responder will have to bid at the three level to show support for one of opener's suits. If opener could have as few as 13 points to make such a bid, the partnership could end up at the three level with as few as 19 (13 + 6) points in the combined hands. To avoid this, opener must have at least 17 points to reverse. With a minimum hand containing clubs and hearts in the above auction, opener would have to rebid 2♣ to describe a hand of minimum strength.

ACTIVITIES

Exercise One — Responder Raises Your Major Suit

With each of the following hands, you open the bidding 1♥, and partner responds 2♥, which is an invitational bid. Add the high-card points and the distributional points. Put each hand in a range of minimum, medium, or maximum. What is your rebid?

1) ♠ 9 7 6	2) ♠ Q 7	3) ♠ 10 7 2
♥ K Q J 9 8 3	♥ A Q 7 6 3 2	♥ A Q J 6 5
♦ A 5	♦ K J	♦ A K Q
♣ A J	♣ J 7 2	♣ A 2

HCP:	15	HCP:	13	HCP:	20
Distr. Points:	2	Distr. Points:	2	Distr. Points:	1
Total Points:	17	Total Points:	15	Total Points:	21
Range:	medium	Range:	minium	Range:	MAximum
Rebid:	3H	Rebid:	Pass	Rebid:	4H

Exercise Two — Responder Raises Your Minor Suit

With each of the following hands, you open the bidding 1♣, and partner responds 2♣, which is an invitational bid. Add the high-card points and the distributional points. Put each hand in a range of minimum, medium, or maximum. What is your rebid?

1) ♠ Q 8 2	2) ♠ 7 3	3) ♠ A 10 8
♥ K J 5 2	♥ K 4	♥ K Q 4
♦ A 6 3	♦ A 4 2	♦ A J
♣ K J 4	♣ A K J 6 3 2	♣ K Q 10 8 4

HCP:	14	HCP:	15	HCP:	19
Distr. Points:	—	Distr. Points:	2	Distr. Points:	1
Total Points:	14	Total Points:	17	Total Points:	20
Range:	Minimum	Range:	medium	Range:	MAximum
Rebid:	Pass	Rebid:	3C	Rebid:	3NT

Exercise Three — Responder Bids 1NT

With each of the following hands, you open the bidding 1♠, and partner responds 1NT. This is an invitational bid, and opener can pass or bid again. The denomination has not yet been decided, so opener has to consider not only the strength of the hand but also the shape. Add the high-card points and the distributional points. Put each hand in a range of minimum, medium, or maximum. What is your rebid?

1) ♠ K J 8 7 3
   ♥ 10 4 2
   ♦ A 9 6
   ♣ A J

HCP:	13
Distr. Points:	1
Total Points:	14
Range:	Min
Rebid:	Pass

2) ♠ A K 9 5 3
   ♥ 6
   ♦ K Q J 5
   ♣ J 4 2

HCP:	14
Distr. Points:	1
Total Points:	15
Range:	Min
Rebid:	2D

3) ♠ A J 9 8 4 2
   ♥ 7 4 3
   ♦ A Q 8
   ♣ 4

HCP:	11
Distr. Points:	2
Total Points:	13
Range:	Min
Rebid:	2S

4) ♠ A Q J 6 4 3
   ♥ A 7 2
   ♦ 9
   ♣ K J 10

HCP:	15
Distr. Points:	2
Total Points:	17
Range:	Med
Rebid:	3S

5) ♠ A K J 4 2
   ♥ K 9
   ♦ A Q 4
   ♣ Q 9 5

HCP:	19
Distr. Points:	1
Total Points:	20
Range:	Max
Rebid:	3NT

6) ♠ K Q J 8 3
   ♥ 9 4
   ♦ A
   ♣ A K 7 6 3

HCP:	17
Distr. Points:	2
Total Points:	19
Range:	Max
Rebid:	3C

Exercise Four — Raising Responder's Suit

With each of the following hands, you open the bidding 1♣, and partner responds 1♠. This is a forcing bid, and opener must bid again. If you can support responder's suit, you need to revalue your hand using dummy points before deciding your rebid. Add the high-card points and the dummy points. Put each hand in a range of minimum, medium, or maximum. What is your rebid?

1) ♠ J 8 7 6	2) ♠ Q 7 4 2	3) ♠ A J 3 2
♥ 8	♥ 10 9	♥ —
♦ A 9 3	♦ A K	♦ Q J 9 6
♣ A K Q 7 6	♣ K 8 7 4 2	♣ A K J 7 2

HCP:	_14_	HCP:	_12_	HCP:	_16_
Dummy Points:	_3_	Dummy Points:	_2_	Dummy Points:	_5_
Total Points:	_12_	Total Points:	_14_	Total Points:	_21_
Range:	_med_	Range:	_Min_	Range:	_MAX_
Rebid:	_3♠_	Rebid:	_2♠_	Rebid:	_4♠_

Exercise Five — Opener Bids a Second Suit at the Two Level

Examine the following auctions:

1)		2)	
OPENER	RESPONDER	OPENER	RESPONDER
1♥	1NT	1♥	1NT
2♦		2♠	

In both cases, opener is showing an unbalanced hand with two suits. Responder usually must make a choice between opener's suits. In which auction, can responder always make the choice at the two level? In which auction, might responder have to go to the three level to show a preference?

Which is higher-ranking on the Bidding Scale: hearts or diamonds? Which is higher-ranking on the Bidding Scale: hearts or spades? What is the difference between the two auctions in terms of the rank of opener's second suit?

When choosing a rebid with an unbalanced hand, opener bids a new suit at the two level that is lower-ranking than the original suit even when holding a minimum hand. If the new suit is higher-ranking than the original suit, opener cannot afford to mention it at the two level unless opener holds a medium hand. Why?

Exercise Six — More Rebids after Responder Bids a New Suit

With each of the following hands, you open the bidding 1 ♦, and partner responds 1 ♠. This is a forcing bid, and you must bid again, further describing your hand. Add the high-card points and the distributional points. Put each hand in a range of minimum, medium, or maximum. What is your rebid?

1) ♠ 9 8
   ♥ K 10 4
   ♦ A J 8 6
   ♣ K Q 5 4

2) ♠ 3
   ♥ K 8 4
   ♦ K Q 9 6 2
   ♣ A J 10 6

3) ♠ K 3
   ♥ A 8 2
   ♦ A K J 8 4 2
   ♣ 9 4

HCP: _____
Distr. Points: _____
Total Points: _____
Range: _____
Rebid: _____

HCP: _____
Distr. Points: _____
Total Points: _____
Range: _____
Rebid: _____

HCP: _____
Distr. Points: _____
Total Points: _____
Range: _____
Rebid: _____

4) ♠ A J
   ♥ A J 10 9
   ♦ A K 7 5 3
   ♣ 10 2

5) ♠ K 6 2
   ♥ 4
   ♦ A K Q 8 3
   ♣ A Q J 2

6) ♠ J 3
   ♥ A Q J
   ♦ A Q 9 6
   ♣ K Q 6 3

HCP: _____
Distr. Points: _____
Total Points: _____
Range: _____
Rebid: _____

HCP: _____
Distr. Points: _____
Total Points: _____
Range: _____
Rebid: _____

HCP: _____
Distr. Points: _____
Total Points: _____
Range: _____
Rebid: _____

Exercise Seven — Responder Jumps

Examine the following auctions:

1)			2)	
OPENER	RESPONDER		OPENER	RESPONDER
1♥	3♥		1♥	2NT

How many points is responder showing in each auction? What is the message given by responder's bid?

Suppose you have the following hand:

♠ 10 6
♥ A J 8 4 2
♦ K 9 5
♣ A 4 2

What would you rebid in the first auction? What would you rebid in the second auction?

Exercise Eight — The Finesse

How many tricks can be developed with each of the following suit combinations if the opponents' cards are as favorably placed as possible? How would you play each combination?

| DUMMY: | 1) K 7 2 | 2) 5 2 | 3) K Q 3 | 4) A 6 3 |
| DECLARER: | 9 4 3 | A Q 3 | 7 4 2 | Q 8 2 |

Exercise Nine — A Finesse Against the Ace
(E-Z Deal Cards: #5, Hand 1 — Dealer, North)

Turn up all of the cards on the first pre-dealt hand. Put each hand dummy style at the edge of the table in front of each player.

Dealer: North

```
                    ♠ A 7 3
                    ♥ A 6 2
                    ♦ A Q 7 5
                    ♣ 5 4 3
     ♠ 9 5 4                      ♠ K Q J 10
     ♥ K Q J 10      N            ♥ 8 7 5
     ♦ 9 8 2      W     E         ♦ 10 6 3
     ♣ Q 10 8        S            ♣ A J 9
                    ♠ 8 6 2
                    ♥ 9 4 3
                    ♦ K J 4
                    ♣ K 7 6 2
```

The Bidding

North is the dealer. Which player would open the bidding? What would the opening bid be?

Look at responder's hand. Can responder support opener's suit? Can responder bid a new suit? What would responder bid? What is the bidding message given by responder's bid? Does opener have to bid again? What would opener rebid? What would the contract be? Who would be declarer?

The Play

Which player would make the opening lead? What would the opening lead be?

How many tricks must declarer take to fulfill the contract? How many sure tricks does declarer have? Which suit provides declarer with the opportunity to develop the additional tricks needed to make the contract? Which suit should declarer play after winning the first trick? Why? What has to happen in order for declarer to make the contract?

Bid and play the deal. Did declarer make the contract?

Exercise Ten — Drawing Trumps with the Help of a Finesse
(E-Z Deal Cards: #5, Hand 2 — Dealer, East)

Turn up all of the cards on the second pre-dealt hand and arrange them as in the previous exercise.

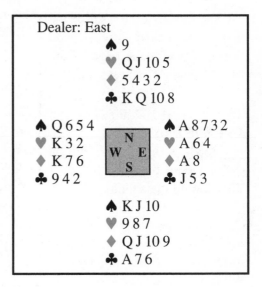

Dealer: East

♠ 9
♥ Q J 10 5
♦ 5 4 3 2
♣ K Q 10 8

♠ Q 6 5 4   ♠ A 8 7 3 2
♥ K 3 2   ♥ A 6 4
♦ K 7 6   ♦ A 8
♣ 9 4 2   ♣ J 5 3

♠ K J 10
♥ 9 8 7
♦ Q J 10 9
♣ A 7 6

The Bidding

East is the dealer. Which player would open the bidding? What would the opening bid be?

Look at responder's hand. Can responder support opener's suit? What is the value of responder's hand? What would responder bid? What is the bidding message given by responder's bid? Does opener have to bid again? What would opener's rebid be?

What would the contract be? Who would be declarer?

The Play

Which player would make the opening lead? What would the opening lead be?

How many tricks must declarer take to fulfill the contract? How many sure tricks does declarer have? Which suit provides declarer with the opportunity to develop the additional tricks needed to make the contract? Which suit should declarer play after winning the first trick? Which card in the suit should declarer play first? Why?

Bid and play the deal. Did declarer make the contract?

Exercise Eleven — Another Finesse against the King
(E-Z Deal Cards: #5, Hand 3 — Dealer, South)

Turn up all of the cards on the third pre-dealt hand and arrange them as in the previous exercise.

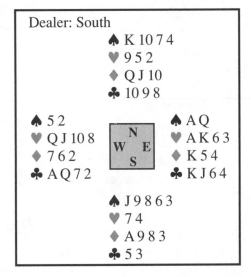

Dealer: South

♠ K 10 7 4
♥ 9 5 2
♦ Q J 10
♣ 10 9 8

♠ 5 2
♥ Q J 10 8
♦ 7 6 2
♣ A Q 7 2

♠ A Q
♥ A K 6 3
♦ K 5 4
♣ K J 6 4

♠ J 9 8 6 3
♥ 7 4
♦ A 9 8 3
♣ 5 3

The Bidding

South is the dealer. Which player would open the bidding? What would the opening bid be?

Look at responder's hand. What is the value of responder's hand? What would responder bid? What is the bidding message given by responder's bid? Does opener have to bid again? What is the value of opener's hand after hearing responder's bid? What would opener rebid?

What would the contract be? Who would be declarer?

The Play

Which player would make the opening lead? What would the opening lead be?

How many tricks must declarer take to fulfill the contract? How many sure tricks does declarer have? Why is declarer unlikely to win a trick with the ♦ K? Which other suit provides declarer with the opportunity to develop the additional trick needed to make the contract? Which suit should declarer play after winning the first trick? How should declarer plan to play the spade suit?

Bid and play the deal. Did declarer make the contract?

Exercise Twelve — The Repeated Finesse
(E-Z Deal Cards: #5, Hand 4 — Dealer, West)

Turn up all of the cards on the fourth pre-dealt hand and arrange them as in the previous exercise.

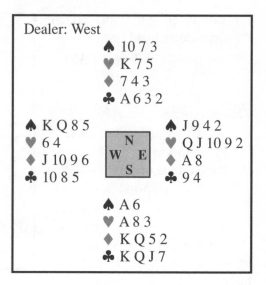

Dealer: West

```
              ♠ 10 7 3
              ♥ K 7 5
              ♦ 7 4 3
              ♣ A 6 3 2
♠ K Q 8 5            ♠ J 9 4 2
♥ 6 4         N      ♥ Q J 10 9 2
♦ J 10 9 6  W   E    ♦ A 8
♣ 10 8 5       S     ♣ 9 4
              ♠ A 6
              ♥ A 8 3
              ♦ K Q 5 2
              ♣ K Q J 7
```

The Bidding

West is the dealer. Which player would open the bidding? What would the opening bid be?

Look at responder's hand. What is the value of responder's hand? Can responder support opener's suit? Can responder bid a new suit? What would responder bid? What is the bidding message given by responder's bid? Does opener have to bid again? What would opener rebid?

What would the contract be? Who would be declarer?

The Play

Which player would make the opening lead? What would the opening lead be?

How many tricks must declarer take to fulfill the contract? How many sure tricks does declarer have? Which suit provides declarer with the opportunity to develop the additional tricks needed to make the contract? In which hand, should declarer win the first trick? Why? Which suit should declarer play after winning the first trick? If declarer wins the second trick, which suit will declarer play next? Why?

Bid and play the deal. Did declarer make the contract?

Answers to Lesson 5 exercises are on pages 304–308.

LESSON 6
Rebids By Responder

Responder's General Approach to the Second Bid

Responder's Decision with 6 to10 Points

Responder's Decision with 11 or 12 Points

Responder's Decision with 13 or More Points

Guidelines for Play

Summary

The Finer Points

Activities

RESPONDER'S GENERAL APPROACH TO THE SECOND BID

Let's consider what has happened by the time responder is ready to make a second bid, *responder's rebid*. Opener started the description of the hand by opening the bidding. Responder made an initial bid asking opener to further describe the hand. Opener then made a rebid, further describing the strength and shape of the hand. For example, the auction might have started like this:

OPENER	RESPONDER
1♥	1♠
1NT	

Responder has now heard two bids from opener and is ready to consider the level and denomination of the contract. The situation is similar to responder's approach when responding to a 1NT opening bid (Lesson 3). Responder usually has a very accurate description of opener's hand. For example, in the above auction, responder knows that opener has a minimum balanced hand with a five-card heart suit and without four-card support for spades. Let's see how responder uses this information.

Responder Categorizes the Strength

Responder decides which of three categories describes the point count value of the hand:

Minimum Hand	6 to 10 points
Medium Hand	11 or 12 points
Maximum Hand	13 or more points

As responder, you consider the point range that opener has described and combine it with your own point count to decide whether the partnership belongs in a partscore or game contract.

Responder Categorizes the Distribution

As responder, you also consider the information that opener has given about distribution when opener made the opening bid and a rebid. You look at your own distribution to determine whether there are any Golden Fits. If you are planning to put the partnership in a game contract, you determine whether there is a Golden Fit in a major suit. Otherwise, you steer the partnership into 3NT. If you are planning to put the partnership in a partscore contract, you look for any available Golden Fit. Otherwise, you place the contract in a notrump partscore.

Responder's Use of the Bidding Messages

Since responder is the captain, responder's bidding messages are important to the opener.

Signoff Bid: Responder may have enough information after hearing opener's rebid to decide on both the level and denomination and to place the contract. Opener is expected to pass when responder makes a signoff bid, since opener has already described the hand.

Invitational Bid: Responder still may not have enough information to determine whether the partnership belongs in partscore or game. If that is the case, responder will make an invitational bid. This bid asks opener to pass if partner's hand is at the bottom of the range that has already been shown or to bid on if at the top of the range.

Forcing Bid: Responder may know the partnership belongs in game but still needs more information from opener to determine the appropriate denomination. In this case, responder will make a forcing bid asking for a further description of opener's distribution.

The Role of the Responder

As responder, you are the captain. You put the pieces of the puzzle together and come up with a solution. Opener's strength usually has been described within 3 or 4 points, and you know the exact strength of your own hand. In addition, you know the partnership needs 26 or more combined points to be in a Golden Game. With fewer than 26 combined points, the partnership should settle for a partscore contract.

You also know that a Golden Fit generally plays one trick better than notrump and that the partnership is trying to uncover an eight-card or longer combined trump suit. If there are 26 combined points but the only Golden Fit is in a minor suit, the contract should be 3NT.

As responder, you put this together and decide:
- What level?   Game or partscore?
- What denomination?   Golden Fit or notrump?

Keep It Simple

It is impossible to reach the best contract on every hand. There will be times that you end up playing in notrump when the hand would have played better in a trump suit. Sometimes, you are playing in a partscore when you can make game. Responder makes the best decision using the information available. Responder tries to answer the questions "What level?" and "What denomination?" and usually ends up placing the partnership in a satisfactory, if not perfect, contract.

RESPONDER'S DECISION WITH 6-10 POINTS

With 6 to 10 points, responder's first bid will have been one of the following: a raise of opener's suit to the two level; a bid of a new suit at the one level; a 1NT response. Opener chooses a descriptive rebid that puts opener's hand into the minimum (13 to 16 points), medium (17 or 18 points), or maximum (19 to 21 points) category.

If opener shows a minimum hand, the partnership will have only enough combined strength for a partscore. If opener has a medium hand, the partnership possibly has enough combined strength for game. If opener has a maximum hand, the partnership definitely has enough combined strength for game. Let's see how responder chooses a rebid in each of these cases.

Opener Has a Minimum Hand

When responder has between 6 and 10 points and opener shows a minimum hand, responder knows the partnership belongs in a partscore. Opener can have at most 16 points. Unless opener has exactly 16 and responder has exactly 10 (a possibility that will be ignored for simplicity's sake), the partnership will always have fewer than 26 combined points. Therefore, responder wants to sign off in the best partscore. This can be accomplished in one of three ways:

- By passing.
- By bidding 1NT if the auction is still at the one level.
- By rebidding at the two level in a suit already mentioned by the partnership.

Suppose the auction starts this way:

OPENER	RESPONDER
1 ♦	1 ♠
1NT	

Opener is showing a minimum balanced hand by rebidding 1NT at the cheapest available level. Here is how responder would handle the rebid when responder also has a minimum hand (6 to 10 points).

♠ K J 6 3
♥ 10 4 2
♦ Q 4 3
♣ K 4 2

With only 9 HCP, responder knows the partnership belongs in a partscore. There might be a Golden Fit in diamonds, but opener may only have a four-card suit. Responder can't be sure. Responder would pass.

♠ K Q J 9 7 3
♥ 6 3
♦ 3 2
♣ 10 7 2

Since opener is showing a balanced hand, responder knows there is a Golden Fit in spades. With only 8 points, responder wants the partnership to play in a partscore and would rebid 2♠. This is a signoff, telling opener to pass.

♠ A 9 7 5
♥ 4
♦ Q 8 6 4 2
♣ 9 3 2

With 7 points, responder knows the partnership belongs in a partscore. Responder also knows that there is a Golden Fit in diamonds. Responder would sign off by bidding 2♦, a suit already mentioned by the partnership.

Suppose the auction starts as follows:

OPENER	RESPONDER
1♦	1♥
2♥	

Opener is showing a minimum hand with four-card support for responder's suit.

♠ K 9 3
♥ K 10 9 7 2
♦ 4 2
♣ 8 6 4

With 7 points, responder knows the partnership belongs in a partscore. The partnership has already found a Golden Fit so responder should pass.

♠ J 3
♥ Q 8 7 5
♦ A 10 8 5 2
♣ 10 3

Responder knows there is a Golden Fit in hearts and, with only 8 points, knows the partnership should play in a partscore. Even though responder knows there is also a Golden Fit in diamonds, there is no reason to disturb the major suit contract. Responder would pass.

Suppose the auction starts as follows:

OPENER	RESPONDER
1 ♣	1 ♥
1 ♠	

Opener could have a minimum or medium hand. It is safer for the responder to assume opener has a minimum hand and choose a rebid accordingly.

♠ K J 2
♥ J 10 7 3
♦ K J 5
♣ 10 7 2

Responder has 9 HCP. No Golden Fit has been uncovered. With a minimum hand, responder wants to stop in partscore and would rebid 1NT. This is a signoff bid.

♠ K 8 6 3
♥ Q 9 5 2
♦ J 4 3
♣ 8 2

Responder initially values this hand at 6 points. When opener bids 1 ♣, responder starts looking for a Golden Fit by bidding 1 ♥ (suits "up the line"). When opener rebids 1 ♠, responder knows there is a Golden Fit in a major suit. Responder now values the hand using dummy points. This brings the total to 7 — 6 HCP plus 1 for the doubleton club. The hand is still in the minimum category, and responder knows the partnership belongs in a partscore. Responder would pass.

♠ 4 2
♥ K 10 6 5
♦ 9 3
♣ A 9 7 6 2

Even knowing there is a Golden Fit in clubs when opener starts the bidding with 1 ♣, responder's first bid is 1 ♥. Responder is looking for a Golden Fit in a major suit. Opener's rebid has told responder that there is no Golden Fit in a major suit. Responder can now sign off in 2 ♣, putting the partnership in a partscore in its Golden Fit.

Suppose the auction starts as follows:

OPENER	RESPONDER
1 ♦	1 ♠
2 ♣	

Again, opener could have a minimum or medium hand. However, responder should assume it is minimum. Opener is also showing an unbalanced hand since, with a balanced hand and no support for responder's suit, opener would rebid 1NT.

♠ A 9 6 4
♥ 9 8 3
♦ K 5 2
♣ 8 6 4

With 7 points, responder wants to stop in partscore in a Golden Fit. There is no spade fit because opener did not raise responder's suit. Since opener has an unbalanced hand with diamonds that are equal in length or longer than clubs, the most likely Golden Fit is in diamonds, opener's original suit, rather than in clubs. Responder would bid 2 ♦, signing off in the likely Golden Fit.

♠ K 10 7 6 3
♥ 8 5
♦ 10 6
♣ Q 10 8 2

Responder prefers opener's second suit. With only 7 points — 5 HCP plus 1 each for the two doubletons — responders would pass

♠ Q J 9 7 6 3
♥ J 7 5 3
♦ 3
♣ Q 4

Responder does not like either of opener's suits and would rebid 2 ♠ to signoff in a suit already bid by the partnership. Bidding a new suit at the two level or bidding 2NT is not one of responder's options with a minimum hand of 6 to 10 points.

Opener Has a Medium Hand

When responder has 6 to 10 points and opener shows a medium hand, the partnership may belong in a partscore or game, depending on whether responder is at the bottom or top of the range. If responder has 6, 7, or 8 points, the partnership belongs in a partscore since opener's maximum is 18 points. Unless opener has exactly 18 and responder has exactly 8 (a possibility that will be ignored for simplicity's sake), the partnership will have fewer than 26 combined points. Therefore, responder wants to sign off in the best partscore. This can be accomplished in one of two ways:

- By passing.
- By bidding a suit already mentioned by the partnership at the cheapest available level.

If responder has 9 or 10 points, the partnership belongs in a game contract since opener's minimum is 17 points. The partnership will have at least 26 combined points. Therefore, responder wants to ensure that the partnership gets to game. Responder can do this in one of two ways:

- By bidding one of the Golden Games.
- By bidding a new suit (forcing) to get a further description of opener's hand.

In each of the following cases, responder has a minimum hand (6 to 10 points), and opener is showing a medium strength hand.

Suppose the auction starts as follows:

OPENER	RESPONDER
1 ♥	1 ♠
3 ♥	

By jumping in the original suit, opener is showing a medium strength, unbalanced hand with no second suit.

♠ K 9 6 5 3
♥ 5 2
♦ Q J 6
♣ 7 4 2

Responder has a hand worth 7 points — 6 HCP plus 1 for the five-card spade suit. Responder knows, therefore, that the partnership does not have enough combined strength for game. Responder would pass.

♠ A 10 4 3
♥ Q 5
♦ K 8 6
♣ 10 9 6 3

Responder, with 9 HCP, knows the partnership belongs in game since opener has at least 17 points. Opener is also showing an unbalanced hand with no second suit, and opener must have at least a six-card heart suit. Responder would bid 4 ♥, placing the partnership in game in its Golden Fit.

♠ K J 8 7
♥ 4
♦ K 10 9 3
♣ Q J 7 5

With 10 HCP, responder knows that the partnership belongs at the game level. With no apparent Golden Fit in a major suit (opener may have only a six-card heart suit), responder would choose the game contract of 3NT.

Suppose the auction starts this way:

OPENER	RESPONDER
1 ♦	1 ♠
2 ♥	

Opener is showing an unbalanced hand of at least medium strength by rebidding at the two level in a higher-ranking suit than the original suit. Opener could also have a maximum hand, so responder should not pass.

♠ Q 10 8 7 3
♥ J 9 5 4
♦ 6 5
♣ Q 2

With support for opener's major suit, responder values the hand using dummy points — 5 HCP plus 1 for each of the doubletons — giving a total of 7 points. Responder would bid 3 ♥. By bidding at the cheapest available level in a suit already mentioned by the partnership, responder shows a hand of 6, 7, or 8 points. With only a medium hand, opener can pass. With a maximum hand, opener will bid on to game.

♠ A J 7 3

♥ 6 5

♦ Q 9 5 4

♣ 7 3 2

With 7 points, responder would like to stop in a partscore. However, responder cannot pass since the partnership would not be playing in a Golden Fit. Instead, responder returns to opener's original suit by bidding 3 ♦ , putting the partnership in a suitable trump fit.

♠ K J 10 9 7 5

♥ 4 3

♦ 9 6

♣ Q 6 2

Responder wants to stop in a partscore but does not like either of opener's suits. Responder would rebid the spade suit at the cheapest available level, 2 ♠ . This tells opener that responder wants to sign off in a partscore.

♠ K Q 8 7

♥ 8 6 2

♦ 7 4

♣ K Q 10 4

With 10 HCP, responder knows the partnership belongs in a game contract. Since responder has not found a Golden Fit in a major suit, responder bids 3NT, putting the partnership in one of the Golden Games.

Opener Has a Maximum Hand

When responder has 6 to 10 points and opener shows a maximum hand, the partnership always belongs in game. Unless opener has exactly 19 and responder has exactly 6 (a possibility that will be ignored for simplicity's sake), the partnership will have at least 26 combined points. Therefore, responder wants to make sure the partnership gets to a suitable game contract. Responder can do this in one of three ways:

- By passing if the partnership is already at the game level.
- By bidding one of the Golden Games.
- By bidding a new suit (forcing) to get a further description of opener's hand.

Suppose the auction starts as follows:

OPENER	RESPONDER
1 ♥	1NT
4 ♥	

♠ Q 9 5
♥ 10 8
♦ A J 7 5 3
♣ J 6 3

Responder has a hand worth 9 points — 8 HCP plus 1 for the five-card diamond suit. Opener's jump to the game level after responder's 1NT bid shows a maximum hand of 19 to 21 points. Since the partnership is already in a game contract, responder would pass.

Suppose the auction starts this way:

OPENER	RESPONDER
1♦	1♠
2NT	

♠ Q J 6 3
♥ A 10 4
♦ 7 5 2
♣ 9 6 3

Responder has 7 HCP. Opener's jump to 2NT shows a maximum balanced hand. Responder knows the partnership belongs in game and, with no available Golden Fit in a major suit, would bid 3NT.

♠ A J 10 8 7 6
♥ 7
♦ Q 8 2
♣ 10 4 2

Responder has 7 HCP plus 2 for the six-card suit. Since opener is describing a balanced hand, responder knows opener has at least two spades. There must be a Golden Fit. Since the partnership belongs in game, responder bids 4♠, a signoff bid.

♠ K Q 9 7 5
♥ J 10
♦ 10 3 2
♣ J 9 7

Responder has 8 points — 7 HCP plus 1 for the five-card suit. Responder knows there is enough combined strength for game but is not sure if there is a Golden Fit in spades. Responder bids 3♠ to get opener to bid 4♠ with three-card support or 3NT with only two spades. 3♠ is a forcing bid. Responder has at least 6 points, and opener has shown a maximum.

Putting It Together

With a minimum hand, 6 to 10 points, responder decides the final contract by combining the value of this hand with the value opener showed when rebidding.

Opener's Range	Responder's Range	Final Level	Responder's Options
13 to 16 (Minimum)	6 to 10	Partscore	• Pass • 1 NT • Two-level bid of a suit already mentioned by the partnership
17 or 18 (Medium)	6 to 8	Partscore	• Pass • Cheapest bid of a suit already mentioned by the partnership
19 to 21 (Maximum)	9 or 10	Game	• Bid a Golden Game • Bid a new suit
	6 to 10	Game	• Pass • Bid a Golden Game • Bid a new suit

Let's see how you would handle the following examples.

OPENER	RESPONDER
1♥	1NT
2♥	

♠ K 10 3
♥ 4 3
♦ J 10 6 5 3
♣ Q 7 4

Opener is showing a minimum unbalanced hand. With 7 points, you know the partnership belongs in a partscore. Pass.

OPENER	RESPONDER
1♦	1♠
3♠	

♠ Q J 9 7 4
♥ K 8 2
♦ 5
♣ J 10 6 5

Opener's jump raise shows a medium hand of 17 or 18 points. With 8 points, it is unlikely there is enough combined strength for game, so pass.

♠ 10 9 7 4
♥ 6 4
♦ A 8 6 3
♣ A Q 9

You have 10 points, enough for game opposite opener's medium-strength hand. Carry on to game in your Golden Fit, 4♠.

OPENER	RESPONDER
1♥	1♠
3♣	

♠ K J 6 2
♥ 5 2
♦ Q 10 4 3
♣ J 9 2

Opener is showing a maximum unbalanced hand by jumping in the second suit (jump shift). Even though you have only 7 points, there is enough combined strength for game. With no known Golden Fit in a major suit, bid 3NT.

OPENER	RESPONDER
1♠	2♠
3♠	

♠ K 9 4
♥ 9 8
♦ 10 9 7 5 2
♣ Q 10 6

Opener's raise to the three level shows a medium-strength hand. With only 6 points — 5 HCP plus 1 for the doubleton heart — pass.

♠ J 9 6 3
♥ K 5
♦ A 7 6 2
♣ 9 6 4

Your hand is worth 9 points — 8 HCP plus 1 for the doubleton heart. There should be enough combined strength for game, so carry on to 4♠.

RESPONDER'S DECISION WITH 11-12 POINTS

With 11 or 12 points, responder's first bid will have been a raise of opener's suit to the three level (invitational) or a new suit at the one level or two level (forcing). If responder raises opener's suit to the three level, opener will either pass with only 13 or 14 points or bid game with more.

If responder bids a new suit, opener will choose a descriptive rebid that puts the hand into the minimum (13 to 16 points), medium (17 or 18 points), or maximum (19 to 21 points) category. When opener has a medium or maximum hand, there will always be enough combined strength for game. Even if opener has a minimum hand, the partnership possibly has enough combined strength for game. Let's look at how responder chooses a rebid in each of these cases.

Opener Has a Minimum Hand

When responder has 11 or 12 points and opener shows a minimum hand of 13 to 16 points, the partnership may belong in either a partscore or game. The final contract depends on whether opener is at the bottom or top of the minimum range. If opener has only 13 or 14 points, the partnership belongs in a partscore. Unless opener has exactly 14 and responder has exactly 12 (a possibility that will be ignored for simplicity's sake), the partnership will have fewer than 26 combined points. If opener has 15 or 16 points, the partnership belongs in game since the partnership will have at least 26 combined points.

Thus, to determine the proper contract, responder needs to get more information from opener. Responder can do this by making an invitational bid — moving toward a game without actually bidding it. Opener can pass the invitational bid if at the bottom of the range, 13 or 14 points, but bid on to game if at the top of the range, 15 or 16 points.

Responder can make an invitational bid in one of two ways:

- By bidding 2 NT.
- By rebidding a suit already mentioned by the partnership at the three level.

Note that these rebids are distinct from those that responder would make with 6 to 10 points when opener shows a minimum hand (pass, 1 NT, rebid at the two level of a suit already mentioned). In this way, opener will know responder is making an invitational bid rather than a signoff bid.

In each of the following cases, responder has a medium hand (11 or 12 points), and opener shows a minimum hand.

Suppose the auction starts as follows:

OPENER	RESPONDER
1 ♦	1 ♠
1NT	

♠ K 10 9 5
♥ Q J 4
♦ J 3
♣ A 10 6 2

Opener showed a minimum balanced hand with the rebid of 1NT. Responder has 11 HCP. The partnership should be in a partscore if opener is at the bottom of the range, or in game if opener is at the top of the range.

Since there does not appear to be a Golden Fit, responder invites game by bidding 2 NT. Opener will pass if at the bottom of the range but carry on to 3 NT if at the top.

♠ A Q 10 9 7 6
♥ 5
♦ J 7 2
♣ K 8 3

Responder has 12 points — 10 HCP and 2 points for the six-card suit. Opener is showing a balanced hand, so responder knows there is a Golden Fit in spades. To make an invitational rebid, responder rebids the suit at the three level, 3♠. Since responder would have bid only 2♠ with 6 to 10 points, opener will know this is an invitational bid, not a signoff bid.

♠ A 9 6 4 2
♥ 5 3
♦ A Q 7 5 2
♣ 6

Responder has 12 points — 10 HCP and 1 point for each of the five-card suits. Responder invites game by bidding 3♦, a suit already bid by the partnership. Responder does not bid 2♦ since that would be a signoff bid showing a hand in the 6 to 10 point range.

Now suppose the auction starts this way:

OPENER	RESPONDER
1♥	2♣
2♥	

♠ A J 10
♥ 4 2
♦ K 10 5
♣ Q J 9 6 3

Responder has a balanced hand without support for opener's major suit. With 12 points, responder makes an invitational rebid of 2NT.

♠ J 10 2
♥ 3
♦ K 10 5
♣ A J 10 9 5 4

With 11 points, 9 HCP and 2 points for the six-card suit and an unbalanced hand with no fit for opener's suit, responder rebids 3♣.

Opener Has a Medium Hand

If responder has 11 or 12 points and opener shows a medium hand of 17 or 18 points, the partnership has at least 28 combined points and belongs in a game contract. Therefore, responder wants to ensure that the partnership gets to game. Responder can do this in one of two ways:

- By bidding one of the Golden Games.
- By bidding a new suit (forcing) to get a further description of opener's hand.

OPENER	RESPONDER
1♣	1♠
3♣	

Opener is showing an unbalanced hand of medium strength (17 or 18) points. Let's look at how responder would handle the following hands, all in the medium range (11 or 12 points).

♠ K Q 10 5 ♥ Q J 7 ♦ A 9 3 ♣ 7 6 3	Responder has 12 HCP and knows there is no Golden Fit in a major suit, although there is a Golden Fit in clubs. Responder puts the partnership in the only available Golden Game, 3NT.
♠ A Q J 9 7 6 3 ♥ J 10 3 ♦ 5 ♣ 4 2	Responder has an unbalanced hand with 11 points. When opener shows a medium hand, responder knows the partnership belongs in game. It looks as if the most probable Golden Game is 4♠. This will be a Golden Fit unless opener has no spades (unlikely).
♠ K J 10 7 3 ♥ 5 4 ♦ A J 9 6 2 ♣ J	Responder has 12 points but is not sure of the best denomination for the contract. In this case, responder bids a new suit, 3♦, to get opener to make a further descriptive bid. After hearing opener's next bid, responder should know whether the partnership should be in a Golden Game in spades or notrump.

Opener Has a Maximum Hand

If responder has 11 or 12 points and opener shows a maximum hand of 19 to 21 points, the partnership has at least 30 combined points and belongs at least in game. Responder can ensure that the partnership gets to a game contract in one of two ways:

- By bidding one of the Golden Games.
- By bidding a new suit to get a further description of opener's hand.

Suppose the auction starts off as follows:

OPENER	RESPONDER
1 ♥	1 ♠
2NT	

Opener is showing a balanced hand of maximum strength (19 to 21 points). Let's see how responder handles the following hands, all in the medium range (11 or 12 points).

♠ J 10 9 5
♥ Q 6
♦ A J 5 3
♣ K 8 2

With 11 HCP and no sign of a Golden Fit in a major suit, responder would put the partnership in the Golden Game of 3NT.

♠ Q 10 9 7 4 2
♥ 3
♦ A Q 3
♣ Q 6 2

Opener has shown a balanced hand. Responder knows there is a Golden Fit in spades and can take the partnership directly to the Golden Game, 4 ♠.

♠ A J 10 8 2
♥ 9 4
♦ K J 3
♣ J 6 2

With only a five-card spade suit, responder is not certain whether there is a Golden Fit in spades. Responder rebids 3 ♠ to get a further description of opener's hand. Opener will bid 4 ♠ with three-card support or 3NT without three-card support for the spade suit.

Putting It Together

With a medium hand of 11 to 12 points, responder combines the value of the hand with the value shown by opener's rebid to decide the contract.

Opener's Range	Responder's Range	Final Level	Responder's Options
13 to 16 (Minimum)	11 or 12	Partscore or game	• Bid 2NT • Make a three-level bid in a suit already mentioned by the partnership.
17 or 18 (Medium)	11 or 12	Game	• Bid a Golden Game. • Bid a new suit.
19 to 21 (Maximum)	11 or 12	Game	• Bid a Golden Game. • Pass in game. • Bid a new suit.

Let's see how you would handle the following examples.

OPENER	RESPONDER
1♣	1♠
2♠	

♠ K 10 9 7 3 2
♥ 5 3
♦ Q 5
♣ A 9 4

Opener is showing a minimum range hand with spade support. You have 9 HCP plus 2 points for the six-card spade suit. This is enough to make an invitational raise to 3♠.

OPENER	RESPONDER
1♦	1♠
2♥	

♠ A Q 10 8
♥ J 8 2
♦ 10 4
♣ K Q 9 6

Opener is showing a medium-strength hand by bidding a second suit at the two level that is higher-ranking than the original suit. With 12 HCP and no Golden Fit in a major suit, bid 3NT.

♠ Q 9 8 6 3
♥ Q J 7 4
♦ 5
♣ K J 3

With four-card support for opener's second suit, you can value your hand using dummy points — 9 HCP plus 3 for the singleton. Opposite opener's medium-strength hand, this is enough to put the partnership in game, 4♥.

OPENER	RESPONDER
1♥	2♣
4♥	

♠ J 8 6
♥ K 3
♦ Q 7 2
♣ K Q 9 7 5

Opener is showing a maximum hand. Since the partnership is already in a game contract, responder can pass.

RESPONDER'S DECISION WITH 13 OR MORE POINTS

With 13 or more points, responder will initially bid a new suit or jump to 2NT over opener's bid of one in a suit.

When responder has 13 or more points, there are enough combined points for game even if opener has a minimum hand. There are some other considerations. In addition to the bonus for bidding and making a game contract, there is a large bonus for bidding and making a slam (a six-level or seven-level contract). A brief discussion of slam bidding is included in the Appendix. For now, it is sufficient to know the partnership needs about 33 combined points to undertake a slam contract. When opener shows a medium hand, there is some possibility for a slam contract. When opener shows a maximum hand, there should always be enough combined strength for slam.

Opener Has a Minimum Hand

If responder has 13 or more points and opener shows a minimum hand of 13 to 16 points, the partnership has at least 26 combined points and belongs in a game contract. Responder can ensure that the partnership gets to game in one of two ways:

- By bidding one of the Golden Games.
- By bidding a new suit at the three level to get a further description of opener's hand.

Suppose the auction starts as follows:

OPENER	RESPONDER
1 ♦	1 ♠
1NT	

Opener is showing a minimum balanced hand. Let's look at how responder handles the following hands, all in the maximum range (13 to 16 points):

♠ A J 9 4 ♥ J 10 ♦ K 9 6 3 ♣ A 4 2	Responder has 13 HCP and knows there is no Golden Fit in a major suit. Responder is certain the partnership belongs in a game contract and takes the partnership directly to game, 3NT.
♠ 1 0 9 7 6 5 2 ♥ A 8 ♦ 6 4 ♣ A K J	Responder has 12 HCP plus 2 points for the six-card suit, a total of 14. Responder knows there is a Golden Fit in spades since opener has shown a balanced hand. Responder's rebid is 4♠.
♠ A Q 8 6 3 ♥ K Q 9 2 ♦ 5 ♣ A 3 2	Responder has 16 points — 15 HCP and 1 for the five-card suit. Responder knows the partnership belongs in game but is not sure of the denomination. Needing further information from opener, responder bids a new suit at the three level, 3 ♥. Opener now has an opportunity to further describe the hand. The partnership may belong in spades, hearts, or notrump.

Opener Has a Medium Hand

If responder has 13 or more points and opener shows a medium hand of 17 or 18 points, the partnership has 30 or more combined points and belongs in at least a game contract.

Since the partnership needs about 33 points for a slam contract, there is also the possibility of a slam when responder has 15 or more points. To keep things simple, we won't consider the possibility of slam for the time being.

Therefore, when responder wants to ensure that the partnership gets to a game contract, the auction proceeds in one of these two ways:

- By bidding one of the Golden Games.
- By bidding a new suit to get a further description of opener's hand.

Suppose the auction starts as follows:

OPENER	RESPONDER
1 ♥	1 ♠
3 ♥	

Opener is showing a medium unbalanced hand. Let's look at how responder handles the following hands, all in the maximum range (13 or more points).

♠ K Q J 2
♥ A 10
♦ 6 5 3
♣ Q J 6 5

Responder has 13 HCP. Since opener has an unbalanced hand with no second suit and at least six cards in his original suit, responder knows there is a Golden Fit in hearts and takes the partnership to game, 4 ♥.

♠ A K Q 6
♥ 5
♦ K 10 9 2
♣ J 10 6 3

There does not appear to be a Golden Fit in a major suit. Responder would put the partnership in the Golden Game of 3NT.

Suppose the auction starts off this way:

OPENER	RESPONDER
1 ♦	1 ♠
3 ♦	

♠ Q J 10 7
♥ K Q 3
♦ 9 8 5 2
♣ A Q

Responder has 14 HCP. Even though there is a fit in diamonds, responder would still bid to a Golden Game, 3NT.

♠ A Q 10 7 6
♥ A 9 6 3 2
♦ 5
♣ K 5

Responder has 15 points — 13 HCP and 1 for each of the five-card suits. Responder knows the partnership belongs in game but is not sure of the best denomination. To get further information from opener, responder bids a new suit, 3 ♥, and waits to hear what opener has to say. Responder should have the information necessary to make a decision after opener's next bid.

Opener Has a Maximum Hand

If responder has 13 or more points and opener shows a maximum hand of 19 to 21 points, the partnership generally will belong in a slam contract. Slam bidding is beyond the scope of this lesson. It is discussed briefly in the Appendix and will be discussed in volume two, *The Diamond Series*.

Putting It Together

With a maximum hand, 13 or more points, responder combines the value of the hand with the value shown by opener's rebid to decide on the final contract.

Opener's Range	Responder's Range	Final Level	Responder's Options
13 to 16 (Minimum)	13 or more	Game	• Bid a Golden Game. • Bid a new suit at the three level.
17 to 18 (Medium)	13 or more	Game or slam	• Bid a Golden Game. • Bid a new suit.
19 to 21 (Maximum)	13 or more	Slam	• Bid a slam.

Let's see how you would handle the following examples.

OPENER	RESPONDER
1♦	1♠
2♦	

♠ A K J 9 7 6 3
♥ —
♦ A 9 7
♣ 6 3 2

Opener is showing an unbalanced hand in the minimum range (13 to 16 points). You have 12 HCP plus 3 points for the seven-card spade suit. That's enough for game. The best game appears to be 4♠, so that's the bid you would make.

♠ A Q 9 7
♥ K J 3
♦ J 9 5
♣ Q 10 7

With 13 HCP and no Golden Fit in a major suit, you take the partnership to game in notrump, 3NT.

♠ A J 8 6 3
♥ A 5
♦ 2
♣ K J 4 3 2

You know the partnership belongs in game, but the best denomination is not clear. Bid a new suit, 3♣, to elicit more information from opener. If opener can show some support for spades, you can play in 4♠. Otherwise bid 3NT.

OPENER	RESPONDER
1♣	1♠
2♥	

♠ A K 9 7 3
♥ A 8 6 4
♦ 10 4
♣ J 5

Opener is showing a medium-strength hand by bidding a second suit at the two level that is higher-ranking than the original suit. With enough for game and support for opener's hearts, bid the Golden Game, 4♥.

♠ Q J 7 6
♥ Q 8 2
♦ K Q 3
♣ Q J 3

With 13 HCP and no Golden Fit in a major suit, rebid 3NT.

GUIDELINES FOR PLAY

The various techniques for developing tricks that have been discussed in previous lessons (promotion, length, finessing) apply to both notrump and trump contracts. In a trump contract, however, when analyzing the alternatives, declarer discovers there are additional ways to develop extra tricks. One way is to take advantage of the trumps in the dummy.

Trumping in the Dummy

NORTH (Dummy)
♠ 4
♥ 9 8 7
♦ 7 6 5 4
♣ 8 7 6 5 4

SOUTH (Declarer)
♠ A 3 2
♥ A K Q J 10
♦ A 2
♣ A 3 2

Suppose South is playing in a contract with hearts as the trump suit. South has eight sure tricks — five heart tricks and the three aces in the other suits. If South takes all the sure tricks, South will be left with five cards, none of which will win a trick. Such cards are called losers.

One of the advantages of playing in a trump contract is that you can occasionally use your trumps to win a trick you would otherwise lose. In the above hand, before playing all the trumps, South could play the ♠A, then lead a small spade and put one of dummy's trumps on it. This is called ruffing (trumping) a loser in the dummy. The advantage of this play is that South ends up with an additional trick. In fact, South could trump both of the losing spades in dummy and end up with two additional tricks, for a total of 10.

Trumping in Declarer's Hand

Trumping losers in dummy is a useful way to get extra tricks. You should look for this possibility in a trump contract whenever there is a short suit (void, singleton, doubleton) in the dummy. It usually does not gain a trick if you trump in your own hand when you are declarer.

Suppose we change the hand slightly:

NORTH
♠ A 3 2
♥ 9 8 7
♦ 7 6 5 4
♣ A 3 2

SOUTH
♠ 4
♥ A K Q J 10
♦ A 2
♣ 8 7 6 5 4

South again starts with eight sure tricks. When South plays the ♠4 to dummy's ace and then leads a small spade from dummy and trumps, there are only eight tricks. Instead, South should plan on establishing the club suit if extra tricks are needed.

The general guideline is to trump your losers in the dummy to get extra tricks, not in your hand. Save the trumps in your hand for drawing the opponents' trumps and for stopping the opponents from taking their tricks in other suits.

SUMMARY

Minimum Hand	6 to 10 points
Medium Hand	11 or 12 points
Maximum Hand	13 or more points

When you make your rebid as responder, you put your hand into one of the following categories according to the point count value (using dummy points if planning to support opener's major suit):

By combining this information with the strength and distribution shown by opener's rebid, you try to decide the level and denomination of the contract. When you have enough information, you sign off in the appropriate contract. If you need more information, you make an invitational or forcing bid using the following guidelines:

Opener's Range	Responder's Range	Final Level	Responder's Options
13 to 16 (Minimum)	6 to 10	Partscore	• Pass • Bid 1NT • Make a two-level bid of a suit already mentioned by the partnership
	11 or 12	Partscore or game	• Bid 2NT • Make a three-level bid of a suit already mentioned by the partnership
	13 or more	Game	• Bid a Golden Game • Bid a new suit at the three level

Opener's Range	Responder's Range	Final Level	Responder's Options
17 or 18 (Medium)	6 to 8	Partscore	• Pass • Make the cheapest available bid of a suit already mentioned by the partnership
	9 or 10	Game	• Bid a Golden Game • Bid a new suit
	11 or 12	Game	• Bid a Golden Game • Bid a new suit
	13 or more	Game	• Bid a Golden Game
19 to 21 (Maximum)	6 to 10	Game	• Pass • Bid a Golden Game • Bid a suit
	11 or 12	Game	• Pass • Bid a Golden Game • Bid a suit
	13 or more	Slam	• Bid slam

THE FINER POINTS

Responder Bids a New Suit

After hearing opener's rebid, the responder can usually determine the appropriate level and denomination. There are times, however, when responder needs further information from opener in order to make a decision. Responder does this by making a forcing bid.

Responder's bid of a new suit at the cheapest level is always forcing (i.e., opener must bid again) unless opener specifically has rebid 1NT. In that case, a bid of a new suit is not forcing if it is lower-ranking than responder's original suit. For example:

OPENER	RESPONDER
1 ♦	1 ♥
1NT	2 ♣

Since responder's second suit, clubs, is lower ranking than the first suit, hearts, opener could pass when preferring clubs to hearts. To make a forcing bid, responder must jump to the three level, 3 ♣. The summary of responder's options reflects this by noting that responder can bid a new suit at the three level with 13 or more points when opener's hand is in the minimum range.

Strictly speaking, responder does not have to bid a new suit at the three level if it is higher-ranking than responder's original suit. For example:

OPENER	RESPONDER
1 ♦	1 ♥
1NT	2 ♠

Since spades rank higher than hearts, responder's rebid is forcing.

Responder does not have to jump to 3♠, which would use up a lot of room on the Bidding Scale. The illustrated auction shows an example of a responder's reverse for which 13 or more points are required.

There are auctions in which even an old suit by responder is forcing. When the partnership has shown enough combined strength for game, any bid below the game level is forcing. For example:

OPENER	RESPONDER
1♦	1♥
3♣	3♥

Opener is showing a maximum hand and responder must have at least 6 points, so the partnership has enough combined strength for game. Based on this logic, responder's 3♥ rebid is forcing.

After Opener's Reverse

In the previous lesson, we learned this principle. When opener bids a second suit at the two level that is higher ranking than the original suit (a reverse), it can show either a medium or a maximum hand. For example:

OPENER	RESPONDER
1♦	1♠
2♥	

Since hearts are higher-ranking than diamonds, opener's rebid of 2♥ shows at least a medium hand of 17 or 18 points. But since a jump shift to 3♥ would use up a lot of room on the Bidding Scale, the rebid could also be used when opener has a maximum hand of 19 to 21 points.

Responder should assume that opener has a medium hand but, because opener may have a maximum hand, responder cannot pass even with 6, 7, or 8 points. Responder must bid again to allow opener to further describe the strength of the hand. With 6, 7, or 8 points, responder can bid an old suit at the cheapest available level (2♠, 3♦, or 3♥ in the above example) or bid 2NT. With a medium hand, opener can pass and, with a maximum hand, opener will carry on to game.

ACTIVITIES

Exercise One — Responder's Rebid Decides What Level

Partner opens the bidding 1♦ and you respond 1♥. What are three rebids opener could make to specifically show a minimum hand?

What strength would a rebid of 1♠ or 2♣ by opener show?

A 1NT rebid by opener shows a balanced hand with 13, 14, or 15 points. What is the minimum number of points responder can hold to decide the partnership should play in game? With what range of points, is responder uncertain whether the partnership should be in game or a partscore? What is the maximum number of points responder can hold to decide the partnership should play in a partscore?

Exercise Two — Responder's Rebid When Opener Shows a Minimum Hand

Suppose the bidding is:

OPENER	RESPONDER
1♥	1♠
2♠	

Add up the high-card points and the distribution points on each of the following hands for responder. Put each hand in a range of minimum (6 to 10 points), medium (11 or 12 points), or maximum (13 or more points). As responder, decide at what level the contract should be played (partscore, possible game, or game), and in what denomination the contract should be played. Use this information to determine your rebid.

1) ♠ 9 8 7 6	2) ♠ Q 10 9 4 2	3) ♠ Q J 7 4 2
♥ A 5	♥ 9 8	♥ K 3
♦ Q 7 4 3 2	♦ A K J	♦ A J 4
♣ 9 3	♣ J 4 3	♣ Q J 3
HCP: _____	HCP: _____	HCP: _____
Distr. Points: _____	Distr. Points: _____	Distr. Points: _____
Total Points: _____	Total Points: _____	Total Points: _____
Range: _____	Range: _____	Range: _____
Level: _____	Level: _____	Level: _____
Denomination: _____	Denomination: _____	Denomination: _____
Rebid: _____	Rebid: _____	Rebid: _____

Exercise Three — Responder's Rebid When Opener Bids a Second Suit

Suppose the bidding is:

OPENER	RESPONDER
1♣	1♥
1♠	

Add up the high-card points and the distribution (or dummy) points on each of the following hands for responder. Put each hand in a range of minimum (6 to 10 points), medium (11 or 12 points), or maximum (13 or more points). As responder, decide at what level the contract should be played (partscore, possible game, or game) and in what denomination the contract should be played. Use this information to determine your rebid.

1) ♠ Q 3 2
   ♥ A 10 9 4
   ♦ Q J 6
   ♣ 7 5 2

HCP: _____
Distr. Points: _____
Total Points: _____
Range: _____
Level: _____
Denomination _____
Rebid: _____

2) ♠ J 5 2
   ♥ A Q 8 3
   ♦ K J 6
   ♣ 10 8 6

HCP: _____
Distr. Points: _____
Total Points: _____
Range: _____
Level: _____
Denomination _____
Rebid: _____

3) ♠ 10 8 3
   ♥ K Q 9 4
   ♦ A J 4
   ♣ K Q 8

HCP: _____
Distr. Points: _____
Total Points: _____
Range: _____
Level: _____
Denomination _____
Rebid: _____

4) ♠ J 7
   ♥ K J 10 8 6 3
   ♦ 9 2
   ♣ 7 5 2

HCP: _____
Distr. Points: _____
Total Points: _____
Range: _____
Level: _____
Denomination _____
Rebid: _____

5) ♠ A 8
   ♥ K Q J 9 7 4
   ♦ 8 6 2
   ♣ 9 5

HCP: _____
Distr. Points: _____
Total Points: _____
Range: _____
Level: _____
Denomination _____
Rebid: _____

6) ♠ K J 8 2
   ♥ A K 8 3
   ♦ 5 2
   ♣ K 7 3

HCP: _____
Distr. Points: _____
Total Points: _____
Range: _____
Level: _____
Denomination _____
Rebid: _____

7) ♠ 6 2
   ♥ Q J 7 5 3
   ♦ 4
   ♣ K 10 9 4 2

HCP:	_____
Distr. Points:	_____
Total Points:	_____
Range:	_____
Level:	_____
Denomination	_____
Rebid:	_____

8) ♠ 8 2
   ♥ K 9 6 2
   ♦ 7 4
   ♣ A Q J 7 4

HCP:	_____
Distr. Points:	_____
Total Points:	_____
Range:	_____
Level:	_____
Denomination	_____
Rebid:	_____

9) ♠ Q 10 7 2
   ♥ A 9 7 4 2
   ♦ K J
   ♣ 10 9

HCP:	_____
Distr. Points:	_____
Total Points:	_____
Range:	_____
Level:	_____
Denomination	_____
Rebid:	_____

Exercise Four — Responder's Rebid When Opener Shows a Medium Hand

Suppose the bidding is:

OPENER	RESPONDER
1 ♥	1 ♠
3 ♥	

What is the range of opener's hand?

Value your hand as responder. Then decide at what level the contract should be played and in what denomination the contract should be played. Use this information to determine your rebid.

1) ♠ K 10 7 4 3
   ♥ 9 2
   ♦ Q J 6 2
   ♣ 10 4

Total Points:	_____
Level:	_____
Denomination	_____
Rebid:	_____

2) ♠ A J 8 2
   ♥ 7
   ♦ K 10 4 3
   ♣ Q 9 8 6

Total Points:	_____
Level:	_____
Denomination	_____
Rebid:	_____

3) ♠ A 10 7 3
   ♥ K 10
   ♦ 7 4 3
   ♣ Q 9 6 2

Total Points:	_____
Level:	_____
Denomination	_____
Rebid:	_____

Exercise Five — Responder's Rebid When Opener Shows a Maximum Hand

Suppose the bidding is:

OPENER	RESPONDER
1 ♦	1 ♥
2NT	

What is the range of opener's hand?

Value your hand as responder. Then decide at what level the contract should be played and in what denomination the contract should be played. Use this information to determine your rebid.

1) ♠ 9 4	2) ♠ 8	3) ♠ K 5 2
♥ K 10 8 4	♥ Q J 10 8 3 2	♥ A J 9 4 3
♦ Q J 9 3	♦ A 6 5	♦ J 10 8
♣ 10 7 2	♣ 9 4 2	♣ 4 3

Total Points: ____	Total Points: ___	Total Points: _____
Level: ____	Level: ___	Level: _____
Denomination ____	Denomination ___	Denomination _____
Rebid: ____	Rebid: ___	Rebid: _____

Exercise Six — Trumping Losers

Construct the following hands for North and South:

NORTH (Dummy)
♠ 8 6 4 2
♥ 5 3
♦ J 7 3
♣ A 9 4 2

SOUTH (Declarer)
♠ A K Q J 10 9
♥ A K 6
♦ 9 4 2
♣ 5

Suppose South is playing in a contract of 4♠. How many sure tricks does South have? How can South get an additional trick?

Could South get an additional trick by leading a club to dummy's ace and then leading a club and trumping it? What conclusion can you draw from this?

Exercise Seven — Developing a Trick by Trumping in Dummy

(E-Z Deal Cards: #6, Hand 1 — Dealer, North)

Turn up all of the cards on the first pre-dealt hand. Put each hand dummy style at the edge of the table in front of each player.

Dealer: North

```
              ♠ Q J 9 3
              ♥ 7 5 3
              ♦ K 3
              ♣ A K 6 2
  ♠ 8 4                    ♠ 6 2
  ♥ K Q 8 4      N         ♥ A 10 9
  ♦ 8 7 5 4    W   E       ♦ Q J 10 6
  ♣ Q 10 9       S         ♣ J 7 5 3
              ♠ A K 10 7 5
              ♥ J 6 2
              ♦ A 9 2
              ♣ 8 4
```

The Bidding

North is the dealer. Which player would open the bidding? What would the opening bid be?

Look at responder's hand. Can responder support opener's suit? Can responder bid a new suit? What would responder bid?

What is the bidding message given by responder's bid? Does opener have to bid again? What is the range of opener's hand? What would opener rebid?

What is the range of responder's hand? At what level, does responder want to play the contract? In what denomination, does responder want to play the contract? What would responder rebid?

What would the contract be? Who would be declarer?

The Play

Which player would make the opening lead? What would the opening lead be?

How many tricks must declarer take to fulfill the contract? How many sure tricks does declarer have? Which suit provides declarer with an opportunity to develop the additional trick needed to make the contract? What must declarer do to develop the additional trick?

Bid and play the deal. Did declarer make the contract?

Exercise Eight — Getting Ready to Trump in Dummy
(E-Z Deal Cards: #6, Hand 2 — Dealer, East)

Turn up all of the cards on the second pre-dealt hand, and arrange them as in the previous exercise.

The Bidding

East is the dealer. Which player would open the bidding? What would be the opening bid?

Look at responder's hand. Can responder support opener's suit? What is the value of responder's hand? What would responder bid?

What is the bidding message given by responder's bid?

```
Dealer: East
                    ♠ K 6 3 2
                    ♥ 8
                    ♦ J 6 4
                    ♣ K Q 7 6 4
    ♠ Q 9 8 5               ♠ J
    ♥ 10 9 7 5    N         ♥ A K Q J 4 3
    ♦ A 9 3    W   E        ♦ 10 8 2
    ♣ 5 2         S         ♣ A 10 9
                    ♠ A 10 7 4
                    ♥ 6 2
                    ♦ K Q 7 5
                    ♣ J 8 3
```

Does opener have to bid again? What is the range of opener's hand? What would opener rebid?

What is the range of responder's hand? At what level, does responder want to play the contract? In what denomination, does responder want to play the contract? What would responder rebid?

What would the contract be? Who would be declarer?

The Play

Which player would make the opening lead? What would the opening lead be?

How many tricks must declarer take to fulfill the contract? How many sure tricks does declarer have? Which suit provides declarer with an opportunity to develop the additional trick needed to make the contract? What must declarer do to develop the additional trick?

Bid and play the deal. Did declarer make the contract?

Exercise Nine — Delaying Drawing Trump
(E-Z Deal Cards: #6, Hand 3 — Dealer, South)

Turn up all of the cards on the third pre-dealt hand, and arrange them as in the previous exercise.

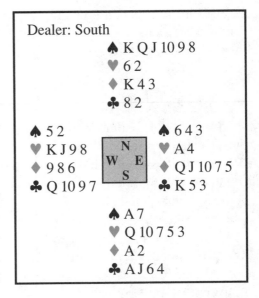

Dealer: South

♠ K Q J 10 9 8
♥ 6 2
♦ K 4 3
♣ 8 2

♠ 5 2   ♠ 6 4 3
♥ K J 9 8   ♥ A 4
♦ 9 8 6   ♦ Q J 10 7 5
♣ Q 10 9 7   ♣ K 5 3

♠ A 7
♥ Q 10 7 5 3
♦ A 2
♣ A J 6 4

The Bidding

South is the dealer. Which player would open the bidding? What would the opening bid be?

Look at responder's hand. What would responder bid? What is the bidding message given by responder's bid? Does opener have to bid again? What is the range of opener's hand? What would opener rebid?

What is the range of responder's hand? At what level, does responder want to play the contract? In what denomination, does responder want to play the contract? What would responder rebid?

What would opener bid next? Why? What would the contract be? Who would be declarer?

The Play

Which player would make the opening lead? What would the opening lead be?

How many tricks must declarer take to fulfill the contract? How many sure tricks does declarer have? Which suit provides declarer with an opportunity to develop the additional trick needed to make the contract? Can declarer draw trumps right away? If not, why not?

Bid and play the deal. Did declarer make the contract?

Exercise Ten — The Repeated Finesse

(E-Z Deal Cards: #6, Hand 4 — Dealer, West)

Turn up all of the cards on the fourth pre-dealt hand and arrange them as in the previous exercise.

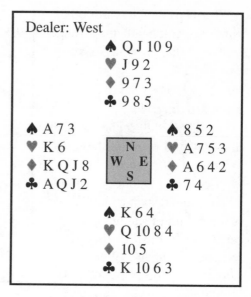

Dealer: West

North
♠ Q J 10 9
♥ J 9 2
♦ 9 7 3
♣ 9 8 5

West
♠ A 7 3
♥ K 6
♦ K Q J 8
♣ A Q J 2

East
♠ 8 5 2
♥ A 7 5 3
♦ A 6 4 2
♣ 7 4

South
♠ K 6 4
♥ Q 10 8 4
♦ 10 5
♣ K 10 6 3

The Bidding

West is the dealer. Which player would open the bidding? What would the opening bid be?

Look at responder's hand. What would responder bid?

What is the range of opener's hand? Is opener's hand balanced or unbalanced? What would opener rebid?

What is the range of re- sponder's hand? Does the partnership have a Golden Fit in a major suit? What would responder rebid?

The Play

Which player would make the opening lead? What would the opening lead be?

How many tricks must declarer take to fulfill the contract? How many sure tricks does declarer have? How can declarer develop additional tricks in the club suit? What does declarer have to hope for? From which hand, should declarer lead clubs? Why?

Bid and play the deal. Did declarer make the contract?

Answers to Lesson 6 exercises are on pages 308–313.

LESSON 7
Overcalls and Responses

Bidding with Competition

The Overcall

Responding to an Overcall

Guidelines for Play

Summary

The Finer Points

Activities

In the first six lessons, you have reached your contract without any bidding by the opponents. Now, it is time to consider what happens when both sides are bidding for the contract.

BIDDING WITH COMPETITION

When your side opens the bidding, you hope to be able to find a Golden Game in either spades, hearts, or notrump. When you can't, you hope to play the contract in a partscore in either a Golden Fit or notrump. You and your partner want to exchange information in an orderly fashion without interruption from the opponents.

When the opponents open the bidding, the likelihood of your side reaching a Golden Game is greatly reduced. Your opponent's opening bid announces at least 13 points. There are only 40 HCP in total in the deck. Even if opener has a minimum hand, that leaves approximately 27 points unaccounted for. (This is only an approximation since players count distributional points in addition to HCP.) You and your partner need most of the outstanding points in order to reach a game contract. This is not impossible, but it means that reaching game is usually not the most important consideration when deciding to take competitive action.

In addition, you probably won't be able to exchange information without interference from the opponents. You are now in a competitive bidding situation. This means that various levels on the Bidding Scale will be taken up by the opponents' opening bid and subsequent auction.

How does this affect the way the partnership thinks about the bidding? Let's look at some of the advantages and disadvantages of coming into the auction when the opponents have opened the bidding.

Advantages of Competitive Bidding

There are several advantages to bidding after your opponents have opened the bidding:

- Your partnership may have enough combined strength to make a partscore or even a game. You should start describing your hand as soon as possible.

- If your side doesn't have the strength to make a contract, you still may be able to interfere with the opponents' exchange of information and make it difficult for them to arrive at their best contract.

- If the opponents do play the contract, the information from your bidding may help your side defend the contract better, including getting a good opening lead.

Disadvantages of Competitive Bidding

There are risks to be considered when your side gets involved in the auction:

- If you are bidding to interfere with the opponents but do not have enough strength in your combined hands, you might end up playing a contract you can't make.

- At the same time you are giving your partner information about your hand, you are also giving information to the opponents that might help them during the play.

Nothing is perfect! You need to balance the advantages and disadvantages when considering a competitive call.

Maybe it sounds like a good idea to enter the auction with the sole purpose of interfering with the opponents' bidding. One player could try to outbid the opponents just to prevent them from playing a contract. However, there are two additional factors to take into account — vulnerability and the penalty double.

Vulnerability

On each hand, your side is said to be either *vulnerable* or *nonvulnerable*. Vulnerability relates to the scoring bonus you get for bidding and making your contract (game or slam) or the scoring penalty for not making your contract. If you are vulnerable, the bonuses and penalties are higher.

How vulnerability is decided depends on the form of scoring. In duplicate bridge, the vulnerability is predetermined for any given hand. Sometimes both sides are nonvulnerable, sometimes both sides are vulnerable, and sometimes one side is vulnerable while the other side is not. It works out that your side is vulnerable on approximately half the hands you play. In rubber bridge, a side is nonvulnerable until it bids and makes its first game. At that time the side becomes vulnerable. There are more details in the Appendix. For now, it is sufficient to know that a side is either nonvulnerable or vulnerable at the start of any deal.

Vulnerability affects the scoring in the following manner:

- The bonus for making a vulnerable game contract is larger than the bonus for making a nonvulnerable game contract (see Appendix).

- The penalty for going down in a nonvulnerable contract is 50 points per trick whereas the penalty for going down in a vulnerable contract is 100 points per trick.

- The bonus for making a small slam or a grand slam contract is larger when vulnerable (see Appendix).

For example, suppose you are in a contract of 4♠. From Lesson 1, you may recall that your trick score for making this contract is 120 points (30 points for each trick in a major suit). If you make the contract in duplicate play or *Chicago-style* rubber bridge, you receive a game bonus in addition to your trick score. If you are nonvulnerable, you get a total of 420 points (120 + 300) for making 4♠. If you are vulnerable, you get

620 points (120 + 500).

If you are defeated in your contract by three tricks (you take only seven tricks instead of 10), however, you lose a penalty of 150 points (3 x 50) if you are nonvulnerable or 500 points (100 for the first trick and 200 each for the next two tricks) if you are vulnerable.

It is more dangerous to bid too high when you are vulnerable. The vulnerability puts a constraint on your competitive actions and must be kept in mind when considering whether or not to interfere with the opponents' auction.

The Penalty Double

There is something else that prevents a player from bidding too much without risking a severe penalty — the *penalty double*. If your opponents bid to a contract that you don't think they can make, you can say "Double" when it is your turn to call. If the contract is doubled and declarer is defeated, the penalties are increased. However, declarer receives additional bonuses for making the contract.

Here are a few pointers about making a penalty double:

- You can double only your opponents' contract. If you don't think your partner can make the contract, keep it to yourself!

- You can double only when it is your turn to call.

- A double does not end the auction — the other players still have an opportunity to call. If there are three passes, then the final contract is said to be doubled. If there is another bid, the auction continues, and the double is no longer in effect.

The effects of the penalty double and the vulnerability combine to determine the size of the penalty as follows:

- The penalty for going down in a doubled contract when nonvulnerable is 100 points for the first undertrick, 200 points for the second and third undertricks and 300 points per undertrick thereafter.

- The penalty for going down in a doubled contract when vulnerable is 200 points for the first trick and 300 points for each subsequent trick.

For example, if you are doubled in a contract of 4 ♠ and defeated by three tricks, the penalty is 500 points (100 + 200 + 200) if you are nonvulnerable, and it's 800 points (200 + 300 + 300) if you are vulnerable. As you can see, the effects of vulnerabilty and the penalty double put a limit on the amount of bidding you can afford to do in competition.

You have been opening the bidding and responding for six lessons without knowing about vulnerability or the penalty double. How do these factors affect what you have learned to this point? All the bids discussed so far are made regardless of the vulnerability or fear of being doubled. It is when everyone gets into the auction (especially when you are bidding merely to interfere with the opponents) that you must keep your eye on the vulnerability and consider whether an opponent might double you.

THE OVERCALL

The simplest form of competitive action when the opponents start the bidding is a bid at the cheapest available level. This is called an *overcall* because you are making a "call" over the opponent's bid.

Here are some examples of overcalls:

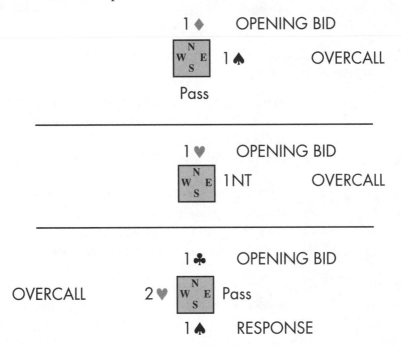

	1♦	OPENING BID
	1♠	OVERCALL
	Pass	

	1♥	OPENING BID
	1NT	OVERCALL

	1♣	OPENING BID
OVERCALL 2♥	Pass	
	1♠	RESPONSE

An overcall can be made at the one level, the two level, or even higher. It can be made in a suit or in notrump. Let's look at some of the requirements for making an overcall.

How Long a Suit Do You Need to Overcall?

When you make an overcall in a suit, you should have at least a five-card suit. This applies whether you are overcalling in a major suit or a minor suit.

One reason for requiring a five-card suit is to minimize the risk of entering the auction when an opponent has opened the bidding. If you are left to play in your suit, you would like to have plenty of trumps. In addition, the longer your suit is, the less likely the opponents are to make a penalty double.

There is another reason for requiring a five-card or longer suit. Your partner will usually lead your suit if the opponents play the contract. You want the suit to be a source of tricks for your side, not the opponents'.

Let's look at some examples. Suppose the opponent on your right has opened the bidding 1 ♦.

♠ A 6
♥ A Q J 10 8
♦ 9 5
♣ K 6 4 2

With a strong five-card heart suit, overcall 1 ♥. Even if you are left to play there, hearts should make a satisfactory trump suit. If the opponents play the contract, you would like partner to lead a heart.

♠ A 8 2
♥ 5 3
♦ 7 4
♣ A K Q 9 7 4

With a good six-card club suit, you want to enter the bidding both to compete and to tell partner something about your hand. Because of the opening bid, you will have to overcall 2 ♣.

♠ A J 10 7 5
♥ A Q 9 6 3
♦ 7
♣ J 10

You have a choice of suits to overcall. Use the same guidelines as when opening the bidding — bid the higher-ranking suit first, 1 ♠. You may have an opportunity to show the heart suit later if the auction continues and the level does not get too high.

You would have opened the bidding with all of the above hands. Does this mean that you need the same strength to overcall as you do to open the bidding? Let's take a closer look at the strength requirements.

The Strength for a One-Level Overcall in a Suit

Consider the following hand:

♠ K Q J 10 5
♥ K 7 2
♦ 5 2
♣ 8 4 3

You have 9 HCP plus 1 for the five-card suit. With only 10 points, you are not strong enough to open the bidding. Your partner would assume that you had at least 13 points, and you might well get the partnership too high on the Bidding Scale during the auction.

However, suppose you are West. South, on your right, is the dealer and opens the bidding 1♦. Your side is nonvulnerable and the opponents are vulnerable. Can a case be made for overcalling 1♠?

Let's look at a possible layout for the entire hand:

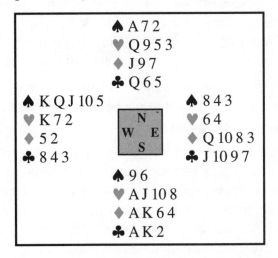

First, consider what happens if North and South are left to bid with no interference from your side. South has a balanced hand with 19 HCP, too strong to open the bidding 1 NT. South would start the auction with 1♦. Holding 9 points, North would respond 1♥. South, with a maximum hand and four-card support for responder's suit, would jump to game. The contract would be 4♥, and it should be successful. North should lose only one spade trick, one heart trick, and one diamond trick.

For making the contract, North and South will get a trick score of 120 points (4 x 30) plus a bonus of 500 points for a vulnerable game — a total of 620 points.

Now, let's see what happens if West interferes with the orderly exchange of information between North and South. South again starts the bidding with 1♦. This time, West overcalls 1♠. Now North has a problem. With only

9 HCP, not enough to bid a new suit at the two level, North can't bid 2 ♥. Instead, with 6 to 10 points, North probably would compromise by responding 1 NT. With only 3 points, East would pass. South, with a maximum balanced hand, might well jump to 3 NT. Notice how the overcall could result in North and South missing their Golden Fit.

Because of the overcall, East would lead partner's suit, spades. After winning the trick, North would have to establish heart tricks to make the contract. West will win a trick with the ♥ K, and, since the contract is notrump, West will take all of the sure spade tricks. With four spade tricks and one heart trick, East and West will defeat the contract.

This shows how an overcall can be effective. It might make it difficult for the opponents to get to the best contract, and it might help the defense make a good opening lead.

What risk does West run by overcalling? Left to play in 1 ♠, West would most likely take five tricks, suffering a penalty of 100 points (50 points per trick when nonvulnerable). Even if the opponents doubled the overcall, the penalty would only be 300 points. In both cases, West would be better off by overcalling rather than by keeping quiet and giving the opponents an easy route to 620 points.

The other risk is that partner would assume West has a stronger hand. On this hand, it doesn't matter, and that will often be the case in a competitive auction. However, some danger exists as we shall see shortly. Partner will have to take this into consideration when responding to a one-level overcall.

In general, an overcall in a suit at the one level can be made on a hand with less than the value of an opening bid, provided the overcaller has at least a five-card suit headed by three of the top five cards in the suit.

The Strength for a Two-Level Overcall in a Suit

It is not always a good idea to overcall on a hand with less strength than an opening bid. Suppose you pick up the following hand:

♠ 8 4 3
♥ K Q J 10 5
♦ K 7 2
♣ 5 2

You have 9 HCP plus 1 for the five-card suit. This hand is very similar to the one in the previous section. Again, you're West, but this time the opening bid on your right is 1 ♠. To show your heart suit, you would have to overcall at the two level. Also, this time your side is vulnerable, and the opponents are nonvulnerable. Can a case be made for overcalling 2 ♥?

Here is a possible layout for the entire deal:

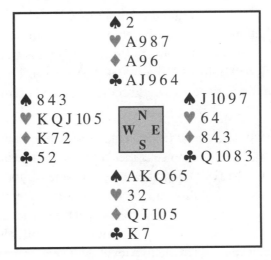

First, let's see what happens if North and South are left to bid with no interference. South would start the auction with 1 ♠, holding an unbalanced hand with a five-card major. With 14 points, enough to bid a new suit at the two level, North would respond 2 ♣. South would rebid 2 ♦ to show a second suit, and North, knowing there was enough combined strength for game and no likely Golden Fit in a major suit, would put the partnership in 3NT. This contract should be successful. North has at least three spade tricks, one heart trick, three diamond tricks, and two club tricks. Even if East were to lead a heart (unlikely since West did not overcall), North can make the contract with the help of a finesse in diamonds.

North and South will get a trick score of 100 points plus a bonus of 300 points for a nonvulnerable game, a total of 400 points.

Now, let's see what happens if West tries to interfere with the exchange of information between North and South by overcalling. Again South starts the bidding with 1 ♠. This time West overcalls 2 ♥. North is in a good position to double for penalty. North knows that with the 13 or more points that South holds, the combined partnership strength should keep West from making the contract.

If left to play in a doubled contract of 2 ♥, West will not fare well. With good defense, West can be held to only four heart tricks and will end up being defeated by four tricks. Since West is vulnerable, the penalty will be 1,100 points (200 + 300 + 300 + 300). This is a heavy price to pay, since the opponents would score only 400 points if West had not interfered.

The strength and shape of the hand is virtually identical to that in the previous section. The difference comes from the change in vulnerability and bidding level. When considering whether to overcall, you must be careful to watch both the vulnerability and the level at which you must overcall. It is alright to overcall with a good five-card suit at the one level with slightly less than opening-bid strength when you are nonvulnerable. However, if you are vulnerable or have to bid at the two level, you need more strength.

1NT Overcall

An overcall of 1NT is similar to a 1NT opening bid. You need a balanced hand with 16 to 18 points. There is one additional consideration. An opening bid in a suit provides information about the shape of opener's hand that will help the opener's partner get off to a good opening lead for their side. Because of this, you generally should have some strength and/or length in the suit bid by your opponent, if you are going to overcall 1NT.

Let's look at a couple of examples. Suppose your right-hand opponent has opened the bidding 1♥.

♠ K 3 ♥ A Q 8 ♦ K Q J 8 ♣ Q 10 6 2	With a balanced hand and 17 HCP, you can overcall 1NT. You have some strength in the opponent's suit, so you don't mind if they lead a heart.
♠ A Q 3 ♥ 6 2 ♦ K Q J 8 7 ♣ A 10 3	You have a balanced hand with 16 HCP. You would tend to open the bidding 1NT. Rather than overcall 1NT with a small doubleton in the opponent's suit, however, you would do better to overcall in your five-card suit, 2♦.

When the Opponents Bid Your Suit

Suppose you pick up the following hand:

♠ A Q J 10 5
♥ 10 7 2
♦ A 9 3
♣ Q 6

You intend to open the bidding 1♠, but the opponent on your right bids 1♠. It make no sense for you to overcall 2♠. There is no advantage in competing with your opponent in the same suit. You will not find much spade support in your partner's hand if your opponent has enough spades to bid the suit.

Should you make a penalty double? It's too soon for that. You would warn the opponents that spades isn't their suit, and they might bid to a better spot. Also, you may not be able to defeat them at such a low level. As we will see in the next lesson, you seldom double a partscore contract if your partner has not bid.

With a hand like this, pass — even though you have an opening bid. You do not have to compete if your hand is unsuitable. Besides, the opponents currently are considering playing with your best suit as trump. Silence is golden!

Putting It Together

When an opponent opens the bidding, consider whether to overcall using the following guidelines:

REQUIREMENTS FOR AN OVERCALL IN A SUIT	REQUIREMENTS FOR A 1NT OVERCALL
• A five-card or longer suit (for both majors and minors). • 13 or more points (occasionally less with a good suit if nonvulnerable and at the one level).	• 16 to 18 points. • Balanced hand. • Some strength in the opponent's suit.

Let's look at some examples. Your side is nonvulnerable, and the opponent on your right opens the bidding 1 ♦ . What would you do with the following hands?

♠ J 9 7 5 3   You have only 9 HCP, and you don't have a good
♥ K 8 5   five-card suit. Pass.
♦ Q 6 3
♣ K 8

♠ A K J 10 7   Overcall 1 ♠ even though you don't have quite the
♥ K 8 3   strength of an opening bid. You do have a good suit,
♦ 7 2   and you are only at the one level, nonvulnerable.
♣ 10 8 5

♠ K Q 3
♥ 7 3
♦ A 2
♣ A J 10 8 7 3

To overcall, you must bid at the two level. With a six-card suit and 14 HCP, overcall 2 ♣. With good strength and a good suit, now is the time to act. You may not get an opportunity later in the auction.

♠ A Q 10
♥ 9 6 2
♦ K Q 10
♣ K Q J 6

With a balanced hand, 17 HCP, and some strength in the opponent's suit, you have the perfect hand to overcall 1NT. This will describe your hand to partner who can take it from there.

♠ A 7 3
♥ J 5
♦ K J 10 8 4
♣ A 9 4

Your opponent has bid your suit. Pass, and see how the auction develops.

RESPONDING TO AN OVERCALL

Responder Raises a Major Suit

Since the overcall promises at least a five-card suit, responder needs only three-card support to raise. This situation is similar to responder's position opposite an opening bid of one in a major suit. Since the auction is competitive, you want to show your support immediately in case you run into interference from the opponents. Because of this, the raises are slightly different from the raises after an opening bid of one of a suit. The single raise, made with 6 to 10 points, remains the same as does the jump (limit raise) with 11 or 12 points. With 13 to 16 points, however, raise directly to game, the four level, instead of bidding a new suit.

Suppose the opponent on your left bids 1♣, and your partner overcalls 1♠. What would you respond with the following hands? Remember to value your hand using dummy points when raising partner's major.

♠ J 10 9   With three-card support for partner's suit, your
♥ 6   hand is worth 8 points — 5 HCP plus 3 for the
♦ K 8 7 6 4   singleton heart. Raise to 2♠.
♣ J 7 4 3

♠ Q J 7 2   With 11 HCP and 1 for the doubleton club, raise
♥ K Q 3   to 3♠ to show 11 or 12 points.
♦ K 8 7 5
♣ 10 9

♠ J 10 9 8   You have 9 HCP and 5 points for the heart void
♥ —   for a total of 14. Raise partner all the way to game,
♦ A 8 5 3   4♠. (If partner had opened the bidding 1♠, you
♣ K J 8 7 3   would have responded 2♣, forcing.)

Responder Raises a Minor Suit

An overcall in a minor suit also promises at least a five-card suit.
Responder needs only three-card support to raise. Raises are similar to
raises of a major-suit overcall. Responder raises to the two level with 6
to 10 points and the three level with 11 or 12 points. However, rather
than raising to the game level of 5♣ or 5♦ with 13 or more points,
responder keeps in mind the Golden Game of 3 NT. To bid 3 NT, responder needs some strength in the opponent's suit. With an unbalanced
hand and no strength in the opponent's suit, responder can bid game in
the minor suit.

Suppose the opponent on your left bids 1♣, and your partner overcalls 1♦. How would you respond with the following hands?

♠ A 9 3   With four-card support for partner's suit and 9
♥ 6 2   HCP, raise to 2♦.
♦ K 10 7 4
♣ Q 7 4 3

♠ K 2
♥ K 7 3
♦ A Q 7 5
♣ 9 7 5 2

With 12 HCP and four-card support for partner's suit, raise to 3♦.

♠ J 10 8
♥ K 9 3
♦ A Q 5
♣ K J 10 7

You have support for partner's suit and are strong enough to raise to game. With some strength in the opponent's suit, choose the Golden Game of 3NT rather than bidding 5♦.

Responder Bids a New Suit

Responder cannot always support partner's overcall — sometimes responder bids a new suit. Whether or not this bid of a new suit is forcing depends on your agreement with partner. To keep the rules consistent with responses to opening bids of one in a suit, we will assume that you and your partner have agreed that a new-suit bid is forcing. Now, you can respond to partner's overcall in the same manner as responding to an opening bid when you do not have support for partner's suit.

One further point. Partner has shown a five-card or longer suit. Generally, you should respond only in a five-card or longer suit. (See the next section for what to do if you can't bid a new suit.) We will see in the next lesson that partner has a different method of competing if partner is interested in hearing about your four-card suits.

Suppose the bidding is opened 1♦, and your partner overcalls 1♥. Let's see what you would do with the following hands.

♠ K J 10 7 3
♥ J 8
♦ 9 4 2
♣ A J 7

You do not have support for partner's suit, but you do have 11 points. That's more than enough to bid. Bid a new suit, 1♠, and wait to hear partner's rebid before deciding what to do.

♠ J 9 7 6 3
♥ 5
♦ 10 9 6 3
♣ Q 4 2

Even though you don't care for partner's suit, you don't have enough strength to bid a new suit at the one level. Pass.

♠ A K 6
♥ 6 3
♦ 10 9 4
♣ A K 10 9 4

You have enough points to go to game, but you don't know where the contract should be played. Bid 2♣, just as you would if partner had opened the bidding, to get a further description of partner's hand.

Responder Bids Notrump

If responder can't raise the overcall and can't bid a new suit, perhaps responder can bid notrump. Responder needs some strength in the opponent's suit to do this. The notrump bids after an overcall are easily remembered. With 6 to 10 points, responder bids 1NT if the one level is still available. With 11 or 12 points, responder bids 2NT. With 13 or more points, responder bids 3NT.

Let's see how this works. Your opponent opens the bidding 1♥, and your partner overcalls 1♠.

♠ 9 8
♥ K J 3
♦ A J 10 8 7
♣ 10 9 3

With 10 points — 9 HCP and 1 for the five-card suit — you aren't strong enough to bid a new suit at the two level. Instead, respond 1 NT, showing a hand in the 6 to 10 point range with some strength in the opponent's suit.

♠ J 3
♥ K Q 10 2
♦ A 9 3
♣ Q 10 8 3

With a balanced hand of 12 HCP and some strength in the opponent's suit, jump to 2 NT. This is similar to the raise of the overcaller's suit to the three level showing 11 or 12 points. If partner had opened the bidding, this response would show 13 to 16 points.

♠ Q 3
♥ A Q J
♦ K 10 8 5
♣ Q 10 7 4

With a balanced hand of 14 HCP, no support for partner's suit, and some strength in the opponent's suit, jump right to 3NT.

Responding to a Two-Level Overcall

When your partner overcalls at the two level, you know that partner has at least a five-card suit and the strength of an opening bid. However, some of the bidding room has been taken up by the opponents' bidding. You are in the position of responding to an opening one-bid starting at the two level. You no longer have the luxury of showing a hand in the 6 to 10 point range by raising partner to the two level, bidding a new suit at the one level, or bidding 1NT.

To compensate, you could modify the range for raising to the three level to 6 to 12 or perhaps 8 to 12 points. For the sake of simplicity, we will leave the ranges the same as when responding to an opening bid. This means that with 6 to 10 points, you pass if partner overcalls at the two level. If you have 11 or 12 points, raise to the three level, bid a new suit, or bid 2NT. If you have 13 or more points, bid game.

Let's see how this works. The opponent on your left bids 1♠, and your partner overcalls 2♥.

♠ Q 9 7
♥ 9 7
♦ J 10 9 4
♣ K J 5 2

You have 7 points. If partner had opened the bidding 1♥, you would respond 1NT, showing a hand in the 6 to 10 point range. There is no room to do this over partner's overcall. A 2NT bid would show 11 or 12 points. Instead, pass.

♠ Q 9
♥ K 8 3
♦ K J 7 4
♣ J 10 7 3

You have support for partner's suit and 11 points — 10 HCP plus 1 for the doubleton. Raise to 3♥, just as you would if partner had overcalled 1♥.

♠ A 8 2
♥ Q 10 7 4
♦ K Q 9 3 2
♣ 5

With 11 HCP plus 3 for the singleton club, raise partner directly to 4 ♥.

Responding to an Overcall of 1NT

A 1NT overcall shows a balanced hand with 16, 17, or 18 points — the same values as a 1NT opening bid. Responder's guidelines are the same as when partner opens 1NT (Lesson 3). Responder, as captain, usually knows enough to sign off in the appropriate contract.

Let's look at a few examples. Your opponent bids 1♣ , and your partner overcalls 1NT.

♠ J 10 9 7 6 3
♥ 9 5
♦ Q 8 2
♣ 6 3

With only 5 points, you know the partnership belongs in a partscore. Since partner has a balanced hand, there is a Golden Fit in spades. Sign off in 2♠.

♠ K 10 4
♥ 10 8 4
♦ K Q J 7 4
♣ 9 6

With 9 HCP plus 1 for the five-card diamond suit, you know there is enough combined strength for game. With no Golden Fit in a major suit, put the partnership in 3NT.

♠ 10 8 4
♥ J 6
♦ K 9 6 3
♣ J 10 7 3

With 5 HCP, you know the partnership belongs in a partscore. Since your hand is balanced, pass.

Putting It Together

In summary, when responding to an overcall, responder categorizes the hand in the same fashion as when responding to an opening bid (minimum, medium, or maximum) and bids accordingly.

With a Minimum Hand (6 to 10 points):
- Pass if already at the two level.
- Raise partner's suit to the two level with three-card or longer support.
- Bid a new suit at the one level.
- Bid 1NT with some strength in the opponent's suit and a balanced hand.

With a Medium Hand (11 or 12 points):
- Raise partner's suit to the three level with three-card or longer support.
- Bid a new suit (even if it is at the two level).
- Bid 2NT with some strength in the opponent's suit and a balanced hand.

With a Maximum Hand (13 or more points):
- Raise partner's suit to game with three-card or longer support.
- Bid a new suit.
- Bid 3NT with some strength in the opponent's suit and a balanced hand.

Your opponent bids 1 ♣, and your partner overcalls 1 ♥. What would you respond with each of the following hands?

♠ Q J 10 8 7 ♥ 3 2 ♦ K 4 ♣ A 8 7 4	You have 10 HCP and 1 point for the five-card spade suit for a total of 11 points. Since you can't support partner's suit, bid your own suit at the one level, 1 ♠.
♠ J 8 2 ♥ 10 5 ♦ K 10 7 6 3 ♣ K 10 4	You have 7 HCP plus 1 for the five-card diamond suit. You can't support partner's suit, and you don't have a suit you can bid at the one level. Respond 1NT.
♠ A 4 ♥ K J 3 ♦ K 9 8 6 4 ♣ 7 5 2	You have support for partner's suit, 11 HCP plus 1 for the doubleton. Raise to 3 ♥ to show 11 or 12 points. Do not bid 2 ♦ in a competitive auction when you have a fit with partner's suit and a medium range hand.

Rebids by the Overcaller

Rebids by the overcaller are similar to rebids by opener (Lesson 5). The overcaller categorizes the hand into minimum (13 to 16 points), medium (17 or 18 points), or maximum (19 to 21 points) and chooses a rebid that describes both the strength and shape of the hand. The opponents' bidding may make this difficult some of the time, but the overcaller can stick with the general principle — the stronger the overcall, the higher on the Bidding Scale the overcaller rebids.

GUIDELINES FOR PLAY

When playing in a trump contract, it is generally a good idea to draw the opponents' trumps before taking your sure tricks in other suits. This is to prevent the opponents from trumping one of your sure tricks. There are times, however, when you have to delay drawing trumps because you have more pressing concerns.

Discarding Losers

Consider the following hand:

NORTH (Dummy)
♠ 6 5 4 3
♥ J 7 4 3
♦ Q 7
♣ A K Q

SOUTH
♠ K Q J 10 9 8 7
♥ A 6
♦ 5 3
♣ 7 4

Suppose you are in a contract of 4♠, and your opponent leads the ♥K. You need 10 tricks, and you start by counting your sure tricks. You have four — the ♥A and the ♣ AKQ. You would plan to promote six additional tricks in the spade suit by driving out the opponents' ace.

Normally, it would be a good idea to lead spades as soon as possible. You want to "take your losses early." But look what happens if you win the ♥A and play the ♠K right away. The opponents can win the ace and take their ♥Q and two diamond tricks to defeat your contract. What went wrong?

In addition to counting your winners, you have to be aware of the potential tricks you might lose if the opponents gain the lead. In the above hand, you have four potential losers once your ♥A is gone — a spade, a heart, and two diamonds.

What can you do about this? You have to look for a way to eliminate one of your losers before giving up a trick to the opponents. You can do this by playing the ♣AKQ and discarding one of your losers (the ♥6, ♦5, or the ♦3). You are running the risk that an opponent will be able to trump one of your club tricks, but you have no choice. You must eliminate one of your losers before giving up the lead.

Once you have discarded one of your losers on dummy's ♣Q, it is safe to drive out the opponents' ♠A. They will only be able to take two other tricks before you regain the lead, draw the remaining trump (if any), and take the rest of the tricks.

In a trump contract, you should always count the losers in your hand (not the losers in the dummy) if you may have to give up the lead before taking all the tricks you need. If you have too many losers, you must look for a way to eliminate one or more of them. One method, as we saw in the last lesson, is to trump losers in the dummy. If this is not possible, you can try discarding losers on extra winners in the dummy. Such considerations help you decide whether you should draw trumps right away or delay drawing trumps because you have more important things to do first.

SUMMARY

When an opponent opens the bidding, you can compete by overcalling if your hand meets the requirements.

REQUIREMENTS FOR AN OVERCALL IN A SUIT
- A five-card or longer suit (for both majors and minors).
- 13 or more points (occasionally fewer with a good suit if nonvulnerable and at the one level).

REQUIREMENTS FOR A 1NT OVERCALL
- 16 to 18 points.
- Balanced hand.
- Some strength in the opponent's suit.

If your partner overcalls in a suit, you may pass, raise, bid a new suit, or bid notrump.

With a Minimum Hand (6 to 10 points):
- Pass if already at the two level.
- Raise partner's suit to the two level with three-card or longer support.
- Bid a new suit at the one level.
- Bid 1NT with some strength in the opponent's suit and a balanced hand.

With a Medium Hand (11 or 12 points):
- Raise partner's suit to the three level with three-card or longer support.
- Bid a new suit (even if it is at the two level).
- Bid 2NT with some strength in the opponent's suit and a balanced hand.

With a Maximum Hand (13 or more points):
- Raise partner's suit to game with three-card or longer support.
- Bid a new suit.
- Bid 3NT with some strength in the opponent's suit and a balanced hand.

If your partner overcalls 1NT, you can respond as if partner opened the bidding 1NT.

RESPONDING TO A 1NT OVERCALL

0 to 7
- Bid 2♦, 2♥, or 2♠ with a five-card or longer suit (2♣ is reserved for the Stayman convention).
- Otherwise, pass.

8 or 9
- Bid 2NT (2♣ can be used to uncover an eight-card major-suit fit.)

10 to 14
- Bid 4♥ or 4♠ with a six-card or longer suit.
- Bid 3 or 3♥ with a five-card suit.
- Otherwise, bid 3NT (2♣ can be used to uncover an eight-card major-suit fit).

THE FINER POINTS

The Strength for an Overcall

The text points out that the overcaller sometimes can have less than the strength of an opening bid for an overcall. The lower limit can be 10 points or fewer depending on how aggressive you and your partner want to be. If the partnership decides to make light overcalls, remember to increase the strength needed for various responses in order to compensate.

Many authorities recommend putting an upper limit on the strength of the overcall at around 17 or 18 points. This is lower than the upper limit of 21 points for opening the bidding at the one level. There are a couple of reasons for this. It is rare to hold a very strong hand when an opponent opens the bidding. If responder knows the overcaller is limited to a maximum of 17 or 18 points, responder does not have to bid with a very minimum hand. In turn, this compensates for the fact that the overcaller could have fewer than 13 points. In addition, the takeout double (discussed in the next lesson) can be used for very strong hands when you want to compete.

When starting out, you can keep things simple by treating an overcall as equivalent to an opening bid. By doing this, you don't have to learn two different sets of responses for partner's opening bids and partner's overcalls. As your experience grows, you and your partner can adopt your own style or adjust your style to fit in with that of bridge players in your area.

The Cuebid Response

It was mentioned in the text that some players treat a new-suit response to an overcall as non-forcing. This is not recommended when starting out, but local practices vary.

One reason why a different framework can be used when responding to an overcall is that responder has an extra response available. Since the partnership is unlikely to want to play in the opening bidder's suit, a bid of this suit by responder can be given a special (artificial) meaning. A bid of a suit bid by the opponents is called a *cuebid*. For example:

NORTH	EAST	SOUTH	WEST
1♥	1♠	Pass	2♥

West's 2♥ bid is a cuebid of the opponent's (North's) suit.

By using a cuebid as an artificial forcing bid when responding to an overcall, you can construct a whole new framework of responses. The cuebid response is beyond the scope of this text, but it may be encountered when you start playing with more experienced players. You can discuss such bids with your partner when the appropriate time comes.

ACTIVITIES

Exercise One — More on Scoring

When you are considering bidding in competition, scoring becomes important. Fill in the following chart. Notice the difference it makes to the score whether or not you are vulnerable or doubled. You are in 3 ♥ and are defeated two tricks.

	Nonvulnerable	Vulnerable
Undoubled		
Doubled		

Exercise Two — The Overcall

The opponent on your right opens the bidding 1 ♦ . What would you bid on each of the following hands?

1) ♠ A Q 8 7 4
   ♥ 7 6
   ♦ J 10 8
   ♣ A K 3

2) ♠ 7 4 2
   ♥ A J
   ♦ A 8
   ♣ K Q 10 9 7 5

3) ♠ A 3 2
   ♥ K Q 8
   ♦ K J 10 2
   ♣ K J 2

Bid: _____   Bid: _____   Bid: _____

Exercise Three — The Strength and Shape for an Overcall

Consider the following hand:

♠ A 7 2
♥ K Q J 9 3
♦ J 5 4
♣ 9 2

If you were the dealer, what would you bid?

If the opponent on your right opened the bidding 1♣, would you consider overcalling 1♥? What would you hope to accomplish?

Would it make a difference if the opponent on your right opened 1♠? Would it make a difference if you were vulnerable?

Consider the following hand:

♠ Q 4
♥ K 8 7 3
♦ A J 2
♣ K 9 6 2

If you were the opening bidder, what would you bid with this hand?

If the opponent on your right opened the bidding 1♣, would you overcall 1♥? If not, why not? What would you do?

Exercise Four — Whether to Overcall

The opponent on your right opens the bidding 1♥. Your side is nonvulnerable. What would you do with each of the following hands?

1) ♠ A Q J 10 8	2) ♠ K 8 4 2	3) ♠ 10 3
♥ 7 3	♥ 8 7 3	♥ 3
♦ A 9 5	♦ 5	♦ A Q J 7 3
♣ 10 4 2	♣ A K Q 10 6	♣ A K 9 4 2

Bid: _____   Bid: _____   Bid: _____

4) ♠ A Q J	5) ♠ K 4	6) ♠ 6 3
♥ K 9 7 3	♥ K Q 10	♥ A K J 8 4
♦ J 8	♦ A J 9 3	♦ A J 8
♣ Q 8 6 3	♣ K J 10 8	♣ 10 7 3

Bid: _____   Bid: _____   Bid: _____

Exercise Five — Responding to a One-Level Overcall

The responses to overcalls are similar but not identical to those after an opening bid. When responding to an overcall, you want to get to the right contract as quickly as possible because everybody is in the auction. If you have support for the overcaller's suit, you bid at the appropriate level — the more you have, the more you bid. You don't mention a new suit first with 13 or more points, as you would in response to an opening bid.

Your opponent bids 1♣, and your partner overcalls 1♠. What would you respond with the following hands?

1)	♠ A 8 7	2)	♠ J 6 3 2	3)	♠ K 10 7 5 3
	♥ 10 9		♥ 9		♥ —
	♦ K 7 6 3		♦ K Q 8 7		♦ A J 8 2
	♣ J 7 5 2		♣ Q 8 7 6		♣ J 10 7 3

Response: _____   Response: _____   Response: _____

Because partner could have less than an opening bid to make an overcall at the one level, responder must be more cautious than when responding to an opening bid. Without support for partner's suit, responder should have at least 8 points to make a bid.

Your opponent bids 1♣, and your partner overcalls 1♥. What would you respond with the following hands?

4)	♠ 9 7 3 2	5)	♠ A Q J 8 5	6)	♠ Q 10 8
	♥ Q 2		♥ 10 4		♥ 7 6
	♦ K 8 6 5		♦ K 8 3		♦ K 10 6 3
	♣ 7 5 3		♣ J 4 2		♣ K J 10 7

Response: _____   Response: _____   Response: _____

Exercise Six — Responding to a Two-Level Overcall

When partner overcalls at the two level, there is no room left for you to show minimum hands of 6 to 10 points. With these hands, you will have to pass.

Your opponent bids 1♠, and your partner overcalls 2♥. What do you respond with the following hands?

	1)	2)	3)
♠	K 10 7 3	A 8 4	J 3
♥	J 4	K J 5	A 10 7 2
♦	Q J 6 2	Q 10 6 2	A K J 8
♣	7 4 2	J 4 2	10 4 2

Response: _____   Response: _____   Response: _____

Exercise Seven — Responding to a 1NT Overcall

When partner overcalls 1NT, you can respond in the same manner as when partner opens the bidding 1NT. You are the captain. It is your role to decide at what level and in what denomination to play the contract.

Your opponent bids 1♦, and your partner overcalls 1NT. What would you respond with the following hands?

	1)	2)	3)
♠	4	K J 3	8 7 5 3
♥	9 7 6 5 3 2	Q 9 6	K 9 6 2
♦	Q J 7	A J 3	10 8 3
♣	6 4 2	7 5 4 2	7 5

Response: _____   Response: _____   Response: _____

Exercise Eight — Discarding Losers

Construct the following hands for North and South:

NORTH (Dummy)
♠ A K 6
♥ J 5 4 3
♦ A 8 3
♣ J 5 4

SOUTH
♠ 3
♥ Q 10 9 8 7 6
♦ 7 6 5
♣ A K Q

Suppose you are in a contract of 4♥, and the opening lead is the ♦ K. How many tricks will you have to lose when developing the trump suit? How many tricks could you potentially lose in the diamond suit? Can you start playing the trump suit right away? If not, why not?

Exercise Nine — Overcalling
(E-Z Deal Cards: #7, Hand 1 — Dealer, North)

Turn up all of the cards on the first pre-dealt hand. Put each hand dummy style at the edge of the table in front of each player.

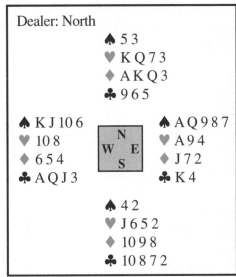

Dealer: North

North:
♠ 5 3
♥ K Q 7 3
♦ A K Q 3
♣ 9 6 5

West:
♠ K J 10 6
♥ 10 8
♦ 6 5 4
♣ A Q J 3

East:
♠ A Q 9 8 7
♥ A 9 4
♦ J 7 2
♣ K 4

South:
♠ 4 2
♥ J 6 5 2
♦ 10 9 8
♣ 10 8 7 2

The Bidding

North is the dealer. What would the opening bid be? What would East bid? What is this bid called?

What would South do in response to partner's opening bid? Has East's bid affected South's response?

What would West bid in response to East's overcall? What does North do now? Does North have an opportunity to finish describing the hand?

What is the bidding message given by West's response. What rebid would East make?

What would the contract be? Who would be declarer?

The Play

Which player would make the opening lead? Which suit would be led? Why?

How many tricks must declarer take to fulfill the contract? How many sure tricks does declarer have? Which suit should declarer play first after winning a trick? Why? What will happen to the two small hearts in declarer's hand?

Bid and play the deal. Did declarer make the contract?

Exercise Ten — Delaying Drawing Trump
(E-Z Deal Cards: #7. Hand 2 — Dealer, East)

Turn up all of the cards on the second pre-dealt hand, and arrange them as in the previous exercise.

```
Dealer: East
                ♠ 9 5 2
                ♥ J 8 7
                ♦ 9 6 4
                ♣ K Q 10 2
    ♠ 8 6                      ♠ K Q J 7 4
    ♥ A Q 4 2       N          ♥ K 6 5
    ♦ 5 3 2      W     E       ♦ A 7
    ♣ J 9 6 3       S          ♣ 8 7 4
                ♠ A 10 3
                ♥ 10 9 3
                ♦ K Q J 10 8
                ♣ A 5
```

The Bidding

East is the dealer. What would the opening bid be?

What would South bid?

What would West do in response to partner's opening bid? Has South's bid affected West's response?

What would North bid in response to South's overcall?

Would North make the same bid if South had opened the bidding at the one level?

What does East do now? Why does East not have to make a rebid?

What would the contract be? Who would be declarer?

The Play

Which player would make the opening lead? Which suit would be led? Why?

How many tricks must declarer take to fulfill the contract? How many sure tricks does declarer have? Which suit should declarer play first after winning the first trick? Why must declarer sometimes delay drawing trumps?

Bid and play the deal. Did declarer make the contract?

Exercise Eleven — Another Fast Discard
(E-Z Deal Cards: #7, Hand 3 — Dealer, South)

Turn up all of the cards on the third pre-dealt hand, and arrange them as in the previous exercise.

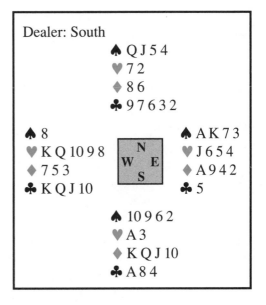

Dealer: South

♠ Q J 5 4
♥ 7 2
♦ 8 6
♣ 9 7 6 3 2

♠ 8
♥ K Q 10 9 8
♦ 7 5 3
♣ K Q J 10

♠ A K 7 3
♥ J 6 5 4
♦ A 9 4 2
♣ 5

♠ 10 9 6 2
♥ A 3
♦ K Q J 10
♣ A 8 4

The Bidding
South is the dealer. What would the opening bid be?

What would West bid?

What would North do in response to partner's opening bid?

What is the value of East's hand in response to West's overcall? What would East bid? Would East make the same bid if West had opened the bidding?

What would the contract be? Who would be declarer?

The Play
Which player would make the opening lead? Which suit would be led? Why?

How many tricks must declarer take to fulfill the contract? How many sure tricks does declarer have? How can declarer avoid losing two diamond tricks? Which suit should declarer play first after winnning the first trick? Why? What will declarer do next?

Bid and play the deal. Did declarer make the contract?

Exercise Twelve — The 1NT Overcall
(E-Z Deal Cards: #7, Hand 4 — Dealer, West)

Turn up all of the cards on the fourth pre-dealt hand, and arrange them as in the previous exercise.

The Bidding
West is the dealer. What would the opening bid be?

What would North bid?

What would East do in response to partner's opening bid?

What is the value of South's hand? Does South know whether the partnership belongs in game or partscore?

What denomination should the partnership play in? What would South bid?

Dealer: West

```
                ♠ A 8 3
                ♥ A K 3 2
                ♦ 7 5 3
                ♣ K Q 6
  ♠ K 10 6               ♠ Q 9 7 5
  ♥ Q J 10 9 7     N     ♥ 5 4
  ♦ A K         W   E    ♦ 8 6 4
  ♣ 10 7 5         S     ♣ J 9 3 2
                ♠ J 4 2
                ♥ 8 6
                ♦ Q J 10 9 2
                ♣ A 8 4
```

What would West do next?

What is the message given by South's bid? What would North rebid? Why?

What would the contract be? Who would be declarer?

The Play
Which player would make the opening lead? Which suit would be led? Why?

How many tricks must declarer take to fulfill the contract? How many sure tricks does declarer have? Which suit can declarer use to develop additional tricks? Why shouldn't declarer take the sure tricks in the other suits first?

Bid and play the deal. Did declarer make the contract?

Answers to Lesson 7 exercises are on pages 313–317.

LESSON 8
Takeout Doubles and Responses

The Takeout Double

Responding to a Takeout Double

Rebids by the Takeout Doubler

Guidelines for Play

Summary

The Finer Points

Activities

THE TAKEOUT DOUBLE

In the last lesson, we saw how a double used for penalties affects the scoring. If you double the opponents' contract and they don't make it, the penalty is increased. If they do make the contract, the number of points the opponents collect is increased.

There is another use for the double. It can be used as a request for partner to bid. This type of double is called a *takeout double*. Like the penalty double, it is used in competitive bidding situations.

Doubling for Takeout

Suppose your opponent opens the bidding 1 ♥ and you have the following hand:

♠ K Q 9 8
♥ 3
♦ A 10 7 6
♣ K Q 4 2

You would like to bid something to show your partner that you have enough strength to compete. To overcall, however, you need a five-card suit. With this type of hand, you aren't sure which suit your side should compete in. You'd like to know partner's best suit, since you have support for clubs, diamonds, and spades. The takeout double is a call that accomplishes this. It announces a hand with the strength of an opening bid that has support for each of the unbid suits. The takeout double asks partner a question — "What is your best suit, partner?"

Penalty or Takeout?

If there are two kinds of doubles, the penalty double and the takeout double, how does your partner know which one you mean? You can't say, "I'd like to make a penalty double of 1 ♥" or "I'd like to make a takeout double of 1 ♥ ." The only word you are allowed to use is *double*.

Two guidelines will help your partner identify the meaning of your double:

- If you and your partner have done nothing except pass, and if the doubled contract is a partscore in a suit, the double is for takeout.

- If either you or your partner has bid, or if the doubled contract is a game, the double is for penalty.

Here are some examples:

NORTH	EAST	SOUTH	WEST
1♥	Double		

Since the double is of a partscore, and since neither East nor West has bid, it is a takeout double.

NORTH	EAST	SOUTH	WEST
1♥	Pass	2♥	Pass
4♥	Double		

Since the double is of a game contract, it is a penalty double.

NORTH	EAST	SOUTH	WEST
1♥	Pass	2♣	Double

Since the double is of a partscore, and since neither East nor West has bid, it is a takeout double.

NORTH	EAST	SOUTH	WEST
Pass	1♠	2♣	Double

West's double is for penalty since East has bid. The question — "What's your best suit, partner?" — no longer applies since West knows that East likes spades.

Distributional Requirements for the Takeout Double

When you make a takeout double, you are asking your partner to pick the suit partner likes best. You must have support for the suit partner chooses. Ideally, when you make a takeout double, you will have at least four cards in each of the unbid suits.

Let's look at our previous example. Your opponent opened the bidding 1 ♥ and you held:

♠ K Q 9 8
♥ 3
♦ A 10 7 6
♣ K Q 4 2

You were ready to accept whichever suit your partner picked.

In competitive situations, however, things aren't always ideal. Every time you want to make a takeout double, you won't hold a singleton and three four-card suits.

Suppose your opponent starts the bidding with 1 ♥, and you hold:

♠ K Q 9 8
♥ 3 2
♦ A 10 7 6
♣ K Q 4

You have four-card support for spades and diamonds but only three-card support for clubs. A takeout double is the best available bid. You hope that partner will not choose clubs but, if that happens, perhaps partner will have five of them, and you will play in a Golden Fit.

Not all hands are suited to a takeout double. Suppose your opponent starts the bidding with 1 ♥, and you have this hand:

♠ 3
♥ K Q 9 8
♦ A 10 7 6
♣ K Q 4 2

This hand looks similar to the earlier example. However, you don't have support for spades, one of the unbid suits. If you ask for partner's best suit, partner may choose spades, and you would be in a bad contract. With this type of hand, you have to pass and await developments.

Let's look at some other examples. Suppose your opponent opens the bidding with 1 ♣.

♠ A 8 5 4 ♥ A 9 7 2 ♦ A 6 3 ♣ Q 5	Make a takeout double. If partner picks hearts or spades, you have four-card support. If partner picks diamonds, partner will have to be satisfied with three-card support. At the very least, you are competing with this hand.
♠ A J 4 ♥ A Q 7 2 ♦ A Q 3 ♣ 9 6 2	You have four-card support for hearts but only three-card support for spades and diamonds. Your extra strength, however, should compensate. Making a takeout double is preferable to bidding 1NT with no strength in the opponent's suit.
♠ A 4 ♥ K 9 3 ♦ Q 7 4 2 ♣ K J 7 3	You have four-card support for only one of the unbid suits, and you have no extra strength to compensate. Pass, since the hand is not suitable for either an overcall or a takeout double.

The Strength of the Takeout Double

Since the takeout double is like opening the bidding for your side, you should have the strength of an opening bid — at least 13 points. However, there is an interesting way of valuing your hand for the takeout double. Count dummy points! You are asking your partner to pick the suit for the contract, so you will be the dummy. Because you can value your hand in this fashion, hands that would be too weak to open the bidding when counting HCP and length may become strong enough for a takeout double.

Suppose the bidding is opened 1 ♥ by the opponent on your right.

♠ K Q 7 6　　　You have only 10 HCP but you can add 3 for the single-
♥ 8　　　　　　ton heart. This gives you a total of 13 dummy points
♦ K 10 4 3　　　— enough to make a takeout double.
♣ Q 9 7 4

♠ A 10 8 5　　　You have 12 HCP plus 1 for the doubleton heart.
♥ 10 6　　　　　Again, this gives you enough to make a takeout
♦ Q 9 4　　　　double.
♣ A Q 6 2

♠ Q 6 5 3　　　You would not open the bidding with this hand. When
♥ —　　　　　　an opponent opens 1 ♥, however, your hand can be
♦ A K 8 2　　　valued with dummy points to give you 10 HCP plus 5
♣ J 10 7 6 3　　for the heart void. Double!

The Bidding Message of the Takeout Double

The takeout double sends a special message in the bidding. The takeout double is a forcing call. It asks partner to pick one of the unbid suits. Partner is not being asked to pass.

Putting It Together

When an opponent opens the bidding, you can make a takeout double of a partscore contract if your partner has not bid and if your hand satisfies the basic requirements.

> ### REQUIREMENTS FOR A TAKEOUT DOUBLE
>
> • 13 or more points (counting dummy points).
>
> • Support for the unbid suits.

Let's look at some example hands. The opponent on your right opens the bidding with 1 ♦.

♠ J 10 9 7
♥ Q 6 4 2
♦ 7
♣ A K 8 6

With 10 HCP and 3 points for the singleton diamond, double. You have four-card support for all the unbid suits.

♠ K Q J 8 6
♥ K 9 3
♦ 4
♣ A 10 6 4

Although you have some support for all the unbid suits, this hand is more suited to an overcall of 1♠. With only three-card support for hearts, you want to emphasize the good five-card spade suit.

♠ Q 8 6
♥ A 4
♦ K Q 7 3
♣ J 9 4 2

Your hand is not strong enough to overcall clubs at the two level. Counting 5 dummy points for the void in diamonds, however, you have enough to double. This is the best way to compete with this hand.

♠ K 8 6 4
♥ A Q 3 2
♦ —
♣ Q 10 8 6 2

Pass. You have neither the required strength nor the distribution to overcall or to make a takeout double.

RESPONDING TO A TAKEOUT DOUBLE

Responder Considers the Bidding Message

After a takeout double, which is forcing, responder must bid even if the hand contains no points. Look at what would happen if responder were to pass:

NORTH	EAST	SOUTH	WEST
1♠	Double	Pass	Pass

North would be pleased to pass since East has announced shortness in spades. It will be very difficult for East-West to prevent North from taking seven tricks and making the contract. Therefore, even when holding a weak hand, West has to consider the consequences of not bidding.

If South bids after the double, however, West may pass.

NORTH	EAST	SOUTH	WEST
1♠	Double	2♠	Pass

In this situation, it is acceptable for West to pass because North-South would be in a contract of 2♠, undoubled. South's bid erases the double by East. In addition, if East wants to bid, there will be an opportunity to do so.

Responder Classifies the Strength of the Hand

There are three ranges for responder when replying to the takeout double. These ranges are almost identical to those we used when responding to an overcall or to an opening bid.

Minimum hand	0 to 10 points
Medium hand	11 or 12 points
Maximum hand	13 or more points

Responder Considers the Distribution

When partner makes a takeout double, the bid describes a hand with support for the unbid suits. Responder wants to pick the suit that is best for the partnership. Responder's first choice is to bid a major suit, since the partnership wants to find a Golden Fit in a major suit. Because the partnership is in a competitive situation, it also wants to get to the best contract as quickly as possible.

Responder's Decision with 0 to 10 Points

With 0 to 10 points, responder wants to make a bid as cheaply as possible. Responder can frequently bid at the one level since a takeout double doesn't use up any room on the Bidding Scale.

As responder, your first choice is a four-card or longer major suit. Your second choice is a four-card or longer minor suit. Your last choice is notrump. Because partner's takeout double denies strength in the suit bid by the opponents, bid notrump only when you have considerable strength in the opponent's suit.

Suppose the opponent on your left opens the bidding with 1♣, and your partner doubles. Assuming the next opponent passes, let's see how you handle the bidding on the following hands.

♠ 8 7 4   You have a very weak hand, only 1 HCP plus 1 for
♥ J 9 6 5 2   the five-card suit. You are obliged to bid, however,
♦ 9 6 2   because partner has doubled. Choose your best suit,
♣ 4 3   hearts, and bid at the cheapest level, 1 ♥.

♠ Q 7 4 3   You have the choice of bidding your five-card dia-
♥ K J 9   mond suit or your four-card spade suit. In a competi-
♦ J 9 7 5 4   tive auction, the partnership is interested in finding a
♣ 3   major suit fit as quickly as possible. Bid 1 ♠ even
                           though your diamonds are longer.

♠ A 7 6 4 2   Bid 1 ♠. You are at the top of your range and will bid
♥ 9 8   again if the opponents continue to compete for the
♦ J 7 6 4   contract. If they bid 2 ♣, you should rebid 2 ♠.
♣ K 3

Responder's Decision with 11 or 12 points

When responder has 11 or 12 points, the partnership may be headed
toward a game contract since the takeout doubler shows a hand worth at
least 13 points. Responder needs to know if the doubler has any extra
strength. To find out, responder invites game by jumping one level.

A jump in response to a takeout double is invitational. It asks partner
to pass with 13 or 14 points and to bid on to game with more strength.

Let's see how responder bids with a medium-range hand of 11 or 12
points. Assume the opponent on your left opens the bidding with 1 ♥,
and your partner doubles.

♠ 10 9 7 4   With 11 HCP, responder wants to invite opener to bid
♥ Q 8 6   on to game. Although the diamond suit looks better
♦ K Q J 8   than the spade suit, responder still prefers to bid the
♣ K 3   major suit. It is more likely that the partnership can
                           make a game contract in spades than in diamonds. To
                           show a medium hand, jump to 2 ♠.

♠ K 6 3
♥ 8 2
♦ A 10 9 7 5
♣ A 6 3

Responder has 11 HCP plus 1 for the five-card suit. To show a medium-range hand, responder jumps to 3 ♦. Note that responder has to bid at the three level with a diamond suit and can stay at the two level with a spade suit.

♠ K 10 7
♥ K Q J 6
♦ 8 4 2
♣ Q J 5

With 12 HCP and no suit to bid, responder can jump to 2NT to invite game. Responder has considerable strength in the opponent's suit and is not worried about playing in notrump.

Responder's Decision with 13 or More Points

With 13 or more points, responder knows that the contract should be played at the game level since partner also has at least 13 points. Responder wants to choose one of the Golden Games, so the contract will be 4 ♠, 4 ♥, or 3NT, whenever possible. Responder's decision is straight-forward on most hands because the doubler has shown interest in the unbid major suit or suits and usually has four-card support.

When responder has 13 or more points, there are many bids that could be made to invite the doubler to give more information about the hand. For now, however, the bidding is made simpler by having responder immediately place the partnership in the best game.

Let's look at some examples. The bidding is opened with 1 ♠ by the opponent on your left, and partner doubles.

♠ 7 2
♥ A 9 7 5 2
♦ A K 3
♣ J 5 2

With 12 HCP plus 1 for the five-card heart suit, responder has a total of 13, enough for game. Because partner has shown support for the unbid suits with a takeout double, responder knows there is a Golden Fit in hearts and can jump directly to game, 4 ♥.

♠ A Q 9
♥ Q 6
♦ J 10 8 2
♣ K Q 8 6

With 14 HCP, responder knows there is enough combined strength for game. The Golden Game is 3NT, even though there is probably a Golden Fit in a minor suit.

♠ K 3
♥ A K 8 4
♦ A 9 2
♣ J 10 7 3

Responder has enough for game. The most likely game is 4♥. It is possible that partner has only three-card support for hearts. Lacking more sophisticated bidding methods, a direct jump to 4♥ is the most reasonable bid on the hand.

REBIDS BY THE TAKEOUT DOUBLER

The rebid by the takeout doubler is similar to the rebid by an opening bidder (Lesson 5). The doubler classifies the hand into one of three categories:

Minimum hand	13 to 16 points
Medium hand	17 or 18 points
Maximum hand	19 to 21 points

Doubler's Decision with a Minimum Hand, 13 to 16 Points

After a double, responder shows a minimum hand, from 0 to 10 points, by bidding at the cheapest level. The takeout doubler should pass partner's minimum response and leave the partnership in a partscore.

If responder shows a medium hand, 11 or 12 points, doubler should take another look at the strength of the hand. If doubler is at the bottom of the range, 13 or 14 points, pass is the right bid. If doubler is at the top, 15 or 16 points, there is a game to be bid.

If responder bids a game to show a maximum hand, 13 or more points, the decision has already been made. The doubler passes at this turn.

Doubler's Decision with a Medium Hand, 17 or 18 Points

When responder shows a minimum hand of 6 to 10 points, the doubler moves up the Bidding Scale one level to show a medium hand of 17 or 18 points. Responder will now know that the takeout doubler has a medium-strength hand, and responder will decide on the final contract.

If responder shows a medium hand of 11 or 12 points, the partnership must have enough combined strength for game. The takeout doubler can now bid a game.

Responder won't hold a maximum hand of 13 or more points very often when the takeout doubler has 17 or 18 points. However, the partnership should be happy in a game contract when this is the case.

Doubler's Decision with a Maximum Hand, 19 to 21 Points

If responder shows a minimum hand of 0 to 10 points, the takeout doubler jumps a level of bidding to show extra strength. This bid won't always get the partnership to a game contract because responder could have a hand with very few points. (Responder will tend to have fewer points when the takeout doubler holds a maximum hand). Alerted to the strength of the takeout doubler's hand, responder can bid accordingly.

If responder shows a medium hand of 11 or 12 points, the takeout doubler will carry on to game.

It would be extremely unusual for responder to have a maximum hand of 13 points when the takeout doubler has a maximum hand. If this occurs, the partnership will bid to a slam contract.

Putting It Together

Suppose the bidding is opened 1 ♥. You make a takeout double, and your partner responds 1 ♠ to show a minimum hand (0 to 10 points). What do you rebid with the following hands?

♠ 10 9 7 4
♥ 10
♦ A J 8 6
♣ A Q 6 4

You have a minimum hand — 11 HCP plus 3 for the singleton heart. Responder has no more than 10 points and may not have any points at all, pass. If the opponents bid again, you will leave any further bidding up to partner.

♠ Q 10 8 3
♥ —
♦ A Q 7 6 2
♣ A 9 5 3

You have 12 HCP plus 5 for the void in hearts, a total of 17. With a medium-strength hand, there is some possibility of game if responder has the top of the range, 9 or 10 points. Raise to 2♠ to tell responder you have 17 or 18 points.

♠ A 9 8 4
♥ —
♦ A K 7 6 2
♣ A 9 5 3

This time you have 20 points, a maximum hand. Jump to 3 ♠ to tell responder you have a hand in the 19 to 21 point range. Responder will pass with 0 to 5 points but will carry on to game with 6 or more.

GUIDELINES FOR PLAY

To improve your play when you are declarer, you should always make a plan. The most important decisions usually come early in the deal. Later, it may be too late! As soon as the dummy comes down, you should take the time to plan the play. By making a plan, you can review what went right and what went wrong after the deal has been played. By going over your plan and the results of your play, you can improve your game.

Making a Plan

To make a plan, declarer goes through four basic steps:

1. **P**ause to consider your objective
2. **L**ook at your winners and losers
3. **A**nalyze your alternatives
4. **N**ow put it together

1. **P**ause to consider your objective. Determine the number of tricks needed to make the contract.

2. **L**ook at your winners and losers. See how close you are to your objective. Count the number of sure tricks you have.

3. **A**nalyze your alternatives. Determine the resources you have available. Look at each suit to see how you can develop additional tricks.

4. **N**ow put it together. Decide how to proceed. Review the various alternatives you discovered in the previous step.

The first two steps were discussed in Lesson 2. From these steps, you know how many additional tricks you must develop to make the contract. If you don't need any more tricks, you can take your tricks and run. The third step encompasses the various techniques discussed in Lessons 3 through 7:

- Promoting high cards.
- Developing tricks in long suits.
- Finessing (leading toward the high card).
- Trumping losers in the dummy.
- Discarding losers.

Often you will discover more than one possible way to defend against your opponent's contract. In the fourth step, you must choose from among your options or perhaps plan to combine them. In doing this, you must be careful to watch your entries, decide whether to draw trumps right away, and so on.

While playing out the hand, watch to see how your plan is working. As you get more experienced, you will learn to formulate better plans and uncover additional possibilities.

Let's look at an example of making a plan.

NORTH (dummy)
♠ A 10 5
♥ 7 6 3
♦ K 9 6 2
♣ 7 4 2

SOUTH (declarer)
♠ 8 6 3
♥ A K 8
♦ A 8 7 3
♣ A Q 5

Suppose you are in a contract of 1NT, and the opening lead is the ♥J. You start by determining your objective: you need to win seven tricks. Next you count your sure tricks: the ♠A, ♥AK, ♦AK and ♣A — a total of six. You need to develop one more trick to make your contract.

What are the possibilities? There are no tricks possible in spades and hearts. You have eight diamonds in the combined hands. It might be possible to develop an extra trick in this suit if the opponents' cards are split 3–2. In clubs, you could take a finesse, hoping East has the king.

Now, you must put it all together. Should you plan to play the diamond suit or the club suit first? In fact, you can combine your options: play the ♦A and ♦K first to see if both opponents follow suit. If they do, the missing diamonds must be split 3–2, and you can lead the suit again to develop a diamond trick. If the missing diamonds are not divided 3–2, you can try the club finesse instead.

You formulate your plan, and then you put it into action. You win the first trick and play the ♦A and ♦K to see if the suit breaks 3–2. If it doesn't, you try the club finesse. If you're defeated, you'll know why — you were unlucky! The diamonds broke 4–1, and West had the ♣K. The play of each hand suddenly turns into an adventure!

SUMMARY

One way to compete in the auction is by making a takeout double. You can tell when a double is for takeout by using the following as a guideline:

GUIDELINES FOR RECOGNIZING A TAKEOUT DOUBLE

- If you and your partner have done nothing except pass, and the doubled contract is a partscore in a suit, the double is for takeout.

- If either you have bid and your partner doubles or your partner has bid and you double, the double is for penalty.

To make a takeout double, you need a hand that satisfies the following criteria:

REQUIREMENTS FOR A TAKEOUT DOUBLE

- 13 or more points (counting dummy points).
- Support for the unbid suits.

RESPONSES BY TAKEOUT DOUBLER'S PARTNER

With a minimum hand (0 to 10 points):
- Bid a four-card or longer major suit at the cheapest level.
- Bid a four-card or longer minor suit at the cheapest level.
- Bid 1NT.
- Pass is not an option.

With a medium hand (11 or 12 points):
- Jump in a four-card or longer major suit.
- Jump in a four-card or longer minor suit.
- Jump to 2NT.

With a maximum hand (13 or more points):
- Jump to game in a four-card or longer major suit.
- Jump to 3NT.

REBIDS BY THE TAKEOUT DOUBLER

With a minimum hand (13 to 16 points):

• Pass if partner bids at the cheapest level.

• Pass with 13 or 14 points if partner jumps a level. Bid a Golden Game with 15 or 16 points if partner jumps a level.

With a medium hand (17 or 18 points):

• Raise one level if partner bids at the cheapest level.

• Bid a Golden Game if partner jumps a level.

With a maximum hand (19 to 21 points):

• Jump raise if partner bids at the cheapest level.

• Bid a Golden Game if partner jumps a level.

THE FINER POINTS

Another Use for the Takeout Double

The text explains the classic use of the takeout double. It shows a hand of opening bid strength with support for the unbid suits. In the finer points at the end of the previous lesson, it was mentioned that some players like to put an upper limit of about 17 or 18 points on the overcall. The takeout double is sometimes used to show a hand too strong to make a simple overcall. With such a hand, you start by doubling. Partner will assume you have made a normal takeout double and respond accordingly. Now, you bid your suit. If partner happens to choose your suit, you can raise.

This is in accordance with the discussion on rebids by the takeout doubler. After partner makes a minimum response, the takeout doubler bids again holding a medium or maximum hand. If the takeout doubler bids a new suit, responder can interpret this to show at least 17 points — a hand too strong to overcall — and generally a one-suited hand.

You must be careful not to abuse the takeout double. If you make a takeout double of 1 ♦ with only a long heart suit, your partner might jump to 4♠, expecting you to have support. That is why you need a strong hand of 17 or more points to double without support for all the unbid suits. The more points you have, the less likely that partner will have enough to jump in response — which would make it difficult for you to show your suit. Also, the extra strength should compensate for the lack of support if partner does jump to a high-level contract.

The Cuebid Response

As discussed at the end of the previous lesson, a partnership will usually not want to play in a suit that has been opened by the opponents. A bid of the opponent's suit, called a cuebid, can be assigned a special meaning. If your partner makes a takeout double, you can use a bid of the opponent's suit to ask for further information from partner. You could make this bid if you have a hand of 13 or more points. You know you want to play a game contract but you don't know in which denomination.

For example, suppose the opponent on your left opens the bidding 1♦. Your partner doubles, and you hold the following hand:

> ♠ A 9 7 5
> ♥ A 9 7 5
> ♦ Q 3
> ♣ A 8 2

With 14 points, you know there is enough combined strength for game. Which contract should you choose? Should you jump to 4♥ or 4♠? Whichever you choose, partner may have only three-card support while having four-card support in the other major. It is even possible that your side belongs in 3NT or 5♣.

You can solve the problem by bidding 2♦, the opponent's suit. This is a forcing bid, asking partner for a further description. If partner bids hearts, you jump to 4♥. If partner bids spades, you jump to 4♠. If partner bids notrump, you raise to 3NT.

The cuebid is useful for responding to takeout doubles and overcalls but it is not essential when first starting out.

ACTIVITIES

Exercise One — Takeout or Penalty?
In the following auctions, is West's double for takeout or penalty?

1)
NORTH	EAST	SOUTH	WEST
Pass	Pass	1 ♦	**Double**

2)
NORTH	EAST	SOUTH	WEST
1 ♣	Pass	1 ♥	**Double**

3)
NORTH	EAST	SOUTH	WEST
Pass	1 ♠	2 ♣	**Double**

4)
NORTH	EAST	SOUTH	WEST
Pass	Pass	1 ♥	Pass
2 ♥	Pass	4 ♥	**Double**

Exercise Two — The Takeout Double
The opponent on your right bids 1 ♥. Using dummy points to determine the value of your hand, decide whether you would make a takeout double with the following hands.

1) ♠ J 8 4 3
♥ 10 9
♦ K Q 7
♣ A Q 10 2

2) ♠ A Q 4 3
♥ 8
♦ A 7 3 2
♣ J 4 3 2

3) ♠ K 9 6 3
♥ —
♦ K 9 8 7 2
♣ A 8 7 3

HCP:	_____	HCP:	_____

HCP: _____   HCP: _____   HCP: _____
Dummy Points: _____   Dummy Points: _____   Dummy Points: _____
Total Points: _____   Total Points: _____   Total Points: _____
Call: _____   Call: _____   Call: _____

Exercise Three — Choosing the Competitive Action

To enter the auction after one of your opponents has opened the bidding, you can overcall or double. What would you do with each of the following hands if the opponent on your right bids 1♣?

1) ♠ A J 10 6 3
   ♥ 4 3
   ♦ K 9 3
   ♣ K Q 6

   Call: _____

2) ♠ A J 5 3
   ♥ Q 10 8 6
   ♦ K J 4 2
   ♣ 9

   Call: _____

3) ♠ Q J 10
   ♥ A J 4 3
   ♦ K 10 2
   ♣ A K 6

   Call: _____

4) ♠ A 3
   ♥ A Q 8 6 3
   ♦ K J 9 5 2
   ♣ 4

   Call: _____

5) ♠ 10 8 7 4
   ♥ A K 8 2
   ♦ A Q 3
   ♣ 8 5

   Call: _____

6) ♠ Q 7 5
   ♥ A J
   ♦ Q 9 7 4
   ♣ K Q 8 3

   Call: _____

Exercise Four — Responding to a Takeout Double
with 0 to 10 Points

Your left-hand opponent opens the bidding 1♠, and your partner doubles. Your right-hand opponent passes. What do you respond with each of the following hands?

1) ♠ 9 8 2
   ♥ J 8 7 5
   ♦ Q 5 4
   ♣ 8 7 2

   Response: _____

2) ♠ J 10
   ♥ K 3
   ♦ Q J 10 8 4
   ♣ 8 6 5 3

   Response: _____

3) ♠ A J 9 3
   ♥ K 10 5
   ♦ J 4 2
   ♣ 10 9 6

   Response: _____

Exercise Five — Responding to a Takeout Double
with 11 or 12 Points

Your left-hand opponent bids 1 ♥, and your partner doubles. Your right-hand opponent passes. What do you respond with each of the following hands?

1) ♠ J 10 7 6 3
    ♥ 9 4 2
    ♦ A Q 6
    ♣ K 3

2) ♠ Q 10 3
    ♥ K J 10 8
    ♦ A 9 2
    ♣ Q 7 3

3) ♠ A 8 2
    ♥ 10 9
    ♦ K Q J 10 8
    ♣ 8 6 2

Response: _____   Response: _____   Response: _____

Exercise Six — Responding to a Takeout Double
with 13 or More Points

Your left-hand opponent bids 1 ♦, and your partner doubles. Your right-hand opponent passes. What do you respond with each of the following hands?

1) ♠ 8 6
    ♥ A K 8 4 2
    ♦ A 9 3
    ♣ J 5 4

2) ♠ A 6 3
    ♥ K 4 2
    ♦ Q J 9 8
    ♣ A 10 3

3) ♠ Q 10 7 6 4 3
    ♥ 9
    ♦ J 8
    ♣ A K J 6

Response: _____   Response: _____   Response: _____

Exercise Seven — Rebids by the Takeout Doubler

Your right-hand opponent bids 1 ♥, and you double. Your partner responds 1 ♠. What do you rebid with each of the following hands?

1) ♠ 9 8 6 2
   ♥ 3 2
   ♦ A 10 6
   ♣ A K J 3

   Bid: _____

2) ♠ K Q J 6
   ♥ —
   ♦ K Q 9 4
   ♣ A J 8 6 2

   Bid: _____

3) ♠ A 9 6 2
   ♥ 4
   ♦ K 8 7 3
   ♣ A K J 2

   Bid: _____

Exercise Eight — Making a Plan

Construct the following hands for North and South:

NORTH
♠ 10 3
♥ A 7 5
♦ 9 8 6 5 3
♣ 9 5 2

SOUTH
♠ A Q 5
♥ K 8 2
♦ A K 4
♣ A K 8 6

Suppose South is playing in a contract of 3NT, and West leads the ♥ Q. How many sure tricks does South have? What are the possibilities of developing additional tricks in each suit? What would South's plan be? How does this help South determine in which hand to win the first trick?

Exercise Nine — The Takeout Double

(E-Z Deal Cards: #8, Hand 1 — Dealer, North)

Turn up all the cards on the first pre-dealt hand. Put each hand dummy style at the edge of the table in front of each player.

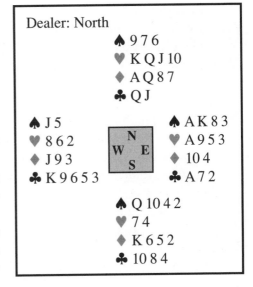

Dealer: North

```
              ♠ 976
              ♥ KQJ10
              ♦ AQ87
              ♣ QJ
♠ J5                        ♠ AK83
♥ 862          N            ♥ A953
♦ J93        W   E          ♦ 104
♣ K9653        S            ♣ A72
              ♠ Q1042
              ♥ 74
              ♦ K652
              ♣ 1084
```

The Bidding

North is the dealer. What would the opening bid be?

Would East like to compete in the auction? How can East compete? Is there any danger?

What would South's response be to North's opening bid? Is South's response affected by East's bid?

What is the bidding message given by East's call? What would West respond?

What would North bid next? What would East bid? Why? What would the contract be? Who would be declarer?

The Play

Which player would make the opening lead? What would the opening lead be?

How many tricks must declarer take to fulfill the contract? How many sure tricks does declarer have? Declarer should look at each suit to decide what possibilities there are for developing tricks. What does declarer plan to do in the diamond suit? What does declarer plan to do in the trump suit? What should declarer's plan be?

Bid and play the deal. Did declarer make the contract?

Exercise Ten — Using Dummy's Trumps
(E-Z Deal Cards: #8, Hand 2 — Dealer, East)

Turn up all of the cards on the second pre-dealt hand, and arrange them as in the previous exercise.

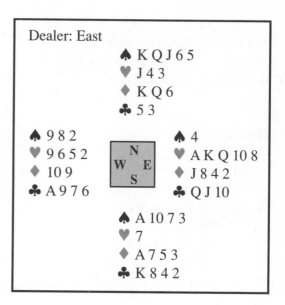

Dealer: East

♠ K Q J 6 5
♥ J 4 3
♦ K Q 6
♣ 5 3

♠ 9 8 2   ♠ 4
♥ 9 6 5 2   ♥ A K Q 10 8
♦ 10 9   ♦ J 8 4 2
♣ A 9 7 6   ♣ Q J 10

♠ A 10 7 3
♥ 7
♦ A 7 5 3
♣ K 8 4 2

The Bidding

East is the dealer. What would the opening bid be?

What would South do?

What would West do in response to partner's opening bid? Has South's call affected West's response?

What would North bid?

What would the contract be? Who would be declarer?

The Play

Which player would make the opening lead? Which suit would be led? Which suit would be led at the second trick?

How many tricks must declarer take to fulfill the contract? How many tricks does declarer have? What possibilities are there in the heart suit? The diamond suit? The club suit? What is declarer's plan? How does declarer's plan affect the play of the trump suit?

Bid and play the deal. Did declarer make the contract?

Exercise Eleven — Careful Play in a Side Suit
(E-Z Deal Cards: #8, Hand 3 — Dealer, South)

Turn up all of the cards on the third pre-dealt hand, and arrange them as in the previous exercise.

Dealer: South

```
                  ♠ Q 8 6
                  ♥ 7 4
                  ♦ 9 8 4 2
                  ♣ 7 6 5 3
   ♠ A J 10 2              ♠ 7 5 3
   ♥ J 9 8 3      N        ♥ K Q 10 6 2
   ♦ A 6       W     E     ♦ 5 3
   ♣ A 8 4         S        ♣ K Q 2
                  ♠ K 9 4
                  ♥ A 5
                  ♦ K Q J 10 7
                  ♣ J 10 9
```

The Bidding

South is the dealer. What would the opening bid be?

What would West do?

What would North do in response to partner's opening bid?

What is the value of East's hand? What would East respond to show this strength?

What is the bidding message given by East's bid? What would West rebid?

What would the contract be? Who would be declarer?

The Play

Which player would make the opening lead? What would the opening lead be?

How many tricks must declarer take to fulfill the contract? How many sure tricks does declarer have? How can declarer develop an additional trick in the spade suit? What is declarer's plan?

Bid and play the deal. Did declarer make the contract?

Exercise Twelve — Careful Play in the Trump Suit

(E-Z Deal Cards: #8, Hand 4 — Dealer, West)

Turn up all of the cards on the fourth pre-dealt hand, and arrange them as in the previous exercise.

The Bidding

West is the dealer. What would the opening bid be?

What would North do?

What would East do in response to partner's opening bid?

What would South respond? What is the point range of South's response?

What would West do next?

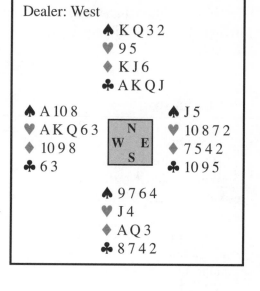

Dealer: West

         ♠ K Q 3 2
         ♥ 9 5
         ♦ K J 6
         ♣ A K Q J

♠ A 10 8   ♠ J 5
♥ A K Q 6 3   N   ♥ 10 8 7 2
♦ 10 9 8   W   E   ♦ 7 5 4 2
♣ 6 3   S   ♣ 10 9 5

         ♠ 9 7 6 4
         ♥ J 4
         ♦ A Q 3
         ♣ 8 7 4 2

What is the value of North's hand? How does North describe the strength of the hand?

What is the bidding message given by North's rebid? What would South rebid? Why?

What would the contract be? Who would be declarer?

The Play

Which player would make the opening lead? Which suit would be led?

How many tricks must declarer take to fulfill the contract? How many sure tricks does declarer have? How should declarer plan to play the spade suit? What role will declarer's ♦ A and ♦ Q play? What is declarer's plan?

Bid and play the deal. Did declarer make the contract?

Answers to Lesson 8 exercises are on pages 317–320.

APPENDIX

A. SCORING

Bridge can be scored in several different ways. All methods follow the same basic scheme. Points and bonuses are awarded for bidding and making contracts, and for defeating contracts but there are minor differences. We will discuss the two most common forms of scoring — duplicate-bridge style and rubber-bridge style.

Duplicate Scoring

In duplicate scoring, each deal is scored independently. The score is a combination of the trick score for bidding and making the contract and appropriate bonuses. The size of the bonus is affected by vulnerability. On each deal, each side has been arbitrarily designated as either nonvulnerable or vulnerable. You know at the start of each hand whether or not your side is vulnerable.

Trick Score

Notrump .... 40 for the first trick
30 for each additional trick

Hearts or spades ...... 30 points per trick

Clubs or diamonds .... 20 points per trick

Doubled contracts ..... Twice the undoubled trick score

Redoubled contracts .. Four times the undoubled trick score

Bonus Points	Nonvulnerable	Vulnerable
Partscore	50 points	50 points
Game	300 points	500 points
Small Slam	500 points	750 points
Grand Slam	1000 points	1500 points
Making a doubled contract	50 points	50 points
Making a redoubled contract	100 points	100 points

Overtricks	Nonvulnerable	Vulnerable
Undoubled	Trick score	Trick score
Doubled	100 per overtrick	200 per overtrick
Redoubled	200 per overtrick	400 per overtrick

Penalties (Undertricks)	Nonvulnerable	Vulnerable
Undoubled	50 per undertrick	100 per undertrick
Doubled	100 for first undertrick	200 for first undertrick
	200 for next two undertricks	300 for additional undertricks
	300 for additional undertricks	

Redoubled	200 for first undertrick	400 for first undertrick
	400 for next two undertricks	600 for additional undertricks
	600 for additional undertricks	

All bonuses are added to the trick score. For example, if you bid and make a slam, you also get the game bonus. Here are some examples:

2 ♥ contract, nonvulnerable, declarer takes nine tricks:

Trick score (30 x 2)	60
Partscore bonus	50
Overtrick bonus	<u>30</u>
Total score	140

4 ♠ contract, vulnerable, declarer takes 10 tricks:

Trick score (30 x 4)	120
Game bonus	<u>500</u>
Total score	620

6 ♦ contract, nonvulnerable, declarer takes 12 tricks:

Trick score (20 x 6)	120
Game bonus	300
Slam bonus	<u>500</u>
Total score	920

2NT contract, doubled, vulnerable, declarer takes 9 tricks:

Trick score (70 x 2)	140
Game bonus	500
Doubled bonus	50
Doubled overtrick bonus	200
Total score	890

Rubber Bridge Scoring

In rubber bridge, points are recorded on a scoresheet divided into four parts by a vertical line and a horizontal line. The vertical line divides the sheet into a column for your points (WE) and the opponents' points (THEY). The horizontal line, called the line, is there so that scores for contracts bid and made can be put below the line and bonuses, overtricks, and penalties can be put above the line.

A rubber is made up of a series of deals which progress until one side wins two games. No bonus is awarded when a partscore or game contract is made. Instead, a bonus is awarded to the side that wins the rubber. A partnership wins a game by scoring 100 points or more from the trick scores recorded below the line. These trick scores can be earned in a single deal or by accumulating them from several partscore contracts. When one side wins a game, a horizontal line is drawn under the trick scores of both sides, and a new game is started. Scores from previous partscores are not counted toward the next game.

When the rubber starts, both sides are nonvulnerable. When a side wins a game, it become vulnerable for the rest of the rubber. The vulnerability affects the bonuses as in tournament scoring.

Bonuses for making overtricks, undertricks, slams, and doubled contracts are the same as for tournament scoring. The bonus for winning the rubber replaces the bonus for making game or partscore in duplicate scoring. The bonus is 700 if the rubber is won by a margin of two games to none and 500 if it is won by a margin of two games to one.

If only one side has a partscore in an unfinished rubber, that side receives a bonus of 100 pts. If only one side has a game in an unfinished rubber, that side a receives a bonus of 300 pts.

A special bonus is awarded in rubber-bridge scoring if one player holds four of the top five cards in the trump suit (100 points for honors), all five of the top trump cards (150 points for honors), or the four aces in notrump (150 points for honors).

At the end of the rubber, the scores are totaled for both sides. The winner is the side with the higher total. If you are playing a series of rubbers, the difference in scores at the end of each rubber is rounded to the nearest 100 points and is carried forward for each partnership to the next rubber.

Here is a sample score sheet:

	WE	THEY	
		150	(f)
(g)	500	30	(f)
(g)	750	500	(d)
(a)	50	60	(c)
			THE LINE
(b)	120		
(e)	90	60	(c)
		40	(f)
(g)	180		
(h)	1690	840	(h)
	−840		
	850		

(a) The opponents bid 3NT and take only eight tricks (down one).

(b) Your side bids 4♥ and takes 10 tricks (game).

(c) The opponents bid 2♠ and take 10 tricks (two overtricks).

(d) Your side bids 2♦. The opponents double, and you take six tricks (down two vulnerable tricks).

(e) Your side bids 3♠ and takes nine tricks.

(f) The opponents bid 1NT and take eight tricks (one overtrick). Declarer holds all four aces (150 points for honors). Their trick score of 40 below the line is added to their previous partscore to give them a game.

(g) Your side bids 6♥ and takes twelve tricks (small slam). You get a slam bonus and also win your second game, winning the rubber.

(h) Your side scored 1690 points, and the opponents scored 840. You win the rubber by 850 points. If you were carrying the score forward, this would be rounded to + 900 for both you and your partner (– 900 for each of your opponents).

B. STAYMAN CONVENTION

When partner opens the bidding with 1NT, responder, as captain, has to decide the level and denomination of the contract. When deciding on the denomination, responder looks for a Golden Fit. The Stayman convention helps responder to uncover a Golden Fit in a major suit.

The Stayman Convention

The Stayman convention, invented by George Rapée and publicized in an article written by Sam Stayman, is an artificial response of 2♣ to an opening bid of 1NT. It is used to ask if opener has a four-card major suit. With a four-card or longer major suit, opener bids it at the two level. Without a four-card major suit, opener artificially rebids 2♦.

When Responder Has 10 or More Points

With 10 or more points, responder knows the partnership belongs in a game contract. With one or two four-card major suits, responder can use the Stayman convention. For example, suppose partner opens the bidding 1NT, and you hold the following hand:

♠ K J 7 3   You respond 2♣, asking if partner has a four-card
♥ K Q 9 3   major suit. If partner rebids 2♥ or 2♠, you can jump
♦ 6 2   directly to game in that suit. If partner bids 2♦, you
♣ K 8 4   know there is no Golden Fit in a major suit. You can
                   jump to 3NT.

When Responder Has 8 or 9 Points

With 8 or 9 points, responder is not sure of the right level and wants to invite game. Responder can start with 2♣, the Stayman convention, when responder is interested in placing the contract in a major suit. For example, opener bids 1NT, and you have the following hand:

♠ 7 4   You respond 2♣ and, if opener bids 2♥, you raise to
♥ A J 4 2   3♥ to invite opener to carry on to game with 17 or 18
♦ K 9 3 2   points. If opener bids 2♦ or 2♠, you know there is
♣ J 7 5   no Golden Fit in a major suit. You can bid 2NT, again
                   inviting game.

Here is a slight variation. Partner opens 1NT, and you have this hand:

♠ K Q 7 4 2   You want to invite game and are interested in a major
♥ 7 6   suit. Start with 2♣. If partner bids 2♠, you can raise
♦ 9 4 2   to 3♠. If partner bids 2♦ or 2♥, you can bid 2♠.
♣ K 8 3   Opener should interpret this as an invitational hand
                   with five or more spades. If you had 0 to 7 points and
                   wanted to sign off in spades, you would have re-

sponded immediately with 2♠. Also, if you held an invitational hand with 8 or 9 points and only four spades, you would bid 2NT when you found that opener did not have four spades. Thus, your bidding shows an invitational hand with five or more spades. Opener can pass or bid 2NT with a minimum hand; opener can jump to 4♠ or 3NT with a maximum hand.

When Responder Has 0 to 7 Points

With 0 to 7 points, you do not have enough bidding room to use the Stayman convention. For example, suppose partner opens 1NT, and you have this hand:

♠ J 3
♥ K Q 6 2
♦ 7 5 3
♣ J 6 4 2

You would like to look for a Golden Fit in hearts. If you use Stayman and respond 2♣, opener might bid 2♠. A 2NT bid by you at this point would be invitational, showing 8 or 9 points. Your only option is to pass over 1NT.

SUMMARY OF STAYMAN CONVENTION

When partner opens the bidding 1NT, you can respond 2♣ (the Stayman convention) if you have 8 or more points and are interested in finding out if opener has a four-card major suit. Opener rebids as follows:

2♦	No four-card major suit.
2♥	Four-card heart suit.
2♠	Four-card spade suit.

C. STRONG OPENING BIDS

Opening bids at the one level show hands with 13 to 21 points. With stronger hands, you can show the extra strength by opening at the two level.

Balanced Hands

With a balanced hand, you open 2NT with 22 to 24 points and 3NT with 25 to 27 points. (Balanced hands of 28 or more points are very rare.) Here are some examples:

♠ A Q 6　　　　With 22 points, open 2NT to show a balanced hand in
♥ K Q 5　　　　the 22 to 24 point range.
♦ Q J 9 3
♣ A K J

♠ A K 3　　　　With 25 HCP plus 1 for the five-card club suit, open
♥ K 8　　　　　3NT to show a balanced hand in the 25 to 27 point
♦ A K J　　　　range.
♣ A Q J 8 3

If your partner opens 2NT, you are the captain. You decide the level and denomination in which to play. With a balanced hand of 0 to 2 points, you pass. Holding three or more points, you take one of the following actions: raise to 3NT with a balanced hand; bid game in a major suit holding a six-card or longer major suit; bid three in a major suit holding a five-card major suit. Opener will now bid 3NT holding only two cards in your major, or opener will bid game in your major holding three or more cards in the suit.

If your partner opens 3NT, there is not much room to explore. Bid 4 ♥ or 4♠ with a six-card or longer major suit. Otherwise, pass (unless you are interested in a slam contract).

Unbalanced Hands

With an unbalanced hand of 22 or more points, open the bidding at the two level in your longest suit. This is called a *strong two-bid*. Here are some examples:

♠ A K Q J 7 3
♥ A K 8
♦ A
♣ K 9 4

With 24 HCP plus 2 for the six-card spade suit, open with 2 ♠.

♠ —
♥ A J 6
♦ A K J 7 4
♣ A K Q 6 3

With 22 HCP plus 1 point for each of your five-card suits, open at the two level. As with opening bids at the one level, you bid the higher-ranking of two five-card suits — 2 ♦.

If someone opens with a strong two bid, the partnership is forced to game. Responder cannot pass. With a weak hand of 0 to 5 points, responder makes an artificial response of 2NT. With 6 or more points, responder can raise opener's suit with three-card or longer support, bid a new suit, or jump to 3NT. For example, suppose your partner opens the bidding with 2 ♥.

♠ 7 6 3
♥ 9 4 3
♦ J 8 6
♣ J 9 7 2

With a weak hand of 2 HCP, respond 2NT. This is artificial and tells opener you have a weak hand. Remember, you must keep bidding until game is reached. If opener rebids 3 ♥, you will carry on to 4 ♥.

♠ A 9 3
♥ J 7 4
♦ K 8 5 2
♣ 7 6 4

With three-card support for opener's suit and 8 HCP, raise to 3 ♥.

♠ K Q 10 9 4   With a good suit of your own and 9 points, respond
♥ J 3   2♠.
♦ Q 7 2
♣ 6 4 3

Weak Two-Bids

> ♠ ♠ ♠ ♠ ♠ ♠ **DUPLICATE PREVIEW** ♠ ♠ ♠ ♠ ♠ ♠
>
> OPENING A WEAK TWO-BID
> - A six-card or longer suit
> - 5 to 10 high-card points
> - No other four-card or longer major

In some areas of the country, many of the players play *weak two-bids*. In this style, the opening bid of 2♣ is used for all strong hands. The real suit is shown when opener rebids at the next opportunity. The opening bids of 2♦, 2♥, and 2♠ are preemptive bids (see Appendix E). They show a six-card suit with 6 to 12 high-card points.

Although it is not recommended that you start off with this bid, you should be aware that a new partner with duplicate experience may have adopted this style. You always can ask your partner, "What kind of two-bids do you play?" Discuss them if necessary.

SUMMARY OF STRONG OPENING BIDS

OPENING BID OF 2NT

- 22 to 24 points
- Balanced hand

OPENING BID OF 3NT

- 25 to 27 points
- Balanced hand

OPENING BID OF TWO IN A SUIT (STRONG TWO–BID)

- 22 or more points
- Unbalanced hand

A strong two-bid is forcing to game, and responder cannot pass. An artificial response of 2NT is used with weak hands of 0 to 5 points.

D. SLAM BIDDING

The discussion in the text covering "What level?" concentrates on the choice between partscore and game since this is the major decision the captain must make. However, large bonuses are awarded in the scoring for bidding and making a slam contract. With considerable extra strength, the partnership should consider bidding a slam.

What Level?

Decisions as to whether or not a partnership has enough combined strength to bid a slam can be based on the points in the combined hands.

With 33 or more combined points, the partnership generally has enough strength for a small slam. With 37 or more points, the partnership should have enough strength for a grand slam.

What Denomination?

At the game level, the partnership usually plays in 3NT, 4 ♥, or 4 ♠. At the slam level, the number of tricks required is the same for every denomination — 12 for a small slam and 13 for a grand slam. Slam can be played in any Golden Fit or notrump. Note, however, that contracts played in a Golden Fit often produce one more trick than those played in notrump.

Bidding a Slam

There are artificial bids (e.g., *Blackwood, Gerber,* cuebids) that are sometimes useful when you are thinking of bidding a slam. However, they are beyond the scope of this text. To keep things simple, jump to small slam in a Golden Fit or notrump if you know the partnership has 33 or more points. Jump to a grand slam if you know the partnership has 37 or more points. For example, suppose your partner opens the bidding with 1NT.

♠ A Q 7 ♥ K J 5 ♦ K 9 3 2 ♣ K J 5	With 17 HCP, you know there is enough strength for slam since opener has at least 16 points. When there is no known Golden Fit, jump directly to 6NT.
♠ A 3 2 ♥ 4 ♦ A K J 7 5 2 ♣ A 7 4	With 16 HCP plus 2 for the six-card diamond suit, there is enough for a slam contract. Opener must have at least two diamonds. Jump to 6 ♦.

If you know there is enough combined strength for slam but are not sure of the denomination, make a forcing bid to get a further description of partner's hand, and then make your decision.

Inviting Slam

Sometimes you know the denomination in which you want to play but are not certain whether there is enough combined strength for slam. In this case, you can invite partner to bid a slam by bidding one level beyond game. Partner can bid again with additional values; partner can pass with a minimum hand. For example, suppose your partner opens the bidding 1NT.

♠ K J 10 ♥ J 9 8 ♦ A K 3 ♣ K J 6 2	Partner has shown 16 to 18 points. With your 16 points, you know there are at least 32 combined points in the hand. There could be 33 or 34. Invite slam by bidding one level beyond game, 4NT. With a minimum hand (16 points), partner will pass. With a maximum (17 or 18 points), partner will accept the invitation and bid 6NT.
♠ A ♥ K Q J 8 6 3 ♦ A 9 5 ♣ 10 8 6	You have 16 points — 14 HCP plus 2 for the six-card heart suit. You know there is a Golden Fit in hearts. Invite slam by jumping one level beyond game, 5 ♥.

There are more sophisticated methods for bidding and inviting slams but they are beyond the scope of this text.

> ## SUMMARY OF SLAM BIDDING
>
> When considering a slam, use the following guidelines:
>
> - 33 or more points: Bid a small slam in a Golden Fit or in notrump.
>
> - 37 or more points: Bid a grand slam in a Golden Fit or in notrump.
>
> When you are not sure there is enough combined strength for slam, you can invite slam by bidding one level beyond game.

E. PREEMPTIVE OPENING BIDS

Opening suit bids are used at the three level or higher to show hands that are too weak to open the bidding at the one level (i.e., fewer than 13 points) and have a long suit, usually at least seven cards in length. These are called preemptive opening bids or preempts.

The Theory Behind Preemptive Bids

Why start the bidding at the three level or higher with a hand that is too weak to open the bidding at the one level? The advantage of a preemptive opening bid is that it takes up a lot of room on the Bidding Scale, and it makes it difficult for the other partnership to exchange information.

For example, if you were planning to open the bidding 1 ♦ and the opponent in front of you opened the bidding with 3 ♥, you would be faced with a difficult problem. How do you show partner that you have an opening bid with diamonds when the auction is already at the three level? A preemptive bid may cause the opponents to reach the wrong denomination, end up too high or too low, or be unable to get into the auction at all.

Of course, there is the possibility that a preemptive opening bid may make it difficult for your partner to bid effectively. There is also a danger that you may be doubled by the opponents and defeated badly! You can minimize the risk and maximize the potential gain by making a preemptive opening bid only with the appropriate type of hand.

Requirements for a Preemptive Opening Bid

An opening preempt at the three level or higher shows:

- A long suit — usually seven or more cards with three of the top five cards in the suit.
- A weak hand — less than the high-card values for an opening bid.

The longer and stronger your suit, the higher the level at which you can open the bidding. Because the penalties for being defeated are greater when you are vulnerable, you should watch the vulnerability when you preempt. If you are nonvulnerable, you may open at the three level with a seven-card suit and at the four level with an eight-card suit.

Here are a couple of examples. Suppose you are nonvulnerable.

♠ 7 3	Open 3 ♥.
♥ K Q J 9 7 6 2	
♦ 5	
♣ 10 6 3	

♠ 3	Open 4 ♣.
♥ 4 2	
♦ 7 6	
♣ A J 10 9 6 5 3 2	

One of the advantages of a preempt is that it is a very descriptive bid. Knowing the type of hand you have, it is easy for partner to respond accordingly.

The advantage of having a good long suit is that it is more difficult for the opponents to double the contract. Even if the opponents do double, the penalty for setting you is likely to be less than the value of a contract they could make.

Responding to a Preempt

If partner opens the bidding in a suit at the three level or higher, you have a good description of partner's hand — a long suit with a weak hand. Unless you have a strong hand of about 16 or more points, there is little chance for a game contract. You should pass.

With a very strong hand, you can bid game in partner's suit or in notrump, or you can bid a long suit of your own (forcing if below the game level). Since partner has at least a seven-card suit, no particular support for partner's suit is required to raise.

Competing Against a Preempt

If an opponent opens the bidding with a preempt, you can still make use of the overcall and the takeout double to compete. Since you are starting the auction at the three level or higher, you need to have a hand stronger than an opening bid if you decide to compete. For example, suppose the opponent on your right opens the bidding with 3 ♦ .

♠ A K J 7 5 3   With a good six-card suit and 16 points, overcall 3 ♠ .
♥ A 9 2
♦ 8 2
♣ Q 3

♠ K J 6 2   With support for the unbid suits, 14 HCP, and 3
♥ A Q 5 3   dummy points for the singleton, you can make a take-
♦ 3   out double.
♣ A J 8 2

♠ Q J 7
♥ K 9 6 3
♦ Q 8 2
♣ A J 5

Even though you have enough points to open the bidding, you do not have enough to start bidding at the three level. Pass.

SUMMARY OF PREEMPTS

A preemptive opening bid shows:

- Seven-card or longer suit.
- Less than the high-card values for an opening bid at the one level.

If partner opens with a preempt, pass unless you have a very strong hand. If the opponents open with a preempt, you can use the overcall and the takeout double to compete.

F. BALANCING

It is beyond the scope of the text to examine all the possibilities that may arise in competitive situations. However, you will learn from experience that you sometimes have to bid in situations where you do not have quite enough strength for the bid you make.

When the Opponents Compete

Suppose your partner opens 1 ♥, and you have the following hand:

♠ 8 3
♥ A 10 9 4
♦ 8 6 5
♣ A 8 3 2

With 8 HCP plus 1 for the doubleton spade, you raise to 2 ♥. Now, suppose the opponent on your left bids 2 ♠, and your partner and the opponent on your right both pass. You have a typical competitive choice — should you pass and let the opponents play the contract or should you bid again to try to buy the contract? With a nearly maximum raise and four–card support for opener's suit, you probably should compete to 3 ♥. Maybe you will make that contract; maybe your bid will push the opponents to 3 ♠ which you might defeat. Even if you go down, the penalty may be less than the value of your opponents' partscore contract. If you had a weaker hand or wanted to defend with spades as the trump suit, you would pass. Partner will not assume that your 3 ♥ bid suddenly shows a strong hand. You already limited your hand to the 6–10 point range with your response of 2 ♥. You are just showing a desire to compete to the three level.

The situation is more awkward if it is your partner who bids 3 ♥. If the opponents had not interfered, this would show a medium hand of 17 or 18 points, inviting you to bid game if you are near the top of your range. However, partner may be stretching a little with 15 or 16 points, unwilling to let the opponents play in 2 ♠. Should you bid on to 4 ♥? This is one of the things that makes the game interesting. As your experience grows, you will find yourself better able to judge what to do in such situations.

When the Auction May Stop

Suppose you have the following hand:

♠ K J 8 4
♥ 9 2
♦ A 6 3
♣ Q 10 6 3

The opponent on your left opens 1 ♥, and your partner and the opponent on your right both pass. You do not have quite enough for a classic takeout double but, if you pass, the opponents will play in a contract of 1 ♥. Looking at your hand, it seems likely they can make that contract. It might be better if your side played a partscore in your best trump suit. It is also possible that if you bid, you may push the opponents to a contract they cannot make. In such a situation, it is usually best to be slightly aggressive and make a takeout double with less than normal strength. The opponent on your left has at most 21 points and probably less. The opponent on your right has fewer than 6 points. Partner must have some of the missing points; so, it should be safe to compete. Since partner passed over the opening bid, it is unlikely partner will have enough strength to get your side too high by jumping to a game contract.

Experience will help you decide when to bid and when not to bid in such situations. For now, you should just be aware of the possibilities of balancing in this situation.

When You Passed Originally

There is one situation where you can always bid on less than normal strength without misleading your partner. If you passed originally, you can't have a hand worth 13 or more points. Look at this hand:

♠ J 3
♥ A J 10 9 7 3
♦ K 8 3
♣ 6 4

You would pass if you were the dealer since you don't have 13 points. However, suppose the bidding now proceeds 1♣ on your left, pass from partner, 1♠ on your right. You can overcall 2♥. Even though you are entering the auction at the two level, partner will not expect you to have a better hand because you passed originally.

Many similar situations arise in competitive auctions where you have limited your strength earlier and enter the auction at a later point. Both you and your partner will have to be on your toes to recognize such opportunities.

G. GLOSSARY OF TERMS

American Contract Bridge League — The National Authority and governing body for organized bridge activities and promotion on the North American Continent. It is usually referred to as the ACBL and is a not-for-profit organization. (Page III)

Auction — A series of bids that determines the final contract. (Page 8)

Balanced (hand) — A hand with no voids, no singletons, and no more than one doubleton. There are three balanced hand patterns: 4-3-3-3; 5-3-3-2; 4-4-3-2. The numbers refer to the number of cards in a suit. (Page 25)

Bid — A commitment to try to take at least the number of tricks named in the specific denomination. (Page 8)

Bidding — The various bids and calls that make up the auction. (Page 5)

Bidding Message — The message given by a bid: either forcing; invitational; or, signoff. (Page 62)

Bidding Scale — The order in which bids can be made. (Page 9)

Blackwood Convention — A convention invented by Easley Blackwood of Indianapolis in 1933 which attained worldwide popularity. It is used when players are on their way to bidding a slam, and one player wants to know the number of aces held by partner. The details are beyond the scope of this book and are discussed in *The Spade Series*. (Page 272)

Bonus — Points scored for making a partscore, a game, a slam, or for defeating the opponents' contract. (Page 12)

Book — The first six tricks won by the declaring side. (Page 8)

Break — The distribution of the outstanding cards in a suit. (Page 96)

Call — Any bid, double, redouble, or pass. (Page 8)

Captain — The partner who knows more about the combined hands and is responsible for directing the partnership to its final contract. Usually the responder is the captain. (Page 29)

Chicago — A form of rubber bridge where a rubber consists of only four deals and vulnerability is not determined by the previously played deals. (Page 198).

Combined (hands) — The cards making up both hands belonging to one partnership. (Page 15)

Contract — The final bid in the auction that commits declarer's side to try to take at least the number of tricks named in the selected denomination. (Page 5)

Convention — A bid that conveys a meaning other than that which would normally be attributed to it. (Page 101)

Convention Card — You are entitled to know the meanings of all bids made by your opponents in tournament bridge. Explanations of all of the partnership's agreements are required to be written on a card called a convention card.

Cuebid — The bid of a suit mentioned by the opponents. It is usually forcing to the game level. (Page 221)

Deal — This term covers the following actions: the even distribution among four players of the fifty-two cards in a deck; the privilege of distributing the cards; the act of dealing; the cards themselves after they have been dealt. (Page 3)

Dealer — The player who distributes the cards. The dealer has the first opportunity to open the bidding. (Page 3)

Declarer — The player who first bid the denomination of the final contract. The player who will try to fulfill the final contract by playing the cards for the partnership. (Page 10)

Defeat — To prevent the declarer from making the contract. (Page 10)

Defense — The side that did not win the contract. (Page 10)

Denomination — The suit or notrump specified in a bid. (Page 8)

Describer — The opening bidder. (Page 29)

Diamond Series — The ACBL lesson series which focuses on the play of the hand, reviews bidding, and introduces defense. (Introduction, VIII)

Discarding — The playing of a card, other than a trump card, of a suit different from the suit led. (Page 5)

Distribution — The number of cards held in each suit by a particular player or by a partnership. The number of cards held in a particular suit by a partnership. (Page 24)

Distribution Points — In hand valuation, points that take the shape of the hand into consideration. (Page 24)

Double — A penalty double increases the scoring value of tricks; a takeout double asks partner to bid the best suit in the hand with a preference for the majors. (Pages 199/232)

Doubleton — A holding of two cards in a suit. (Page 25)

Drawing Trumps — The playing of trumps until there are none in the opponents' hands. (Page 39)

Dummy — Declarer's partner. The hand that is placed face up on the table after the opening lead. (Page 11)

Dummy Points — In hand valuation, points used when planning to support partner's suit. A void is given 5 points, a singleton is given 3 points, and a doubleton is given 1 point. (Page 82)

Duplicate Bridge — The form of bridge in which the same deal is played more than once. (Page 2)

Entry — A card that provides a means of winning a trick in a particular hand. (Page 140)

Finesse — An attempt to win a trick with a card that does not rank as high as one held by the opponents. (Page 138)

Five-card Major System — A method of bidding which requires the opening bidder to have at least five cards in a major to bid the suit. (Page 43)

Follow Suit — Play a card in the suit that is led. (Page 5)

Forcing (bid) — A bid that forces partner to bid again. (Page 62)

Forcing (jump) **Raise** — A double raise of partner's suit. This bid is forcing to game. (Page 101)

Four-card Major System — A method of bidding that permits the opening bidder to have four cards in a major suit to bid the suit. (Page 43)

Game — A total trick score of 100 points or more. (Page 12)

Game Contracts — 3NT; 4♥; 4♠; 5♣; 5♦. (Page 13)

Game Raise — A raise to one of the five game contracts: 3NT; 4♥; 4♠; 5♣; or 5♦. (Page 28)

Gerber Convention — A convention invented by John Gerber of Houston, Texas in 1938. Like the Blackwood convention, it is used by players on their way to bidding a slam to find out the number of aces, and sometimes kings, held by partner. *The Spade Series*, ACBL's fourth beginning bridge book, has more details. (Page 272)

Going Down — Being defeated in a contract. (Page 13)

Golden Fit — At least eight cards in the same suit between your hand and your partner's hand. (Page 27)

Golden Game(s) — 3NT, 4♥, 4♠. (Page 28)

Grand Slam — A contract to take all 13 tricks. (Page 13)

Hand — The cards held by one of the players, a deal of bridge, the position at the table (e.g., second hand). (Page 3)

Hand Valuation — The number of total points, adding both high-card points (A=4, K=3, Q=2, J=1) and distribution points (1 point for each card in a suit over four). (Page 24)

HCP — The abbreviation for high-card points. (Page 24)

Heart Series — ACBL's third beginning bridge book which focuses on defense and reviews bidding and play. (Introduction, VIII)

High-Card Points (HCP) — The value of the high cards in a hand: ace=4; king=3; queen=2; jack=1. (Page 24)

Higher-ranking (suit) — A suit higher on the Bidding Scale. Spades is the highest ranking suit; clubs is the lowest ranking suit. (Pages 7,32)

Honor (card) — One of the five top cards in a suit — an ace, king, queen, jack, or ten. (Page 264)

Honors —Special bonuses in rubber - bridge scoring. (Page 264)

Invitational (bid) — A bid that invites partner to bid again. (Page 62)

Jump Raise — A bid in partner's named suit which jumps one level of the bidding. If you jump two levels, it is a double jump. (Page 101)

Jump Shift — A bid in a new suit at a level one higher than necessary. (Page 102)

Lead(ing) — The first card played to a trick. (Page 5)

Left–hand Opponent — The player on your left, often abbreviated LHO. (Page 11)

Length Points (distribution points) — The value of long suits in a hand: five-card suit=1; six-card suit=2; seven-card suit=3; eight-card suit=4. (Page 24)

Level — The number of tricks a player contracts to take when making a bid. It includes an assumed six tricks (book). (Page 8)

Limit Raises — The raise of a one-level opening bid to the three level. It shows a hand with about 11 or 12 points and support for opener's suit. (Page 101)

Loser — A card in a player's hand that could lose a trick to the opponents. (Page 6)

Lower-ranking (suit) — A suit lower on the Bidding Scale. The lowest ranking suit is clubs. (Page 9)

Major Suits — Hearts and spades. (Page 12)

Make — To take enough tricks to fulfill the contract. (Page 10)

Minor Suits — Clubs and diamonds. (Page 12)

Nonvulnerable — State of the scoring where neither side is vulnerable. (Page 198)

Notrump — A contract with no trump suit. The highest card played in the suit led wins the trick. (Page 7)

Offense — The partnership that wins the contract. (Page 10)

Opener's Rebid — The second bid by opener. (Page 65)

Opening Bidder — The player who makes the first bid in the auction. (Page 10)

Opening Lead — The card led to the first trick by the player on declarer's left. (Page 11)

Overcall — A bid made after an opponent has opened the bidding. (Page 201)

Overtrick — A trick won by declarer's side in excess of the contract. (Page 261)

Partnership — The two players seated opposite each other at the table. (Page 2)

Partscore — A contract with a trick score worth less than 100 points. (Page 13)

Pass — A call indicating that a player does not want to bid at that turn. (Page 8)

Penalty — The bonus awarded to the defending side for defeating a contract. (Page 12)

Penalty Double — A double with the intention of increasing the penalty bonus for defeating the opponents' contract. (Page 199)

Plan — The four steps declarer goes through before deciding how to play a hand. They are: (1) pause to consider your objective; (2) look at your winners and losers; (3) analyze your alternatives; (4) now put it together. (Page 37)

Play (of the cards) — The part of a deal following the auction during which the declarer tries to make the contract. (Page 5)

Pointcount — The high-card valuation introduced by Bryant McCampbell in 1915 and publicized by Milton Work and Charles Goren. Ace=4, K=3; Q=2; J=1. (Page 24)

Preemptive (bid) — A bid made to interfere with the opponents' auction. It usually is made with a long suit and a weak hand. (Page 101)

Promotion — The increase in the trick-taking potential of a card as the higher-ranking cards are played. (Page 66)

Raise — To support partner's suit by bidding that suit at a higher level. (Page 57)

Rank (of cards) — The ace is highest, followed by the king, queen, jack, ten ... down to the two. (Page 3)

Rebid — A second bid by any player. (Page 65)

Responder — The partner of the opening bidder, the partner of the player who overcalls or makes a takeout double. (Page 29)

Responder's Rebid — Responder's second bid. (Page 156)

Reverse — Any rebid in a suit higher ranking than the original one. (Page 145)

Right-hand Opponent — The player on your right, often abbreviated RHO. (Page 11)

Rubber Bridge — The form of bridge in which a deal is not played more than once. The unit in scoring is a rubber, which denotes the winning of two games by one side. (Page 2)

Ruff(ing) — To play a trump on a trick when you are void in the suit led. (Page 7)

Set — To defeat the contract. (Page 10)

Shuffling — Shuffle the cards. (Page 3)

Signoff — A bid that asks partner to pass. (Page 62)

Singleton — A holding of one card in a suit. (Page 25)

Small Slam — A contract to take 12 tricks. (Page 13)

Spade Series — ACBL's fourth beginning bridge book which focuses on duplicate bridge and reviews bidding, play, and defense especially as they apply to duplicate tactics. (Introduction, VIII)

Split — The distribution of the outstanding cards in a suit. (Page 96)

Stayman Convention — A convention invented by George Rapée and publicized in an article written by Sam Stayman. An artificial response of 2♣ to an opening bid of 1NT asks opener to bid a four-card major suit if there is one. (Pages 55, 201)

Strong Raise (forcing jump raise) — The raise of a one-level opening bid to the three level. It shows a hand with about 13 or more points and support for opener's suit. (Page 101)

Strong Two-Bids — The traditional use of an opening two-bid in a suit to show a hand which can virtually guarantee game, or even slam. (Page 269)

Suits — The four groups of cards in the deck each having a characteristic symbol: clubs; diamonds; hearts; spades. (Page 3)

Support — The number of cards held in a suit that partner has bid. (Page 81)

Sure Trick — A trick that can be taken without giving up the lead to the opponents. (Page 38)

Takeout Double — A double of an opposing bid that asks partner to bid. (Page 232)

Touching — Cards that are adjacent in rank (e.g., the queen and the jack). (Page 14)

Treatment — An approach to bidding or a special way of handling certain hands that is beyond the scope of a basic bridge course. (Page 101)

Trick — The unit of play consisting of four cards, one contributed by each player in clockwise rotation, which starts with the player on lead. (Page 5)

Trick Score — The points scored for contracts bid and made, not including any overtricks. (Page 12)

Trump (suit) — The suit named in the contract. (Page 7)

Trumping — Playing a trump on a trick when one is void in the suit led. (Page 7)

Unbalanced (hand) — A hand containing a void, a singleton, or more than one doubleton. (Page 25)

Valuation — The method of determining the value of a particular hand during the auction. Usually a combination of values for high cards held and length. (Page 24)

Void — The absence of cards in a specific suit. (Page 25)

Vulnerability — The condition of the scoring that affects the size of the bonus for making or defeating the contract. Bonuses and penalties are higher if the declarer is vulnerable. (Page 198)

Weak Two-Bid — The use of an opening bid of two in a suit other than clubs as preemptive. Classically, this bid describes a hand with 6 to 12 high card points and a six-card suit. (Page 270)

H. ANSWERS TO EXERCISES

Lesson One: Getting Started

Exercise One
Sometimes one of your high cards doesn't take a trick. This happens
when an opponent has a higher card that captures it. It also happens because
you can't get the lead and end up having to throw it away on one of the
opponents' winners. However, low cards sometimes will take tricks, especially when they are part of a long suit. Your low card may be the only card
left in the suit, and the opponents have to discard since they can't follow
suit.

Exercise Two
There are always surprises — that's what makes the game so interesting. A card may be a winner depending on when you get to play it. For
example, if you have a king and are the last to play to the trick, you have a
good chance of making your king a winner. If the ace is played before you,
then your king is high — all you have to do is get the lead and enjoy your
winner later. If the ace isn't played, then your king is a winner on that trick.
Predicting the cards you think will be winners helps improve your memory.

Exercise Three
Lead a diamond. You want your opponent to play the ace so that your
remaining diamonds will be winners. Keep your aces in the other suits so
that you can win the next trick and have the opportunity to play your diamonds. You can expect to take eight tricks.

Exercise Four
West will lead from length. This means West has at least three other
cards in the suit led. If West leads an honor, then it is the top of a sequence.
A low card means there is no sequence in the suit, but there may be one or
two high cards nevertheless.
    Working with a partner has both advantages and disadvantages. It is

pleasant because you now are on a team; you have someone sitting opposite you who is helping you take tricks. It is more difficult because you can't see each other's cards. You would like to know not only the long suits partner has but where partner's strength lies.

Exercise Five

Short suits are important when playing in a trump contract;, when you have no cards left in a suit, you can use the trump cards to trump the opponents' winners.

Exercise Six

- North and South like the spade suit best.
- South would suggest spades first.
- North has only three spades and might find it difficult to agree that spades should be trump.
- North could estimate taking three tricks.
- South could estimate taking six tricks at least and maybe seven.
- North and South can predict taking nine tricks — perhaps 10.
- East and West like the diamonds best.
- West would likely suggest diamonds first.
- East could estimate one or two tricks.
- West could estimate three or four tricks.
- E–W could predict six or seven tricks.
- N–S predicted the higher number of tricks.
- The contract would be 3 ♠ or 4 ♠.

Exercise Seven

- South mentioned the suit that ended up being trump. South will be the declarer.
- West, the player to the left of the declarer, will lead.
- North's hand is the dummy and is placed face up on the table.
- South starts by drawing the opponents' trump cards. Then South takes the winners in the partnership's combined hands. South should end up with 10 tricks.

Exercise Eight
- No, N–S do not have a suit they would like to have as trump.
- E–W also have no suit they would like to name as trump.
- The denomination would be notrump.
- North could estimate two or three tricks.
- South could estimate one trick — maybe.
- N–S could predict only three or four tricks.
- East could estimate four tricks.
- West could estimate five tricks.
- E–W could predict nine tricks.
- E–W predicted the higher number of tricks.
- The contract would be 3NT.
- East or West would first mention the denomination of the contract.
- The declarer (East or West) should end up with nine tricks.

Exercise Nine

1) eight tricks	2) 10 tricks	3) 13 tricks
4) nine tricks	5) 11 tricks	6) seven tricks
7) 12 tricks		

Exercise Ten

1) 60 points	2) 120 points	3) 120 points
4) 100 points	5) 60 points	6) 30 points
7) 100 points	8) 80 points	9) 100 points

- Game contracts: 3NT (7), 4♥ (2), 4♠ (3), 5♣ (4) and 5♦ (9)

Lesson Two: Objectives

Exercise One

1) 12 HCP	2 distribution points	14 total points
2) 8 HCP	1 distribution point	9 total points
3) 19 HCP	0 distribution points	19 total points

Exercise Two

Hands one, two and five are balanced.

Exercise Three

You need 26 combined points to make 3NT, 4 ♥, or 4 ♠ and slightly more, 29 combined points, to make 5 ♣ or 5 ♦.

Exercise Four

- The partnership needs seven cards in the combined hands to have the majority of cards in the suit.
- No. A minimum majority would not be adequate since the opponents would have six trump cards, nearly as many as you.
- When the partnership holds eight or more trumps, they can be comfortable with the trump suit.
- The eight cards could be divided in this manner: eight in one hand and none in the other, although this is very rare; seven in one hand and one in the other (also rare); six in one hand, two in the other; five in one hand, three in the other; four in one hand, four in the other.
- The specific high cards are not as important as the length of the trump suit.

Exercise Five

1) 17 HCP	0 distribution points	17 total points	1NT
2) 12 HCP	1 distribution point	13 total points	1 ♠
3) 9 HCP	1 distribution point	10 total points	Pass
4) 16 HCP	2 distribution points	18 total points	1 ♥
5) 14 HCP	0 distribution points	14 total points	1 ♣
6) 13 HCP	0 distribution points	13 total points	1 ♦
7) 20 HCP	0 distribution points	20 total points	1 ♣
8) 13 HCP	0 distribution points	13 total points	1 ♦
9) 13 HCP	3 distribution points	16 total points	1 ♣

Exercise Six

      1) Game   2) Partscore   3) Possibly Game

Exercise Seven

      1) No   2) Yes   3) Possibly

Exercise Eight

    1) One sure trick   2) Three sure tricks   3) Two sure tricks
    4) Three sure tricks

Exercise Nine
The bidding

- N–S have 27 combined points.
- E–W have 14 combined points.
- N–S have enough for a Golden Game.
- N–S do not have a Golden Fit in a major suit.
- North opens the bidding with 1NT.
- North is the describer.
- South is the responder and the captain.
- The contract should be 3NT.
- North would be declarer.

The play

- East makes the opening lead.
- East leads the ♠K.
- Declarer needs nine tricks.
- Declarer has nine sure tricks.
- Take your tricks and run is good advice because declarer can be assured of making the contract by taking the nine winners.
- If the defenders get the lead, they could take four spades and the ♥A — that is more tricks than declarer can afford to lose.

Exercise Ten
The bidding

- N–S have 18 combined points.
- E–W have 23 combined points.

- Neither partnership has enough strength for a Golden Game.
- Neither partnership has a Golden Fit.
- E–W have the majority of the strength.
- East opens the bidding with 1 ♦.
- East is the describer.
- West is the responder and the captain.
- E–W should be in a partscore.
- The denomination should be notrump.
- 1NT would be a reasonable contract.
- The opening bidder does not necessarily end up as the declarer.
- West could be the declarer by first mentioning the denomination of the contract. For example, West could mention notrump first.

The play

- North makes the opening lead.
- North leads a small card from hearts, the longest suit.
- Declarer needs seven tricks to fulfill the contract.
- E–W have seven sure tricks.
- Play the high card from the short side applies to the spade suit. This is good advice because, if declarer wins the first trick with the ♠Q, declarer still has a small card to get over to the ♠AKJ. If declarer wins the first trick with the high cards from East's hand, the dummy, then declarer may take the ♠Q when spades have been played three times. There is still a good trick in the dummy but declarer has no way to get to it.

Exercise Eleven

The bidding

- N–S have 24 combined points.
- E–W have 18 combined points.
- Neither partnership has enough strength for a Golden Game.
- N–S have a Golden Fit in spades and the majority of the strength.
- E–W have a Golden Fit in diamonds.
- The dealer does not have to open the bidding.
- North opens the bidding with 1 ♣.

- N–S want to reach a partscore contract in spades.
- A reasonable contract is 2♠.

The play
- West makes the opening lead.
- West leads the ♥Q.
- Declarer has to take eight tricks.
- There are eight sure tricks between North and South.
- The advantage of playing in a Golden Fit is that you can stop the opponents from taking too many tricks in any one suit.
- If N–S played this hand in notrump, the opponents could take four tricks in hearts and five tricks in diamonds.

Exercise Twelve
The bidding
- N–S have 15 combined points.
- E–W have 28 combined points.
- E–W have enough points for a Golden Game.
- E–W have a Golden Fit in hearts.
- N–S have a Golden Fit in clubs.
- E–W have the majority of strength.
- West opens the bidding with 1NT.
- East knows that there is enough combined strength for a game contract because East has 11 total points and West has at least 16 points — a combined total of at least 27 points.
- East knows there is a Golden Fit in hearts because West has at least two hearts to open the bidding with 1NT.
- The contract should be 4♥.

The play
- South leads the ♣Q.
- Declarer needs 10 tricks.
- There are 10 sure tricks.
- Declarer should draw trumps to take away the opponents' trump cards.

- If declarer did not do this, the opponents could score a small trump when South trumps the third diamond trick.

Lesson Three: Responses to 1NT Opening Bids

Exercise One

1) 4 total points	partscore	spades	2♠
2) 6 total points	partscore	notrump	pass
3) 7 total points	partscore	notrump	pass — 2♣ is a conventional response.

- All of the hands are in the 0 to 7 point range, so responder knows that the partnership belongs in partscore.

Exercise Two

1) 11 total points	game	spades	4♠
2) 11 total points	game	maybe hearts	3♥
3) 13 total points	game	notrump	3NT

- All of the hands have at least 10 total points so responder knows that the partnership belongs in game.

Exercise Three

Any hand with 8 or 9 total points.

Exercise Four

- Seven signoff responses are: pass; 2♦; 2♥; 2♠; 3NT; 4♥; 4♠.
- The invitational response is 2NT.
- Two forcing responses are 3♥ and 3♠.

Exercise Five

- It is important for responder to steer the partnership into a Golden Fit whenever possible because the trump cards prevent the opponents from taking winners in their strong suits.

Exercise Six

    1) two tricks   2) one trick   3) one trick   4) one trick

Exercise Seven

The bidding

- North opens the bidding with 1NT.
- North is the describer.
- South is the responder and the captain.
- The contract should be in game.
- The denomination is notrump.
- The response should be 3NT
- Responder makes a sign-off bid and opener should pass.
- The contract is 3NT.
- North is declarer.

The play

- East makes the opening lead.
- East leads the ♣Q.
- Declarer needs nine tricks.
- Declarer has six sure tricks.
- Diamonds provide the best opportunity to develop the additional tricks needed to make the contract.
- Declarer should play diamonds after taking the first trick because declarer wants to set the suit up right away while there are still winners in the other suits.
- Declarer should make the contract.

Exercise Eight

The bidding

- East opens the bidding with 1NT.
- East is the describer.
- West is the responder and the captain.
- The contract should be in game.
- The denomination should be spades.
- The response should be 4♠.
- The responder gives a sign-off message.

- Opener should pass.
- The contract would be 4♠.
- West is declarer.

The play

- North leads the ♣Q.
- Declarer needs 10 tricks, but has only four sure tricks.
- Declarer can develop the extra tricks in spades (four) and hearts (two).
- Declarer should play the spades first because that is the trump suit.
- If declarer plays other suits first, declarer's winners may be trumped by the opponents.
- Declarer should make the contract.

Exercise Nine

The bidding

- South opens the bidding with 1NT.
- Maybe the contract should be a game.
- The denomination would be notrump.
- The response would be 2NT.
- Responder makes an invitational bid.
- Opener would bid again holding 18 points — the maximum 1NT range.
- The contract is 3NT.
- South is declarer.

The play

- West makes the opening lead.
- West leads the ♠Q.
- Declarer needs nine tricks and has six sure tricks.
- The extra tricks can be developed in diamonds.
- Diamonds should be played after winning the first trick.
- Declarer should play the ♦Q first — the high card from the short side.
- If declarer plays the suit differently, declarer may not be able to get back over to the dummy to enjoy the diamond winners.
- Declarer should make the contract.

Exercise Ten
The bidding
- West opens the bidding with 1NT.
- The level of the contract should be a partscore.
- The denomination should be diamonds.
- The response is 2♦.
- Responder gives a signoff bid.
- Opener must pass.
- The contract is 2♦.
- East is declarer.

The play
- South makes the opening lead.
- South leads the ♠Q.
- Declarer needs to take eight tricks to fulfill the contract.
- Declarer has five sure tricks.
- The extra tricks can be developed in diamonds, the trump suit.
- After winning the first trick, declarer plays diamonds.
- Declarer will have to give up the lead three times before developing sure tricks in the diamond suit.
- The hand will play better in diamonds because there is not enough protection in the other suits. Declarer would lose too many tricks in notrump.
- Declarer should make the contract.

Lesson Four: Responses to Opening Bids of One in a Suit.

Exercise One

1) 6 HCP	3 dummy points	9 total points	2♥
2) 8 HCP	1 distribution point	9 total points	1♠
3) 7 HCP	1 distribution point	8 total points	1NT

- All three hands fall in the 6 to 10 point range.
- Count dummy points for the first hand because you can support partner's major suit.

Exercise Two

    c) Raise partner's major suit to the two level with at least three-card support.

    b) Bid a new suit at the one level.

    a) Bid 1NT.

    b) Bid a new suit at the one level.

    a) Raise partner's minor suit to the two level with at least five-card support.

    c) Bid 1NT.

Exercise Three

    1) 1♠   2) 1NT   3) 1♥

Exercise Four

    1) 2♥   2) 3♠   3) 2♦

- Responder is the captain.
- Opener will further describe the hand on the next bid.

Exercise Five

- The level will be game.
- Responder will force opener to bid until game is reached.

    1) 2♦   2) 2NT   3) 2♦

- A new suit by responder is a forcing bid, and opener has to bid again.

Exercise Six

    1) three tricks   2) three tricks   3) four tricks
    4) five tricks

Exercise Seven

The bidding

- South opens the bidding with 1♦.
- Responder cannot support the opening bid nor bid a new suit.
- The response would be 1NT.
- Responder has 6 to 10 points and no four-card major.

- Opener does not need to bid again.
- The contract would be 1NT.
- North is declarer.

The play
- East makes the opening lead.
- The opening lead would be the ♠Q.
- Declarer needs seven tricks to fulfill the contract.
- Declarer has six sure tricks.
- The additional trick could be developed in clubs.
- Declarer should play clubs after winning the first trick to develop the extra trick needed as quickly as possible. Meanwhile declarer keeps the winners in the other suits to prevent the opponents from taking tricks.
- Declarer should make the contract.

Exercise Eight

The bidding
- The opening bid would be 1♠ by West.
- Responder can support opener's suit.
- The value of the hand is 6 points.
- Responder would bid 2♠.
- This is an invitational bid, and opener does not have to bid again.
- The contract would be 2♠, and West would be the declarer.

The play
- North makes the opening lead.
- The lead would be the ♦Q.
- Declarer needs to take eight tricks.
- Declarer has five sure tricks.
- The best opportunity to develop additional tricks is in the spade suit.
- After winning the first trick, declarer should play the spades.
- Declarer needs to be lucky to make the contract because he can afford to lose only one trick in the spade suit. The opponents' spades need to be divided 2–2.
- Declarer should make the contract.

Exercise Nine
The bidding
- South opens the bidding with 1♥.
- The value of responder's hand is 14 total points — 1 point for the doubleton spade.
- Responder first bids 2♦.
- This bid is forcing.
- Opener would show a second suit by raising to 3♦.
- The final contract would be 4♥ because responder puts the contract back into hearts.
- South is the declarer.

The play
- West makes the opening lead.
- The lead would be the ♠K.
- Declarer needs to take 10 tricks to make the contract.
- Declarer has nine sure tricks.
- The diamond suit provides the best chance for the extra trick.
- After winning the first trick, declarer should draw the trump. That will take two rounds on this deal. Then, declarer goes about trying to get the extra trick in the diamond suit.
- Declarer should make the contract.

Exercise Ten
The bidding
- The opening bid would be 1♣ by West.
- Responder has 13 points.
- Responder can't support the opening minor suit because responder holds only four cards in the club suit.
- Responder has no suit to show.
- Responder would bid 2NT.
- This is a forcing bid and opener must bid again.
- Opener is likely to continue on in notrump, making the contract 3NT with East as the declarer.

The play
- South makes the opening lead.

- The lead would be the ♠J.
- Declarer needs to take nine tricks.
- Declarer has eight sure tricks.
- Believe it or not, the club suit provides declarer with the opportunity to develop an extra trick.
- A club should be played right after winning the first trick.
- For declarer to make the contract, the clubs have to be divided 3–2.
- Declarer should make the contract.

Lesson Five: Rebids by Opener

Exercise One

1)	15 HCP	2 distribution points	17 total points
	medium	3 ♥	
2)	13 HCP	2 distribution points	15 total points
	minimum	pass	
3)	20 HCP	1 distribution point	21 total points
	maximum	4 ♥	

Exercise Two

1)	14 HCP	0 distribution points	14 total points
	minimum	pass	
2)	15 HCP	2 distribution points	17 total points
	medium	3♣	
3)	19 HCP	1 distribution point	20 total points
	maximum	3NT	

Exercise Three

1)	13 HCP	1 distribution point	14 total points
	minimum	pass	
2)	14 HCP	1 distribution point	15 total points
	minimum	2 ♦	
3)	11 HCP	2 distribution points	13 total points
	minimum	2♠	

4) 15 HCP   2 distribution points   17 total points
    medium   3♠
5) 19 HCP   1 distribution point   20 total points
    maximum   3NT
6) 17 HCP   2 distribution points   19 total points
    maximum   3♣

Exercise Four
1) 14 HCP   3 dummy points   17 total points
    medium   3♠
2) 12 HCP   2 dummy points   14 total points
    minimum   2♠
3) 16 HCP   5 dummy points   21 total points
    maximum   4♠

Exercise Five
- In the first auction, responder could make the choice at the two level.
- In the second auction, responder might have to go to the three level.
- Hearts is higher ranking.
- Spades is higher ranking.
- In the first auction the second suit is lower ranking than the first suit.
- In the second auction, the second suit is higher ranking than the first suit.
- Without extra values, opener does not want to force the responder to make a choice at the three level.

Exercise Six
1) 13 HCP   0 distribution points   13 total points
    minimum   1NT
2) 13 HCP   1 distribution point   14 total points
    minimum   2♣
3) 15 HCP   2 distribution points   17 total points
    medium   3♦
4) 17 HCP   1 distribution point   18 total points
    medium   2♥

5)	19 HCP maximum	1 distribution point 3♣	20 total points
6)	19 HCP maximum	0 distribution points 2NT	19 total points

Exercise Seven

- Responder is showing 11 or 12 points in the first auction, 13 or more in the second auction.
- The first response is invitational, the second is forcing.
- Pass
- 3NT

Exercise Eight

1) one trick 2) two tricks 3) two tricks 4) two tricks
- In each case, lead toward the card you hope will take a trick.

Exercise Nine
The bidding

- North opens the bidding with 1♦.
- Responder cannot support opener's minor suit, nor can he bid a new suit, so he would reply 1NT.
- Responder's bid is invitational; opener does not have to bid again.
- Opener would pass.
- The contract would be 1NT. South would be the declarer.

The play

- West makes the opening lead.
- The opening lead would be the ♥K.
- Declarer needs seven tricks to make the contract.
- Declarer has six sure tricks.
- The club suit provides the best opportunity for an extra trick.
- After taking the lead, the declarer should lead toward the ♣K.
- Declarer should make the contract.

Exercise Ten
The bidding
- East opens the bidding with 1♠.
- Responder can support opener's suit. The hand is worth 8 points; so responder bids 2♠.
- The bid is invitational and opener does not have to bid.
- Opener would pass.
- The contract would be 2♠.
- East is declarer.

The play
- South makes the opening lead.
- South leads the ♦Q.
- Declarer needs eight tricks to make the contract.
- Declarer has five sure tricks.
- The spade suit provides the best chance to take additional tricks.
- After winning the first trick, declarer should play the ♠A and then a small spade toward the queen — the card declarer hopes will take a trick.
- Declarer should make the contract.

Exercise Eleven
The bidding
- East opens the bidding with 1♣.
- Responder has 9 points and bids 1♥.
- This is a forcing bid. Opener has to bid again.
- Opener's hand is now worth 21 points.
- Opener would rebid 4♥.
- The contract would be 4♥.
- West is declarer.

The play
- North makes the opening lead.
- North leads the ♦Q.
- Declarer needs 10 tricks to fulfill the contract.
- Declarer has nine sure tricks.
- Declarer is unlikely to win a trick with the ♦K because it is trapped

between North's ♦ QJ10 and South's ♦ A.
- The spade suit provides the opportunity to get an extra trick.
- After declarer gets the lead, declarer plays the trump suit, drawing the opponents' trump cards. Then declarer leads a spade toward dummy's ♠ AQ, planning to finesse dummy's ♠ Q.
- Declarer should make the contract.

Exercise Twelve
The bidding
- South opens the bidding with 1 ♦.
- Responder has 7 points. Since responder can't support opener's suit or bid a new suit at the one level, responder bids 1NT.
- This is an invitational bid — opener does not have to bid again.
- Since opener's hand is strong, opener jumps to game in notrump (3NT).
- The contract is 3NT.
- North is declarer.

The play
- East makes the opening lead.
- East leads the ♥ Q.
- Declarer needs nine tricks.
- Declarer has seven sure tricks.
- The diamonds provide the best opportunity to develop additional tricks.
- Declarer should win the first trick in hand with the king in order to lead toward the ♦ KQ.
- If declarer wins the first diamond trick with a high diamond, declarer should lead a small club to the ace. Now, declarer plays another diamond toward the remaining high diamond in dummy.
- Declarer should make the contract.

Lesson Six: Rebids by Responder

Exercise One
- 2 ♥; 2 ♦; 1NT.
- 1 ♠ would show either a minimum or medium hand. 2 ♣ would show

at least 13 points and an unbalanced hand.
- Responder needs at least 13 points to be sure the partnership should be in game.
- With 11 or 12 points, responder is uncertain whether the partnership should be in game or partscore.
- If responder has 10 points (or fewer), the decision should be to play in partscore.

Exercise Two

1)	6 HCP minimum pass	1 distribution point partscore	7 total points spades
2)	11 HCP medium 3♠	1 distribution point possible game	12 total points spades
3)	14 HCP maximum 4♠	1 distribution point game	15 total points spades

Exercise Three

1)	9 HCP minimum 1NT	0 distribution points partscore	9 total points notrump
2)	11 HCP medium 2NT	0 distribution points possible game	11 total points notrump
3)	15 HCP maximum 3NT	0 distribution points game	15 total points notrump
4)	5 HCP minimum 2♥	2 distribution points partscore	7 total points hearts
5)	10 HCP medium 3♥	2 distribution points possible game	12 total points hearts

6)   14 HCP   1 dummy point   15 total points
      maximum   game   spades
      4♠

7)   6 HCP   2 distribution points   8 total points
      minimum   partscore   clubs
      2♣

8)   10 HCP   1 distribution point   11 total points
      medium   possible game   clubs
      3♣

9)   10 HCP   2 dummy points   12 total points
      medium   possible game   spades
      3♠

Exercise Four

- Opener's hand has 17 or 18 points. (Medium range.)

1)   7 total points   partscore   hearts   pass
2)   10 total points   game   notrump   3NT
3)   9 total points   game   hearts   4♥

Exercise Five

- Opener has 19 to 21 points. (Maximum range.)

1)   6 total points   game   notrump   3NT
2)   9 total points   game   hearts   4♥
3)   10 total points   game   possibly hearts   3♥

Exercise Six

- South has nine tricks.
- An additional trick could be developed by trumping the third heart in the dummy.
- There would not be an additional trick since you have counted six spade winners already.
- The conclusion is that you get an extra trick by trumping in the short hand (dummy) rather than in the long hand.

Exercise Seven

The bidding

- North opens the bidding with 1♣.
- Responder cannot support opener's suit, but can bid a new suit at the one level, 1♠.
- Responder's bid is forcing and opener has to bid again. Since opener's hand is in the minimum range, opener rebids 2♠.
- Responder's hand is maximum. It's at the game level in spades.
- Responder would rebid 4♠.
- 4♠ is the contract, and South is declarer.

The play

- West makes the opening lead.
- The opening lead would be the ♥K.
- Declarer needs 10 tricks to make the contract.
- Declarer has nine sure tricks.
- The diamond suit provides the opportunity to develop an additional trick because the third round can be trumped in the dummy.
- Declarer has to leave a trump in the dummy to trump the third diamond.
- Declarer should make the contract.

Exercise Eight

The bidding

- East opens the bidding with 1♥.
- Responder can support opener's suit and has 7 dummy points.
- Responder bids 2♥.
- Responder's bid is invitational, and opener does not have to bid again.
- Opener's hand is medium so opener bids 3♥.
- Responder's hand is minimum. Responder wants to play in partscore in hearts.
- Responder passes the 3♥ bid.
- The contract is 3♥.
- East is declarer.

The play

- South makes the opening lead.

- South leads the ♦ K.
- East needs nine tricks to fulfill the contract.
- Declarer has eight sure tricks.
- The clubs provide an opportunity for an extra trick if declarer plays the clubs twice so that there are none in the dummy. Declarer has to leave at least one heart in the dummy to trump the third round of clubs.

Exercise Nine

The bidding

- South opens the bidding with 1 ♥.
- Responder cannot support the hearts but can bid a new suit — 1 ♠.
- Responder's bid is forcing, and opener has to bid again.
- Opener's hand is minimum. Since the hand is unbalanced, opener rebids a lower-ranking new suit — 2 ♣.
- Responder's hand is medium.
- Responder might want to play in a game in spades.
- Responder rebids 3 ♠.
- Opener bids 4 ♠ because opener knows responder has at least six spades and 11 or 12 points.
- The contract is 4 ♠, and North is declarer.

The play

- East makes the opening lead.
- The opening lead is the ♦ Q.
- Declarer needs to take 10 tricks.
- Declarer has nine sure tricks.
- The diamonds provide the opportunity for an extra trick.
- Declarer cannot draw all of the trumps right away because one spade must be kept in the dummy to trump the third round of diamonds.
- Declarer should make the contract.

Exercise Ten

The bidding

- West opens the bidding with 1 ♦.
- Responder bids 1 ♥.

- Opener's hand is in the maximum range and is balanced.
- Opener rebids 2NT.
- Responder's hand is minimum.
- The partnership does not have a Golden Fit in a major suit, only in diamonds. Responder bids 3NT.

The play
- North makes the opening lead.
- The opening lead is the ♠Q.
- Declarer needs nine tricks to make the contract.
- Declarer has eight sure tricks.
- Declarer can hope to develop an extra club trick either by playing the ace and queen so that the jack is good or by trying the finesse — leading toward the ♣AQJ combination and hoping that South has the ♣K.

Lesson Seven: Overcalls and Responses

Exercise One

	Nonvulnerable	Vulnerable
Undoubled	100 points	200 points
Doubled	300 points	500 points

Exercise Two

1) 1♠   2) 2♣   3) 1NT

Exercise Three
- Pass
- Yes. You would interfere with the opponents' bidding, compete for the contract, tell partner something about your hand, and perhaps push the opponents too high.
- Yes. If the opponent opened 1♠, you would have to overcall 2♥ rather than 1♥. This is more dangerous since you would need eight tricks to make the contract rather than seven.
- It would be more costly if you didn't make your contract if you were

vulnerable. Therefore, it is more dangerous to overcall when you are vulnerable.
- Open 1♣.
- You would not overcall 1♥ because the suit is not long enough. You would have to pass.

Exercise Four

1) 1♠	2) 2♣	3) 2♦
4) Pass	5) 1NT	6) Pass

Exercise Five

1) 2♠	2) 3♠	3) 4♠
4) Pass	5) 1♠	6) 1NT

Exercise Six

1) Pass	2) 3♥	3) 4♥

Exercise Seven

1) 2♥	2) 3NT	3) Pass

Exercise Eight
- You have to lose two tricks in the trump suit.
- There are two potential losers in diamonds.
- You can't draw trumps right away because the opponents would take two diamond tricks and two trump tricks. Instead, you must first discard one of your diamond losers on the extra spade winner in the dummy.

Exercise Nine
The bidding
- North opens the bidding with 1♦.
- East bids 1♠. This is an overcall.
- South passes. East's bid did not affect this response.
- West, with 12 total points, jumps to 3♠.
- North, with a minimum hand, passes.

- West's response is invitational.
- East bids game since East has 15 points and West has shown at least 11.
- The contract is 4♠.
- East is declarer.

The play
- South makes the opening lead of the ♦10, partner's bid suit.
- Declarer needs 10 tricks.
- Declarer has 10 sure tricks.
- Declarer draws the trumps first since declarer doesn't have to give up the lead to do this.
- The two small hearts in declarer's hand will be discarded on the clubs in the dummy.
- Declarer should make the contract.

Exercise Ten

The bidding
- East opens the bidding with 1♠.
- South overcalls 2♦.
- West would pass, because West can no longer bid 1NT.
- North passes. If South had opened 1♦, North could have responded 1NT.
- East passes, since East has a minimum opening bid.
- The contract would be 2♦. South would be the declarer.

The play
- West leads the ♠8, the suit partner bid.
- Declarer needs eight tricks and has four sure tricks. However, declarer has six losers — two in spades, three in hearts, and one in diamonds.
- Declarer should play clubs first, discarding one of the losers on the extra club winner in dummy. Declarer sometimes must delay drawing trumps because there are too many quick losers if a trump trick has to be lost.
- Declarer can expect to make the contract.

Exercise Eleven
The bidding
- South opens the bidding with 1 ♦.
- West overcalls 1 ♥.
- North passes.
- East has 12 HCP and 3 distribution points — 15 in total.
- East bids 4 ♥.
- If West had opened the bidding, East would bid a new suit, 1 ♠, forcing, since East is too strong to bid 3 ♥.
- The contract is 4 ♥.
- West is declarer.

The play
- North leads the ♦ 8, top of a doubleton in partner's suit.
- West needs 10 tricks and has three sure tricks. However, West also has four losers — one in hearts, two in diamonds, and one in clubs.
- Declarer can avoid losing two diamond tricks by discarding a diamond on the extra spade winner in dummy.
- After winning the first trick, declarer plays the spades in order to discard one diamond loser right away. Declarer can then draw trumps.
- Declarer should make the contract.

Exercise Twelve
The bidding
- West opens the bidding with 1 ♥.
- North overcalls 1NT.
- East passes.
- South has 9 points. South does not know whether the partnership belongs in game or partscore. The denomination should be notrump.
- South would bid 2NT, showing 8 or 9 points.
- West passes.
- South made an invitational bid. North passes with a minimum hand, 16 points.
- The contract is 2NT.
- North is declarer.

The play
- East leads the ♥ 5, top of a doubleton in the suit partner has bid.
- Declarer has six sure tricks and needs eight tricks to make the contract.
- Declarer can develop extra tricks in diamonds by playing them right away. If declarer plays the sure tricks in other suits first, it will be too late to develop the diamond winners. The opponents will get the lead, and they will have enough winners in the other suits to defeat the contract.
- Declarer should make the contract. Declarer will only take eight tricks if West (correctly) continues leading hearts after winning the first diamond trick.

Lesson Eight: Takeout Doubles and Responses

Exercise One
1) takeout   2) takeout   3) penalty
4) penalty

Exercise Two

1) 12 HCP	1 dummy point	13 total points	double
2) 11 HCP	3 dummy points	14 total points	double
3) 10 HCP	5 dummy points	15 total points	double

Exercise Three
1) 1 ♠   2) Double   3) 1NT
4) 1 ♥   5) Double   6) Pass

Exercise Four
1) 2 ♥   2) 2 ♦   3) 1NT

Exercise Five
1) 2 ♠   2) 2NT   3) 3 ♦

Exercise Six
   1) 4♥   2) 3NT   3) 4♠

Exercise Seven
   1) Pass   2) 3♠   3) 2♠

Exercise Eight
   • South has seven sure tricks.
   • South could get one extra trick in spades, if East has the king; two extra tricks in diamonds, if the missing diamonds are divided 3–2; one extra trick in clubs, if the missing clubs are divided 3–3.
   • South should try to develop the diamonds since there is a possibility of two extra tricks.
   • South should win the first trick with the ♥K. Dummy's ♥A will be needed later as an entry to the established diamond tricks.

Exercise Nine
The bidding
   • North opens the bidding with 1♦.
   • East can compete by making a takeout double. There is some danger that West will have no points and no suit to bid.
   • South passes. South's bid is not affected by East's call.
   • East's call is forcing, and West has to respond. West bids 2♣.
   • North passes.
   • East passes with a minimum hand after hearing West make a minimum response.
   • The contract is 2♣. West is declarer.
The play
   • North leads the ♥K, top of a sequence.
   • Declarer needs eight tricks to make the contract.
   • Declarer has five sure tricks.
   • Declarer wants to trump a losing diamond in the dummy.
   • Declarer wants to draw the opponents' trumps, hoping they divide 3–2.

- Declarer needs to trump the losing diamond first before drawing trumps.
- Declarer should take eight tricks.

Exercise Ten
The bidding
- East opens the bidding with 1 ♥.
- South would make a takeout double.
- West passes. West's call is not affected by South's double.
- North bids 4 ♠.
- The contract is 4 ♠, and North is declarer.

The play
- East leads the ♥ A. Next, East would lead the ♣ Q.
- Declarer needs to take 10 tricks and has eight sure tricks.
- There is a possibility of an extra trick if the missing diamonds are divided 3–3. In clubs, there is the possibility that East has the ace.
- The best chance is to trump the hearts in the dummy.
- Declarer has to leave two trumps in the dummy to do this.
- Therefore declarer must delay drawing the opponents' trumps.
- Declarer makes the contract.

Exercise Eleven
The bidding
- South opens the bidding with 1 ♦.
- West would make a takeout double.
- North passes.
- East bids 2 ♥ with a hand worth 11 points.
- East's bid is invitational.
- With 14 HCP plus 1 for the doubleton diamond, West would bid 4 ♥, knowing that East has at least 11 points.
- The contract is 4 ♥.
- East is declarer.

The play
- South leads the ♦ K.
- Declarer needs 10 tricks to make the contract.
- Declarer has five sure tricks.
- Declarer can get an extra trick in spades by leading twice toward the A-J-10 combination if South has either the king or the queen or both the king and the queen.
- Declarer's plan is to draw the trump and then try to get an extra trick in spades.
- Declarer makes the contract.

Exercise Twelve
The bidding
- West opens the bidding with 1 ♥ .
- North would make a takeout double.
- East would pass.
- South's hand is in the minimum range and would respond 1 ♠ .
- West passes.
- North has a maximum hand and describes the hand by jumping the bidding.
- North bids 3 ♠ .
- North is making an invitational bid. South will go on to game knowing that North has 19 to 21 points.
- The contract will be 4 ♠ .
- South is declarer.
The play
- West leads the ♥ A.
- Declarer needs to take 10 tricks.
- Declarer has seven sure tricks.
- Declarer should plan to lead toward the ♠ KQ.
- Declarer's ♦ AQ will provide the entries to do this.
- Declarer should make the contract.

INDEX
(Also see Glossary)

Join the fun!

Thank you for your interest in the game of bridge. The American Contact Bridge League (ACBL) is happy to extend you a special invitation to join our organization.

We know you will enjoy the game of bridge, and we believe you'll enjoy it even more once you become a member of the largest bridge club in North America.

ACBL membership includes

- *The Bridge Bulletin*, our monthly magazine
- Local, regional, national and international tournament *(choose from more than 1000 each year)*
- Access to 3800 clubs throughout North America
- Discounts off purchases of merchandise offered in our Product Catalogs
- Opportunity to obtain a major credit card through ACBL's affinity program
- Discounts on airline fares, hotel rates and car rentals
- Group insurance
- Friendly Competition and fun!

Please join us today!

When we receive your paid membership application, you will receive your player number and a new member packet. You will be on your way to greater enjoyment of the game we all love.

MEMBERSHIP APPLICATION

American Contract Bridge League • 2990 Airways Boulevard, Memphis, TN 38116-3847

Send to: ACBL - Membership

☐ **NEW MEMBER $14* (1 year)**   ☐ **STUDENT $10* (in school & under age 26)**

☐ **2nd YEAR $28* (Single)**   ☐ **HOUSEHOLD $50* (1 year)**   **$ Enclosed** _____   ☐ U.S.   ☐ Canadian

☐ Ms. ☐ Miss
☐ Mrs. ☐ Mr. _____
First Name   (Please Print)   Last Name

Address _____
City

Province/
State _____ Postal Code _____ Phone(s) ( ) _____ ( ) _____
Day   Evening

Date of Birth _____   ☐ Male   ☐ Female
month/day/year

Signature _____ **Date** _____

* Based on 1996 prices in U.S. fares

Software for bridge lovers!

CLUB SERIES ON COMPUTER DISK —
Interactive program ideal for new players to practice. Great graphics. Complements Audrey Grant *Club Series*. IBM compatible, any Windows, 3 Meg HD.

Disk/Manual	# 230510	*Member*	$14.95
Disk/Manual/			
Club textbook	# 230515	*Member*	$19.95

AUDREY GRANT'S BETTER BRIDGE EDITION BY BRIDGE MASTER — Easily
leads new player from basic concepts of play into more difficult levels. Additional deals available for beginner (basic) and intermediate players at $13.45 for members.

Audrey Grant *(needs Bridge Master)*   # 370264
   List $44.95   *Member* $40.45
Audrey Grant *(without Bridge Master) DOS*   # 370263
   List $59.95   *Member* $53.95
Audrey Grant *(Windows)*   # 370258
   List $59.95   *Member* $53.95

BRIDGE MASTER — Lesson hands teach
proper dummy play technique. Written analyses follow interactive deals. Good graphics/user friendly. Basic to advanced (5 levels). More disks available for all skill levels $13.45 for members. 117 deals. IBM compatible.
Bridge Master DOS   # 370266   List $59.95
   Member $53.95
Bridge Master Win   # 370261

MEADOWLARK BRIDGE
— Versatile bidding system generates 70 different hand types for bidding practice. Other disks of actual tournaments available. Your results will be match-pointed with actual tournament results. Needs 386,4 Meg RAM, Windows 3.1 or higher.

Meadowlark Bridge 1.10
230400   List $59.95
   Member $53.95

BRIDGE BARON VI —
Most popular. Improved bidding with flow charts. Library for saving deals/match replay. Hands for bidding and play. Windows 3 +, 1.5 Meg on HD, 1 Meg RAM.
Bridge Baron (Windows)
   # 230435   List $59.95
   Member $53.95
Bridge Baron (MAC) *New version*
   # 230440   List $59.95
   Member $53.95
Bridge Baron (DOS)
   # 230430   List $9.95
   Member $53.95

COUNTING AT BRIDGE — Gain confidence, reach your potential as a bridge
player. Avoid silly mistakes by learning to count at the bridge table. Interactive program has 100 problems to transform average player's game.
Counting at Bridge   # 230451   List $34.95   *Member* $31.45

CREDIT CARD ORDERS:

Call our toll-free order line
1(800) 264-2743 (U.S.)
1(800) 264-8786 (CANADA)
Fax (901) 398−7754

ACBL ORDER FORM

2990 Airways Boulevard • Memphis, TN 38116-3847

WE WILL BE UNABLE TO ACCEPT ORDERS UNDER $10.00 DUE TO RISING POSTAL COSTS AND PROCESSING FEES.

Credit Card Holders Call Toll-Free
1-800-264-2743 United States
1-800-264-8786 Canada
FAX: 901-398-7754
8 - 4:30 Central Time 901-332-5586, ext. 272

1
ORDERED BY: ACBL # _____

NAME _____

ADDRESS _____

CITY _____ STATE _____

ZIP _____ DAYTIME PHONE _____

2
SHIP TO: (IF DIFFERENT FROM BOX 1)

NAME _____

ADDRESS _____

CITY _____ STATE _____

ZIP _____ DAYTIME PHONE _____

ACBL GUARANTEES Your Satisfaction!

3

ITEM #	QUANTITY	DESCRIPTION	SIZE	COLOR	PRICE	TOTAL

SAME DAY SERVICE UPON REQUEST

We are proud to offer you "same day" service. Phone before 12:00 noon Central time and request it and your order will be shipped that same day.

Sorry, no discount allowed on ACBL scrip, Computer-Dealt Hands, Bid Boxes/Bidding Boxes or The ACBL Handbook.

4 Subtotal		
5 Subtract appropriate discounts	-
6 TN residents add 8.25% sales tax	+
7 Shipping & Handling	+
8 TOTAL	

7 SHIPPING & HANDLING

ORDER AMOUNT	ADD
Up to $10.00	$3.50
$10.01 to $20.00	$4.25
$20.01 to $30.00	$5.00
$30.01 to $40.00	$5.75
$40.01 to $50.00	$6.50
$50.01 to $75.00	$7.75
$75.01 to $100.00	$9.00

9 METHOD OF PAYMENT

(U.S. Funds only)

☐ Check or Money Order *(payable to ACBL)*
☐ Discover   ☐ MasterCard   ☐ Visa

Acct. # _____

MC Bank # _____ Exp. date: ____

Cardholder Signature _____

All orders within the contiguous 48 states over $100.00 will be billed actual freight.
Shipments outside the contiguous 48 states will be charged actual freight plus handling fee.
Shipping/handling fee will be added to all orders unless otherwise stated.

Please see that we have all the information we need to provide you with satisfactory and speedy service:
- Check or money order or credit card information enclosed
- Complete "ship to" address when different from your own
- Correct and complete item numbers, quantities and descriptions for items ordered

PRICES SUBJECT TO CHANGE WITHOUT NOTICE